SCOTLAND

SCOTLAND

AN ANTHOLOGY

COMPILED BY PAUL HARRIS

CADOGAN PUBLICATIONS
LONDON

First published 1985

ISBN 0 947754 05 9

Published by Cadogan Publications Ltd.
16 Lower Marsh, London SE1
(Holding Company – Metal Bulletin PLC)

Phototypeset on Linotron in 11 on 12pt Baskerville
by Photocomp Ltd

Printed and bound in Great Britain by
Biddles Ltd, Guildford, England

ACKNOWLEDGMENTS

Grateful acknowledgment is made to the following for permission to reprint copyright material in this anthology:

CHAPTER 1 THE NATURE OF THE SCOT

The Estate of Moray McLaren for 'Who are the Scots?' from UNDERSTANDING THE SCOTS by Moray McLaren.

John Murray Publishers Ltd for 'Damn Scotch!' from A CHILDHOOD IN SCOTLAND by Christian Miller.

Canongate Publishing Ltd and Alasdair Gray for 'The Spread of Ian Nichol' from UNLIKELY STORIES by Alasdair Gray.

Alan Bold for 'Song of a Small Nation' from TO FIND THE NEW by Alan Bold.

Mainstream Publishing Co (Edinburgh) Ltd for 'A Country without Future?' from SCOTTISH JOURNEY by Edwin Muir.

Alexander Scott for 'Scotched' from DOUBLE AGENT by Alexander Scott.

Paul Harris Publishing for 'The Red Fellows' from WHAT DO YOU THINK YOURSELF? by Naomi Mitchison.

CHAPTER 2 EDINBURGH

James Thin Ltd for an extract from EDINBURGH'S CHILD by Eleanor Sillar.

Alasdair Alpin MacGregor and Methuen & Co for 'Cable Car Days' from AULD REEKIE by Alasdair Alpin MacGregor.

The Executors, MacDiarmid Estate for TALKING WITH FIVE THOUSAND PEOPLE IN EDINBURGH by Hugh MacDiarmid.

Paul Harris Publishing for 'A View from Calton Hill' from A SUBURB OF BELSEN by Stanley Roger Green.

CHAPTER 3 GLASGOW

Iain Crichton Smith for 'You Lived in Glasgow' from COLLECTED POEMS by Iain Crichton Smith.

David Higham Associates Ltd for 'Trial Trip' from THE SHIPBUILDERS by George Blake.

John Farquarson Ltd and William McIllvanney for an extract from THE PAPERS OF TONY VEITCH by William McIllvanney.

The Salamander Press for 'Greensleeves' from ITS COLOURS THEY ARE FINE by Alan Spence and for an extract from THE SLAB BOYS by John Byrne.

Polygon Books for 'George Square' from DREAMING FRANKENSTEIN AND COLLECTED POEMS by Liz Lochhead.

Oliver & Boyd for 'Sweet Saturday Night' by R. N. Biles from SCOTLAND 1938.

The Souvenir Press for 'The Streets of Glasgow' from THE ALBANNACH by Fionn MacColla.

Mainstream Publishing Co (Edinburgh) Ltd for an extract from SCOTTISH JOURNEY by Edwin Muir.

Clifford Hanley for 'The Glasgow Underground'.

International Literary Management for an extract from POINT OF DEPARTURE by James Cameron.

CHAPTER 4 THE LOWLANDS

Paul Harris Publishing for 'Kelso Horse Show' from COLLECTED POEMS by Maurice Lindsay.

Methuen & Co and Dodd, Mead & Co for an extract from IN SEARCH OF SCOTLAND by H. V. Morton.

CHAPTER 5 THE HIGHLANDS AND ISLANDS

The Estate of Moray McLaren for 'The Real Gaels' from UNDERSTANDING THE SCOTS.

Canongate Publishing Ltd for 'Shores' from SPRING TIDE AND NEAP TIDE by Sorley Maclean.

Faber & Faber Ltd for 'The Herring Fishers' from THE SILVER DARLINGS by Neil M. Gunn.

Macdonald & Co (Publishers) Ltd and Richard Scott Simon Ltd for extracts from CROWDIE AND CREAM by Finlay J. Macdonald.

The Estate of Compton Mackenzie, Chatto & Windus and Houghton Mifflin Co Inc for an extract from WHISKY GALORE by Compton Mackenzie.

Dairmid Gunn for an extract from A HIGHLAND RIVER by Neil M. Gunn.

Mainstream Publishing Co (Edinburgh) Ltd for 'Orkney' from SCOTTISH JOURNEY by Edwin Muir.

George Mackay Brown and The Hogarth Press for 'Death of a Community' from GREENVOE by George Mackay Brown.

CHAPTER 6 THE GRANITE CITY AND THE GOLDEN HAIRST

Curtis Brown Ltd and the Estate of Lewis Grassic Gibbon for extracts from A SCOTS HAIRST and SUNSET SONG.

Paul Harris Publishing for 'Aikey Brae' by David Toulmin and 'Fun on the Green' from THE WHITE BIRD PASSES by Jessie Kesson.

Century Publishing Co Ltd for 'The Games' from FARMER'S BOY by John R. Allan.

Flora Garry for 'Bennygoak' from BENNYGOAK AND OTHER POEMS by Flora Garry.

David Kerr Cameron and Victor Gollancz Ltd for 'Lament for a Lost Landscape' from THE CORNKISTER DAYS by David Kerr Cameron.

The Charles Murray Trust and Aberdeen University Press for 'Bennachie' from THE COMPLETE POEMS OF CHARLES MURRAY by Charles Murray.

Methuen & Co and Dodd, Mead & Co for 'The Aberdeen Joke Factory' from IN SEARCH OF SCOTLAND by H. V. Morton.

CHAPTER 7 THE SABBATH

John Murray Publishers Ltd for 'The Kirk' from A CHILDHOOD IN SCOTLAND by Christian Miller.

Methuen & Co and Dodd, Mead & Co for 'Dressed for the Sabbath' from IN SEARCH OF SCOTLAND by H. V. Morton.

Alasdair Alpin MacGregor and Methuen & Co for 'A Capital Sabbath' from AULD REEKIE by Alasdair Alpin MacGregor.

Sussex University Press for 'A Jewish Sabbath in Edinburgh' from TWO WORLDS by David Daiches.

Polygon Books for 'Sunday Song' from DREAMING FRANKENSTEIN AND COLLECTED POEMS by Liz Lochhead.

James Thin Ltd for 'An Edinburgh Sunday' from AN EDINBURGH CHILDHOOD by Eleanor Sillar.

CHAPTER 8 OF REBELLIONS PAST AND PRESENT

The Estate of Moray McLaren for 'Glorious Failure' from UNDERSTANDING THE SCOTS by Moray McLaren.

Alasdair Alpin MacGregor and Methuen & Co for 'Scottish Nationalism' from AULD REEKIE by Alasdair Alpin MacGregor.

Bernard MacLaverty and Jonathan Cape Ltd for 'A Time to Dance' from A TIME TO DANCE AND OTHER STORIES by Bernard MacLaverty.

CHAPTER 9 OF DAILY BREAD AND THE WATER OF LIFE

Richard Drew Publishing Ltd for the two recipes Sassermaet and Petticoat Tails by Catherine Brown.

Curtis Brown Ltd and the Estate of Lewis Grassic Gibbon for 'An Aberdeen High Tea' from A SCOTTISH SCENE by Lewis Grassic Gibbon.

Oliver & Boyd for 'Food in these Parts' by Will Y. Darling from SCOTLAND 1938.

Paul Harris Publishing for 'Ballade of Good Whisky' from COLLECTED POEMS by Norman MacCaig.

CHAPTER 10 THE ARTS

Stephen Mulrine for 'A Gude Buke' from NOISE AND SMOKY BREATH.

Paul Harris Publishing for 'At the Orphanage' from THE WHITE BIRD PASSES by Jessie Kesson.

The Society of Authors on behalf of the Bernard Shaw Estate for 'Shaw on Barrie' by George Bernard Shaw.

A. D. Peters & Co Ltd for 'James Bridie' from THE ART OF ADVENTURE by Eric Linklater.

Macdonald Publishers for 'Embro to the Ploy' from COLLECTED POEMS by Robert Garioch.

Mrs McBey for 'The First Etchings' and 'The First Exhibition' from THE EARLY LIFE OF JAMES McBEY: AN AUTOBIOGRAPHY 1883-1911.

Jay Landesman for 'Meeting a Scottish Painter' from WHO IS EDDIE LINDEN by Sebastian Barker/Eddie Linden.

Edwin Morgan and Carcanet Press Ltd for 'To Joan Eardley' from POEMS OF THIRTY YEARS by Edwin Morgan.

George Mackay Brown andThe Hogarth Press for 'The Burning Harp' from HAWKFALL by George Mackay Brown.

Gordon Wright Publishing Ltd for 'To an Aberdeen Poet who writes solely in English' from MORE COLLECTED POEMS by Helen B. Cruickshank.

CHAPTER 11 THE SCOT AT PLAY AND AT REST

Paul Harris Publishing for 'The Benefactor' from COLLECTED POEMS by William J. Tait.
Paul Harris Publishing for 'Zandra' by Donald Campbell.

The Scotsman Publications Ltd for THE RULES OF OLD-FASHIONED GOLF by Anthony Troon.

Methuen & Co and Dodd, Mead & Co for 'The Hunter Home from the Hill' from IN SEARCH OF SCOTLAND by H. V. Morton.

Robin Chapman-Campbell for 'The Country Gentleman's Tweed Suit' from CATALOGUE OF SOME TRADITIONAL CLOTHES AS WORN AT BLAIR AWFOLL, HOME OF MAJOR FROST-BYE OF THAT ILK by Robin Chapman-Campbell.

The Glasgow Herald and Ronald Mavor for 'The Highland Meeting' by Ronald Mavor.

If, through inability to trace the present copyright owners, any copyright material is included for which permission has not specifically been sought, apologies are tendered in advance to proprietors and publishers concerned.

INTRODUCTION

For the tourist from abroad or, indeed, for the resident of that southern appendage tacked on to the bottom of Scotland below Hadrian's Wall, Scotland is a romantic country of cloud-capped mountains, mist-shrouded glens, mysterious lone pipers, canny caber tossers and holidaying Royals. Not that this picture is necessarily inaccurate – the fierce, rugged beauty of the scenery cannot be disputed, especially beyond the Highland line – it is just that it is woefully incomplete.

The historical explanation for this romanticised view of a once proud and independent nation can be adequately explained by the historians and a potted version might go something like this. Following the collapse of the rebellion of 1745 'Bonnie' Prince Charlie takes to the heather and flees the dreaded English Redcoats. After many adventures he is saved by his trusty Highlanders and takes ship to France; but now the English sweep through the glens, burning, pillaging and carrying off the menfolk; the clan system has broken down, the kilt is worn no more and the pipes no longer play; the people are replaced by sheep and the great emigration begins. But Scotland's reputation is restored in 1822 when King George IV steps ashore at the port of Leith resplendent in kilt (and pink hose to warm his Hanoverian legs) and is greeted by Sir Walter Scott who, through his books, has already embarked upon a campaign for the glorification of Scotland's heritage. King George is followed by other Royals to Scotland and a grand house takes shape at Balmoral. And Balmorality is born.

All of a sudden Scotland becomes fashionable. Every English drawing room boasts at least an engraving of *The Stag at Bay*, 'Rabbie' Burns or a scene from Sir Walter Scott, if not a huge heavy oil painting of lugubrious Walt Disney-like Highland cattle against a backdrop of towering peaks. Artists and writers of the Victorian era besiege Scotland and serve up to an eager public exactly the sort of picture that endures to this day. The Scots themselves are a little puzzled by all this but take it very much in their stride. The West of Scotland has become the workshop of the British Empire and most people are busily engaged building ships, equipment and tools to perpetuate an Empire on which the sun shows no sign of setting. Of course, The Boer War and, later, the First World War puts paid to all that and the sun starts to slip below the horizon in an alarmingly rapid fashion. By the mid-thirties depression has arrived with a vengeance and, so far as Scotland is concerned, it is not to lift to any real degree. Alas, all does not end happily ever after.

This is not a historical essay, and it is not really my intention to sum up 250 years of Scottish history in as many superficial words in an attempt to explain the deficiencies in perception of Scotland as both a nation and a country. Suffice to say, I think, that after more than a century of repression Scotland adopted the mantle fashioned by others and has been the prisoner of it ever since. Her self esteem was further undermined by the collapse of her economic foundations in the twentieth century.

What is of real concern here is the effect this has had on indigenous writers and visiting writers. The eighteenth and nineteenth centuries brought English and continental writers swarming to Scotland. Some are complimentary – some are not. Most are downright patronising. In this anthology I have given most of them pretty short shrift. You will find here the Boswells and names like Burt, Defoe, Topham, Simond, Nodier, Stendhal, Byron and William Hazlitt. Their contributions are representative and not quite as odious as many of their fellow travellers'. Meantime, Scotland had discovered some great writers of her own and figures like Robert Burns and Sir Walter Scott entertained in the drawing rooms of Edinburgh. I have also given them fairly short shrift. It is, I fear, one of the easiest things in the world for the anthologiser to stuff his anthology of 'good things Scottish' full of Burns and Scott and those published, especially during the Thirties and Forties, bear ample witness to this. Perhaps, though, the reader will enjoy the works of lesser known writers like Peter Still, William Thom and the remarkable Christian Watt.

But it is the writers of the twentieth century I wish to commend to the reader above all, and it is upon them that there is the emphasis – if, indeed, there is any discernible emphasis. For these are the writers who are able to see this country in a historical perspective; who have been, and are, writing at the time of probably the most significant change in the last half millenium. For it is these fine twentieth century writers who sketch in so much of the picture left incomplete by their forbears in their concern for the pursuit of a romantic ideal; who write of a real

Scotland which those of us who live and work in the country know to be a truer and fairer representation. And, above all, there are some very good writers indeed working in Scotland today.

My selection here is, inevitably, highly personal. I have striven for some kind of balance – whether it be geographical or in terms of time, setting or choice of subject matter. I have sought to exclude the old, tired chestnuts which seem to crop up time and again in other collections. I have tried to beware of the caricature or pastiche which so often passes as 'typical'. And, above all, I have been conscious of the temptation to draw upon writers I have published in the last fifteen years of publishing in Scotland. Ultimately, I trust I have not fallen foul of this particular temptation and I certainly do not think the book would have been complete without the David Toulmins or Jessie Kessons. Some of my choices may be regarded as bizarre – in selection of extract if not author. I would hope that this is quite deliberate in an attempt to come forward with some new discoveries rather than the tired and tested samples. In the selection of extracts from prose writers I have sought pieces which should be if not exactly self-contained then certainly not tantalisingly incomplete. It is remarkable how many (quite well known) writers are difficult to anthologise. Of course, the most hazardous part of the course for any anthologiser is not so much whom to put in but who is left out. I am sorry if your favourite writer is not here. I am even sorrier if you are the writer. But, I would be the first to admit, this is all highly subjective.

I should like to thank Christopher Burness, on this occasion *my* publisher, for giving me the opportunity to compile this anthology. It has been a real delight: a voyage of rediscovery around my own bookshelves and those of others as I have re-read so many books which have given me pleasure over the years (and, indeed, some discovered for the first time). The role of the compiler is a modest one – the stars of this operation are the writers – and so I know it cannot be construed as a fine conceit if I say that I know I shall enjoy reopening this book time and again. I just hope that, as they used to say a hundred years ago, you, Dear Reader, will enjoy similar pleasure.

Paul Harris, Edinburgh (Spring 1985)

FOR

CAROL ANN

CONTENTS

ACKNOWLEDGMENTS

INTRODUCTION

THE NATURE OF THE SCOT, 1

EDINBURGH, 19

GLASGOW, 35

THE LOWLANDS, 61

THE HIGHLANDS AND ISLANDS, 79

THE GRANITE CITY AND
THE GOLDEN HAIRST, 109

THE SABBATH, 147

OF REBELLIONS PAST & PRESENT, 161

OF DAILY BREAD AND
THE WATER OF LIFE, 183

THE ARTS, 197

THE SCOT AT PLAY AND AT REST, 221

BIBLIOGRAPHY, 245

INDEX, 248

A NEW
and Accurate Map of
SCOTLAND
from the latest
SURVEYS.
ATLANTIC OCEAN
NORTH SEA
WESTERN ISLANDS
ORKNEY ISLANDS
Westra Firth
Sanda Sound
Pentland Firth
Wick
CAITHNESS SHIRE
SUTHERLAND SHIRE
ROSS SHIRE
INVERNESS SHIRE
MURRAY SH.
BAMFF SH.
ABERDEEN SHIRE
Aberdeen
MEARNS SHIRE
ARGYLE SHIRE
PERTH SHIRE
ANGUS SHIRE
FIFE SH.
KINROSS
Firth of Tay
St. Andrews
FIRTH of FORTH
STIRLING SH.
EDINBURGH
HADDINGTON SHIRE
BERWICK SH.
Berwick
Holy I.
RENFREW SHIRE
Glasgow
BUTE ARRAN SHIRE
AIR SHIRE
DUMFRIES SH.
ROXBURGH SHIRE
KIRKUDBRIGHT SHIRE
WIGTOWN SHIRE
NORTHUMBERLAND
CUMBERLAND
Newcastle
Cheviot Hills
Mull of Cantire
Mull of Galloway
Burrow Head
Rathlin I.
Giants Causway
IRELAND
Sound of Jura
Sound of Mull
ISLA
JURA
MULL ISLE
Rum
Egg
Barra
LEWIS ISLAND
Stornaway
St. Kilda
DORNOCH FIRTH
MURRY FIRTH
Cromarty
British Statute Miles
5 10 20 30 40 50
Long. West from London.

circa 1760

CHAPTER 1

THE NATURE OF THE SCOT

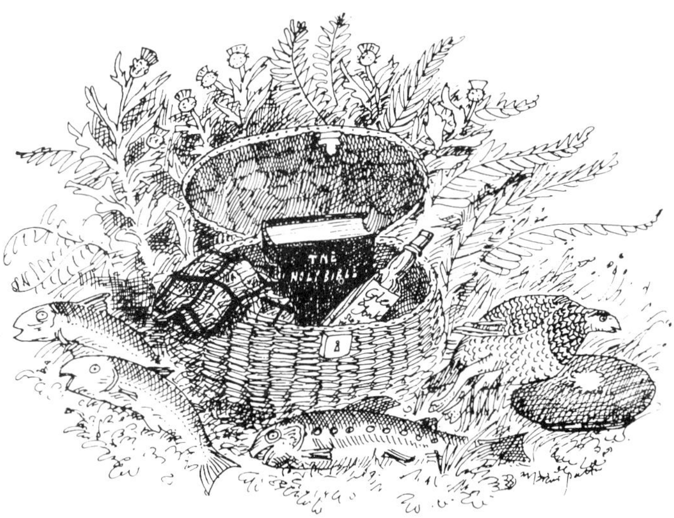

Mixed Feelings

The Scots are as diligent, as industrious, as apt for Labour and Business, and as capable of it, when they are abroad, as any People in the World; and why should they not be so at Home? and, if they had Encouragement, no doubt they would.

Daniel Defoe (1661-1731)

Trust yow no Skott.

Andrew Boorde, Suffragan Bishop of Chichester,
Letter to Thomas Cromwell, 1 April 1536

A Scottish accent is very nearly as good as a testimonial.

The Rt. Hon. David Lloyd George (1863-1945)

There never came a fool out of Scotland: they all stay at home.

Anonymous

The Scotch are proverbially poor and proud, we know they can remedy their poverty when they set about it. No one is sorry for them.

William Hazlitt (1778-1830)

A land of meanness, sophistry and lust.

Lord Byron (1788-1824)

WHO ARE THE SCOTS?

Moray McLaren addresses himself, and the reader, to some elementary truths on the matter . . .

The first thing to understand about the Scots is that they are not English. This may seem a somewhat unnecessary statement for most of my own compatriots and for many English, particularly those living in the North of England. But it is a point worth making for a number of foreign visitors to these shores who are inclined to think of this main island of ours, with its adjacent archipelago of nearly a thousand other islands, as England, and of all the inhabitants as English.

The second thing to understand is that the Scots are not British, neither are the English (no self-respecting Englishman calls himself a Briton – does he?). Nor, for that matter, is anyone British. A Briton and British were uneasy terms disinterred after centuries to get round an awkward corner of description when the Parliaments of England and Scotland were united in 1707. But apart from George III who, poor man, before he went mad, went about the place, gutturally and proudly proclaiming himself to be the 'first King born a Briton', the terms didn't take on.

For some time, it is true, the English called Scotland North Britain, and in my own lifetime I have received letters from English friends addressed to me on the envelope at 'Edinburgh, N.B.'. This has invariably been effectively countered and stopped by replying with letters addressed to 'London, S.B.'.

The truth is that the best and most distinctive things in Britain are not British. Cricket is an English game, and no matter how many Scots, Welsh or Irish may be playing in it, the national team is the All England Eleven. Shakespeare is an English poet and not a British one. And so, though golf may have become something like a world-wide epidemic, it was and radically remains a Scottish not British game. Burns, by the way, is not a British poet, nor was Harry Lauder a British comedian. And who in the whole wide world ever asked for a double 'British and soda'?

Moray McLaren (1901-71)

'Damn Scotch!'

One bright day in late spring, my father was dressing to go to Edinburgh. Normally, for a journey so far south, he would abandon the kilt that he wore at home and put on an ordinary trouser suit, because, although Edinburgh was the capital of Scotland, to us northern highlanders it ranked as lowland, and in the lowlands we wore English clothes. We called ourselves 'Scotch' (never 'Scottish'), and we referred to men who wore kilts in Edinburgh – or, horror of horrors, outside Scotland – as 'damn Scotch'. Men who got married in London wearing highland dress were also 'damn Scotch', and so were people who (except at the Caledonian Ball in Park Lane) danced reels south of the border. Whether from politeness or a less commendable feeling of superiority, we never criticized the dress of foreigners, in which category we included the English. They could wear tartan whenever or however they liked.

Christian Miller (1920-)

The Kilt's My Delight

A somewhat more fanciful and romantic view of the kilt.

Wool from the mountain, dyes from the vale;
  Loom in the clachan, peat-fires bright;
To every strand of it some old tale –
  Oh the tartan kilt is my delight!
Went to its spinning brave songs of Lorn,
  Its hues from the berry and herb were spilt;
Lilts of the forest and glee of morn
  Are in his walking who wears the kilt.

For priest, nor clerk, nor merchant men,
  Nor biders at home was the pleating pressed,
But for the loins of those who ken
  Hill-wandering; offspring of the mist,
Wood-trackers, waders of wild streams,
  The world their pillow, their roof the night;

Who sleeps in tartan has high dreams,
Oh the kilt of the Highlands is my delight!

I will put on me that gallant gear,
Brave first garb of the human kind,
Travel the moors and the hills of deer,
And feel on my body the kiss of the wind.
Be it melting heat or the driven sleet,
Kings to stand with or foes to fight,
Dance in the shieling or death to meet,
Oh the darling kilt is my delight!

Neil Munro (1864-1930)

'A Particularly Disagreeable Nation'

Among ourselves, the Scotch, as a nation, are particularly disagreeable. They hate every appearance of comfort themselves and refuse it to others. Their climate, their religion, and their habits are equally averse to pleasure. Their manners are either distinguished by a fawning sycophance (to gain their own ends, and conceal their natural defects), that makes one sick; or by a morose, unbending callousness, that makes one shudder.

William Hazlitt (1778-1830)

The Puddock

The reader must draw his own conclusion as to why this brilliant satirical piece is included in this chapter . . .

A puddock sat by the lochan's brim,
An' he thocht there was never a puddock like him,
He sat on his hurdies, he waggled his legs,
An' cockit his heid as he glowerd throu' the seggs,
The bigsy wee cratur' was feelin' that prood,
He gapit his mou' an' he croakit oot lood:

'Gin ye'd a' like tae see a richt puddock,' quo' he,
'Ye'll never, I'll sweer, get a better nor me.
I've fem'lies an' wives an' a weel-plenished hame,
Wi' drink for my thrapple an' meat for my wame.
The lasses aye thocht me a fine strappin' chiel,
An' I ken I'm a rale bonny singer as weel,
I'm nae gyaun tae blaw, but the truth I maun tell –
I believe I'm the varra MacPuddock himsel'.'

* * *

A heron was hungry an' needin' tae sup,
Sae he nabbit th' puddock and gollup't him up;
Syne runkled his feathers: 'A peer thing,' quo' he,
'But – puddocks is nae fat's they eesed tae be.'

bigsy: *conceited*
cratur':*creature*
glowerd: *scowled*
hurdies: *haunches*
peer: *poor*
runkled: *ruffled*
syne: *then*
chiel: *fellow*
eesed: *used*
gollup't: *gobbled*
nabbit: *seized*
puddock: *frog*
seggs: *reeds*
thrapple: *throat*
wame: *belly*

J. M. Caie (1878-1950)

THE SPREAD OF IAN NICOL

As a result of the publication of his novel Lanark, *Alasdair Gray has not only won wide ranging critical acclaim but also, quite possibly unwittingly, established himself as something of a Scottish guru. This is one of his unlikely short stories. I like to think it says something quite important about the Scots.*

One day Ian Nicol, a riveter by trade, started to split in two down the middle. The process began as a bald patch on the back of his head. For a week he kept smearing it with hair restorer, yet it grew bigger, and the surface became curiously puckered and so unpleasant to look upon that at last he went to his doctor. 'What is it?' he asked.

'I don't know,' said the doctor, 'but it looks like a face, ha, ha! How do you feel these days?'

'Fine. Sometimes I get a stabbing pain in my chest and stomach but only in the morning.'

'Eating well?'

'Enough for two men.'

The doctor thumped him all over with a stethoscope and said, 'I'm going to have you X-rayed. And I may need to call in a specialist.'

Over the next three weeks the bald patch grew bigger still and the suggestion of a face more clearly marked on it. Ian visited his doctor and found a specialist in the consulting room, examining X-ray plates against the light. 'No doubt about it, Nicol,' said the specialist, 'you are splitting in two down the middle.'

Ian considered this.

'That's not usual, is it?' he asked.

'Oh, it happens more than you would suppose. Among bacteria and viruses it's very common, though it's certainly less frequent among riveters. I suggest you go into hospital where the process can complete itself without annoyance for your wife or embarrassment to yourself. Think it over.'

Ian thought it over and went into hospital where he was put into a small ward and given a nurse to attend him, for the specialist was interested in the case. As the division proceeded more specialists were called in to see what was happening. At first Ian ate and drank with a greed that appalled those who saw it. After consuming three times his normal bulk for three days on end he fell into a coma which lasted till the split was complete. Gradually the lobes of his brain separated and a bone shutter formed between them. The face on the back of his head grew eyelashes and a jaw. What seemed at first a cancer of the heart became another heart. Convulsively the spine doubled itself. In a puzzled way the specialists charted the stages of the process and discussed the cause. A German consultant said that life was freeing itself from the vicissitudes of sexual reproduction. A psychiatrist said it was a form of schizophrenia, a psycho-analyst that it was an ordinary twinning process which had been delayed by a severe case of prenatal sibling rivalry. When the split was complete, two thin Ian Nicols lay together on the bed.

The resentment each felt for the other had not been forseen or guarded against. In bed the original Ian Nicol could be recognized by his position (he lay on the right of the bed), but as soon as both men were strong enough to walk each claimed ownership of birth certificate, union card, clothes, wife and National Insurance benefit. One day in the hospital grounds they started fighting. They were evenly matched and there are conflicting opinions about who won. On leaving hospital they took legal action against each other for theft of identity. The case was resolved by a medical examination which showed that one of them had no navel.

The second Ian Nicol changed his name by deed poll and is now called Macbeth. Sometimes he and Ian Nicol write to each other. The latest news is that each has a bald patch on the back of his head.

Alasdair Gray (1934-)

Song of a Small Nation

We Scots are thought a sullen race
Who dwell on evils Calvin made.
Our beauty was *never* Knox's face:
There's far too much that's left unsaid.

'The North's as barren as our mud'
Proclaim the sages who can feel
A nation's pulse without its blood:
They still insuit us while they steal.

If Scots are now frustrated men
It took the Englishmen to raid
A great indigenous culture when
England was thriving in the shade.

The 'hard facts' tell of battles lost –
We lost a good deal more, I feel.
Now we can *use* our past, but first
Let's say: the feudal wound won't heal.

There's far too much that's left unsaid.
They still insult us while they steal;
England was thriving in the shade
Let's say: the feudal wound won't heal.

Alan Bold (1943-)

A Country Without Future?

These gloomy observations were made by Edwin Muir in the mid-thirties and seem to have been amply borne out by subsequent events. Certainly, the reader cannot fail to experience an overpowering feeling of deja vu reading about his return to the shipyard.

He paints a picture of a people who have suffered much with an extraordinary degree of stoicism.

But I should like to put here my main impression, and it is that Scotland is gradually being emptied of its population, its spirit, its wealth, industry, art, intellect, and innate character. This is a sad conculsion; but it has some support on historical grounds. If a country exports its most enterprising spirits and best minds year after year, for fifty or a hundred or two hundred years, some result will inevitably follow.

England gives some scope for its best; Scotland gives none; and by now its large towns are composed of astute capitalists and angry proletarians, with nothing that matters much in between. Edinburgh is a partial exception to this; but Edinburgh is a handsome, empty capital of the past. And as no civilisation that is composed merely of exploiters and exploited can endure for long, Glasgow, Dundee, Aberdeen, and Greenock are now following Edinburgh. They are monuments of Scotland's industrial past, historical landmarks in a country which is becoming lost to history.

Edwin Muir (1887-1959)

Scotched

Scotch God
Kent His
Faither.

Scotch Religion
Damn
Aa.

Scotch Education
I tellt ye
I tellt ye.

Scotch Queers
Wha peys wha
– For what?

Scotch Prostitution
Dear,
Dear.

Scotch Liberty
Agree
Wi me.

Scotch Equality
Kaa the feet frae
Thon big bastard.

Scotch Fraternity
Our mob uses
The same razor.

Scotch Optimism
Through a gless,
Darkly.

Scotch Pessimism
Nae
Gless.

Scotch Initiative
Eftir
You.

Scotch Generosity
Eftir
Me.

Scotch Sex
In atween
Drinks.

Scotch Passion
Forgot
Mysel.

Scotch Free-Love
Canna be
Worth much.

Scotch Lovebirds
Cheap
Cheap.

Scotch Fractions
A hauf
'n' a hauf.

Scotch Afternoon-Tea
Masked
Pot.

Scotch Drink
Nip
Trip.

Scotch Poets
Wha's the
T'ither

Alexander Scott (1920-)

The Red Fellows

Naomi Mitchison is justly regarded as a shrewd observer of her fellow human beings against all sorts of international backgrounds. Here she is very much at home as she superbly distills the Highland character – both male and female – in a tale of guile outwitted by a very clever but far from untypical Scots lassie.

"An so they are giving five pounds a head for the red fellows! Well, well." Toddlebonny sank his nose in the glass. It was likely that he was doing his bit of thinking. Even today a good pound note, weary with handling maybe, but the name of an ancient and reputed Scots Bank over it, is gey handy in a bar, and five of them would stretch the best part of a week. And a bar was Toddlebonny's favourite place. Not that he might not be found among the brackens at odd times or leaning against a dyke considering. Ploys came in and out of his mind. It had only been the evening before that the farmers had decided that if they could all get together and give a right good-going bonus, they would get rid of the foxes altogether and be easier in their minds about the lambs. For the lambing would begin any day now in the lower fields and the hill ewes a fortnight later. And why should this good money find its way only into the pockets of certain ones? Toddlebonny began to think aloud on this matter, after a look around the bar. For it had become public knowledge by now.

"I was thinking that Big Willie was getting well above himself, speaking the way he'd have the money in the bank!" said a crony of his. He, the same as Toddlebonny, had been in the merchant navy in the old days, and later on at the fishing – Cod Eye he was mostly called.

"Ah, keepers! Big Willie MacDonald and they smart visitors in their tweeds and all."

"Big Willie would be the first to know where the vixens could be, if there were one or two in the plantings. Would you say now, Toddlebonny, that they would pay the five pounds right enough for the young ones? A vixen is a bonny beast, so she is, and a shame to be killing her. She might have thirty pounds inside of her, aye, that she might."

Toddlebonny considered. "Aye, now, I was thinking, the schoolmaster was after telling me – oh, a whilie back before any word of all this. Nature, he called it. There was this vixen he had sighted. I'd kept it in mind, for a wee fact will come in handy one day or another. Aye. So if one had a place. Kind of quiet. Like yon old shed of yours at the back. You would hardly be needing it today."

"Where I have my nets lying." Cod Eye smiled to himself. "Aye, aye, a nice soft place is a tangle of old nets."

"So long as you're not coorying down to the fish hooks!"

"Ah, but I always had a sweet regard for a nice wee bot! And it was never myself on the under side. Sure as you're there, many a pleasant hour – aye, thanks, Toddlebonny, I'll take a wee hauf. But what at all had you in mind?"

"Well, one could make good use of a shed. Cod Eye, though I'm loath to distract you from pleasing memories of torn knickers. We could be doing the thing between us."

"Aye, so we could. But what thing?"

"Man, are you not hearing me right? The money's the same for the cubs and I know well enough that Big Willie is keeping back a vixen maybe this one the schoolmaster had a sight of, and why wouldn't he?"

"Aye, so he would if you were him, Toddlebonny. But is a keeper the same made as ourselves?"

"Ah, don't be daft, Cod Eye! We'll need a noose and gloves and a strong sack. And to watch. We must choose our night and go cannily about it. We can't have her strangled and her so useful to us." They had moved down from the bar now to one of the wee tables. There was nobody listening, nobody at all.

"But if he sees?" Cod Eye whispered into his glass.

"I said watch. And he has his weaknesses."

"Aye indeed. And one is for my own niece. Dugaldina, the one that's in the Glasgow office. And she forever coming down for the weekend. And cleaning! You'd think she wanted to make a hospital out of me."

"Well now, isn't that the Lord's Providence at work!"

Indeed that was the way it seemed to both of them, and now it was the weekend. Cod Eye had taken his niece Dugaldina with him to the kirk. He himself had been in the choir now for the best part of forty years and his voice was not just what it had been once, but they were a kindly lot and nobody wanting to say a word to hurt him. Dugaldina was getting the dinner ready, for she and her chum Sheila from the same office would need to get the afternoon bus back to Glasgow. "What's the matter with your wrist, Uncle Dougal?" asked Dugaldina. She hadn't noticed it till just now, but some way it had been a full weekend. This chum of hers, Sheila, had been trying to persuade Big Willie to read *Lady Chatterley's Lover* and the both of them in mad giggles, for there was Willie trying to get round Sheila to tell him just what it was about the book that would do him good to read, for he was not that keen on reading. Ach, what a Saturday evening and a nice change from the office! Most weekends when she came, she managed to give her uncle's house a bit clean out, but not this time; she'd barely lifted a brush.

"I'd a bit scrape on a barbed wire" her uncle said, "but it's nothing. No, no, you've no need to look, I put plenty on it." He was fond of the lassie and it had been great the way she and Big Willie had spent the whole evening together, but some way he was wishing she would say goodbye. In case she heard anything. But why should she? They had gone about it cannily and no one to see. The poor beastie had been half strangled, but quick enough with her teeth till they got her tied right. And now she was in the shed with plenty warm bedding and as many soup bones from the butcher's as she could get her teeth into, and soon there'd be wee five pound notes popping out of her.

It was two weekends after and a great feel of spring and scent of flowers and young leaves, and the first lambs crying out for their mothers and the clumsy, clot-fleeced lumps of black-face ewes butting their way through to the right lamb. But Big Wille was in the worst of tempers. Dugaldina couldn't make out at all what was wrong or why he was miscalling the whole glen, for he had not exactly explained to her about the fox bounty nor how that vixen had gone missing. It could have upset a lassie the like of her. Dugaldina had looked forward to a long, sunny Saturday afternoon and into the evening and a certain spot a wee bit up the burn, where you could stare up through the young leaves once you were lying easy there. Ah well, it hadn't gone right. He had seemed – nasty. You felt you couldn't trust him if he had you alone. He'd try and work something off on you. No, she wouldn't go with him in the mood he was in. They had words and she'd gone off saying she was through unless he'd come over and say he was sorry. So she was back early. She came to the back and there was her uncle and his old crony Toddlebonny unlocking the shed at the end of the garden beyond the blackcurrant and raspberry bushes and the rhubarb. She though she might as well get a few sticks of rhubarb for the supper; maybe she would get a drop of cream from the farm. See there, the old man hadn't even bothered himself to take out the old raspberry canes! He was slipping, him. And what at all were they looking at in the shed? She'd just go along. Well! Weren't they the cutest, sweetest, darlingest wee things – "Uncle Dougal, where did they come from?"

"Quick now!" And Toddlebonny was quickest. "Well now, 'Dina, this is the way it was. We found the poor mother hurt, someone must have had a shot at her so we brought her in – near dead, was she no', Cod Eye? We fed her, for one couldn't let her starve, but neither of us expecting she'd live, and now, see, the bonny wee red fellows she's brought us!"

The vixen flattened her ears, growling and showed sharp teeth. She was used more or less to Cod Eye and Toddlebonny, but here was a new one and her cubs were not to be touched! Dugaldina moved back quickly: "What are you going to do with them, Uncle Dougal?"

"Well now, I haven't just thought right, but mind, not a cheep to yon Willie MacDonald. He'd be black angry, two poor old men the like of ourselves taking care of one of his foxes."

"Aye, that's the God's truth," said Toddlebonny, "so you'll not let slip a word?"

"It's not likely I'll be speaking to Willie MacDonald," she said, with a cold kind of look, "he's none of mine."

"Never tell me he thinks more of yon Sheila than of yourself!"

"No, it's not that. Not at all." She looked away at the rhubarb. "I'm just fed up with him. Let him come and find me if he wants!"

Toddlebonny glanced at Cod Eye; clear as day the two had quarrelled and the one thing they couldn't have was Big Willie coming round after her. "No, no," said Cod Eye, "keep you your pride, lassie. Tell him, just, if he comes smelling after you, that he'll not set foot inside the gate! Aye, that'll fix him."

She didn't answer. Did she want to unfix him? Men! If she'd had Sheila with her they could have talked it over, but Sheila needed to go and see her folks an odd weekend. She made supper, the old man doing his best to cheer her up talking of the years he'd been in the merchant navy and the ploys he was on in foreign ports, and she wondering all the time how different the stories would have been if he'd been telling them to another man. For indeed there was this hiding and cheating going on half the time and fine if it didn't go too far, but could you count on that?

Maybe she'd be best not to think of Big Willie for a while. After all there were boys in the office she could go out with. But some way they hadn't the same feel.

Sure enough, Big Willie came the next day when she was just finished with the Sabbath dinner dishes. He stood at the gate, pressed on the latch, was coming in as though he owned the place! But she went out to meet him and her uncle Dougal watched anxiously from behind the front room curtains. The man had his dog with him and if the dog was to smell – but 'Dina was standing her ground, good lassie! Aye, even with the window shut, he could hear her voice, sharp and angry. He licked his lips. And there, the man was away.

She came back in. "Uncle Dougal!" she said, "Willie has told me about the fox bounty and he's accusing you of stealing the vixen and I, Lord forgive me, I said I'd cleaned out the whole place and not a trace of a fox."

"That's my clever lassie," he said, "my good, loyal lassie!"

But didn't she burst into tears: "I lied to him, I'm as bad as yourself, I'm worse! He'll never – we'll never – go away Uncle Dougal, don't touch me, I've seen through you and I hate you!"

Och the lassies! What is a man to do? If himself had been forty years younger or thirty even, and her not his sister's lassie – but, Lord in Heaven, such thoughts were not seemly! Not a word out of her till bus time and then another month till she came back, this time with her chum, the Sheila lassie. Tight-lipped, she seemed. He had tried to make his peace and listened for a sign of it – aye, there they were giggling away in the toproom! "Did you like what I got for you, then?" he asked, for she was carrying the big box of chocolates – and, Lord Almighty, the price of it, but there, it came out of the five pounds, his share of the ten! – with yon bonny picture of roses and a pink ribbon. And then the wee bonnet. "I though, just, with the bit of tartan and yon feather, you would suit it great!"

"Uncle Dougal," she said, "you shouldn't have – you with just your pension! But – " And here she stopped and looked round at Sheila and made a face. "– but I suppose it was –"

"Och, not all all," he said, "not at all! Aren't you my own good, kind lassie!"

"Well," she said, "I'll wear it to the kirk tomorrow, but you'll not mind if I take off the tartan and pin on a piece of material I've got by me. It's just a thought too bright for my costume."

"Anything at all!" he said, "And come your ways over to the table. I've these lettuces from my own wee patch and a bit fish, better than you'll get in Glasgow." He kept wondering, had she said a word to Sheila? Maybe not. Ah, the craft of the creatures!

After their tea anyway, Sheila went off to pick flowers; there was a carpet, just, in the woods. And Dugaldina said to her uncle: "Now we'll go and see the red fellows."

"Ach well –"

"That's what we'll do," said his niece and gave him a hard look. He got the key and they went down the path past the rhubarb; he unlocked the door. "There were seven last time," she said, counting the cubs. Bright-eyed, pretty, soft, making baby growls and pounces.

"Ah well, two of them died, a pure shame it was," lied Cod Eye. But she did not soften, not at all, just stood looking in a daft kind of way. "You'll not say a word –" he began anxiously.

But she shut him up. "Willie would have killed them just the same as yourself." They were playing together now, twenty-five pounds worth of wee foxes. She turned her back.

It was a grievous weekend for Cod Eye and no chance of speaking to Toddlebonny until the Monday. But they got together at last. "Man," said Toddlebonny, "what at all has gone wrong?"

"Well, this is it," said Cod Eye. "The besom must have watched where I put the key in below the sugar in my blue tin. Aye, she saw and she must have gone out in the night and let them all out. And you and me giving her those sweeties and the bonnet – I wish it might burn her ears off!"

"The wicked, ungrateful lassie! When did you get to know, Cod Eye?"

"Och, just before church time and she and her chum were already down the kirk road and not possible for a thing to be said. But the psalm nigh choked me! And when we were back there was little enough I could say in front of her chum, for they'd the dinner ready and then left together for the bus."

"Thirty pounds," said Toddlebonny, shaking his head, "and all our troubles feeding her, the ungrateful brute, just to skedaddle when the door was opened! Ach, I'm half hoping Big Willie will shoot her, it would serve her right!"

"And me with my wrist bitten and a new lock on my shed and all," mourned Cod Eye. Sadness fell on them both.

"But I've a notion," said Toddlebonny, "surely we might start breeding dogs? There's the shed and all. If we sold the pups it would be away nicer than killing them."

"Aye, there's that. If I had not kept my mind steady on the money it would have been beyond me, the poor wee fellows. Pups? If there was a market. But Big Willie is forever getting them off yon Labrador bitch of his –"

"Ah, but the summer visitors will go for wee terriers, half the price to feed. But did she say nothing, the lassie? I can scarcely credit it, and you her own uncle."

Cod Eye shook his head. "Ach, all she said was: 'cheatery will never thrive' – and her going off to Glasgow with my wee bonnet and the great box of sweeties under her arm!"

Naomi Mitchison (1897-)

CHAPTER 2

EDINBURGH

The Beauty of Edinburgh

Living in Edinburgh there abides, above all things, a sense of its beauty. Hill, crag, castle, rock, blue stretch of sea, the picturesque ridge of the Old Town, the squares and terraces of the New – these things seen once are not to be forgotten. The quick life of to-day sounding around the relics of antiquity, and overshadowed by the august traditions of a Kingdom, makes residence in Edinburgh more impressive than residence in any other British city. I have just come in – surely it never looked so fair before! What a poem is that Princes Street! The puppets of the busy, many-coloured hour move about on its pavements, while across the ravine Time has piled up the Old Town, ridge on ridge, grey as a rocky coast washed and worn by the foam of centuries; peaked and jagged by gable and roof; windowed from basement to cope; the whole surmounted by St. Giles's airy crown. The New is there looking at the Old. Two Times are brought face to face, and are yet separated by a thousand years. Wonderful on winter nights, when the gully is filled with darkness, and out of it rises, against the sombre blue and the frosty stars, that mass and bulwark of gloom, pierced and quivering with innumerable lights. There is nothing in Europe to match that, I think.

Alexander Smith (1830-67)

Another Beauty of Edinburgh

But though the bleak air of this Climate may give, as it is said to do, that keen penetrating look to the inhabitants, which they certainly possess, as well as great activity of body, they are far from being healthy in general. I have scarce met with one instance of remarkable longevity amongst all the people I have seen, and there are very few places where you observe more funerals. Whether this is to be attributed entirely to the climate, or in some part to the College of Physicians, who are very eminent in their profession, I leave you to determine for yourself.

There is one circumstance here which certainly deserves notice, as it is a contradiction to all the rules which are laid down in regard to climates; I mean, the early maturity of their women. It is generally imagined that cold has the same degree of influence over the animal, as it has over the vegetable world; but in this country they are in direct opposition; for the plants are very late, and the girls extremely forward.

Edward Topham (1751-1820)

Northern Goddesses

The ladies of Edinburgh possess a more graceful deportment than those of London; they are at once slenderer and more fragile. Up to the present time I have found among them fewer laughing Hebes than haughty Junos and stately-walking Dianas . . . To grace of figure the young ladies of Edinburgh add, for the most part, the charm of some agreeable talents. There are few of them who are not musicians, and who are deficient in extraordinary skill in the labours of the needle; there are few of them also unacquainted with French.

Amedée Pichot (1822)

One cannot but be conscious of an underlying melancholy in Scotswomen. This melancholy is peculiarly attractive in the ballroom, where it gives a singular piquancy to the enthusiasm and earnestness that they put into their national dances.

Stendhal (1783-1842)

Edinburgh after Flodden

When news of the defeat of Flodden reached the capital, most of the women, and all the men left, were pressed into service to defend the threatened city.

Forasmuch as there is great rumour now lately risen within this town, touching our Sovereign Lord and his army, of which we understand there has come no verity as yet, wherefore we charge strictly and command in our said Sovereign Lord the King's name, and in that of the Presidents for the Provosts and Baillies within this burgh, that all manner of persons, townsmen within the same, have ready their arms of defence and weapons for war, and appear therewith before the said Presidents at the tolling of the common bell, for the keeping and defence of the town against them that would invade the same. And we also charge that all women, and especially vagabonds, that they pass to their labours, and be not seen upon the street clamouring and crying, under the pain of banishing of their persons without favour, and that the other women of better sort pass to the kirk and pray, when time requires, for our Sovereign Lord and his army, and the townsmen who are with the army; and that they hold them at their private labours off the streets within their houses, as becometh.

Municipal Proclamation, September 10, 1513

Welcome to Harriet Beecher Stowe

As sung at the Banquet given her in Edinburgh, on Wednesday, 20th April 1853.

Come, Scotland, tune your stock and horn,
And hail with song this joyous morn,
When on Love's eagle pinions borne,
Harriet Beecher Stowe's come.

Chorus: Freedom's angel now's come,
Mercy's sister now's come,
Grim Oppression drees his doom:
Harriet Beecher Stowe's come.

Through hostile ranks our sires of yore,
Fair Freedom's flag unsullied bore,
And still she fills our bosom's core:
Harriet Beecher Stowe's come.

A woman's arm Truth's falchion bears,
A sweet low voice stern Conscience fears,

And stony hearts dissolve in tears:
      Harriet Beecher Stowe's come.

And far as rolls the ocean wave,
Is heard that voice now raised to save,
Alike the slaver and the slave:
      Harriet Beecher Stowe's come.

And tyrants scared the writing scan,
O'er-arching heaven with rainbow span,
MAN HATH NO PROPERTY IN MAN:
      Harriet Beecher Stowe's come.

Then welcome be that honoured name,
So dear to freedom and to fame;
Come, rend the welkin with acclaim:
      Harriet Beecher Stowe's come.

James Ballantine (1808-77)

AN AMERICAN TRAVELLER

Salvation by Hume

Dear Friend, Edinburgh, Oct. 27. 1771

Thro' Storms and Floods I arrived here on Saturday night, late, and was lodg'd miserably at an Inn; But that excellent Christian David Hume, agreable to the Precepts of the Gospel, has *received the Stranger,* and I now live with him at his House in the new Town most happily. I purpose staying about a Fortnight, and shall be glad to hear from you. I congratulate you on certain political Events that I know give you Pleasure. Let me know how it is with you and yours, how my Wife does, and Sir John Pringle, and our other Friends. With sincerest Esteem I am, my dear Friend, Yours most affectionately

B FRANKLIN
Benjamin Franklin (1706-90)

An Edinburgh Childhood

This is taken from a delightful book, published when the author was over 90 years of age, and which vividly recalls an Edinburgh childhood in the last quarter of the nineteenth century. The author's father followed the legal profession, becoming a Sheriff, and they lived in a grand Georgian house in the centre of Edinburgh.

A little girl of three, both her hands stretched up and held by a grown-up person on either side, gazed along what seemed an endless vista of broad grey street. Such is an early, vague memory of myself and of what I came to know as 'York Place'. As the years passed, that memory became the background of many memories, more definite, more solid, indelible, perhaps eternal.

61 York Place, Edinburgh, the home of my youth, with the shallow, stone steps leading up to the wide, dignified door. A wide front door has ever to me a welcoming air, a promise of hospitality, kindly and generous. And indeed up those steps came, through the years, many a gay guest, passing on through the wide door flung open to receive them, into the warm and gracious hall, and upstairs to the bright lights, the voices and laughter, of the drawing-room.

Immediately opposite to the house, across what to my childish eyes was an immense width, paved with grey stone 'setts', stood St. Paul's church – our church, to which, even when very young, we were taken every Sunday by my father, the Sheriff. St. Paul's was on the sunny side of the street, facing the south. '61' faced the cold north, and if St. Paul's had not been there we could have seen, from our drawing-room windows, down the long slope of trees and houses away to the grey Forth and across to the Fife hills. On many a cold autumn night have I stood at one of those windows and watched the flashing and flickering of the Northern Lights above St. Paul's.

The street ran east and west, the north side on a lower level than the south, and its tall grey houses had, I think, a greater air of aristocratic aloofness than those on our side, where some had been made into flats, and had common stairs. One of these common stairs was next door to '61', leading up to a flat which by rights should have been the top part of our house. The people living in that flat used to have dances, and as our nursery was just below the room they danced in, often and often have I lain awake through the long evening listening to the strumming of a piano overhead, and the thumping of feet, which so shook the ceiling that I lay in constant dread lest it should come crashing down on me and Louis. But these York Place houses were built with walls so solid, with floors so strong and yet so elastic, that not even a crack showed in the plaster.

The two tall windows of the big nursery looked south, over the backgreen to a lane, ever to me mysterious, for the high wall hid it, and the door in the wall was never open that I can remember. But there were sounds that came from the lane: the rattle of the coal carts on dark winter mornings, and the coalman's harsh cry, in untuneful seconds, 'Ca-ool! Ca-ool!'

At the far side of the lane, just beyond our wall, could be seen the side-wall and windows of the Roman Catholic pro-cathedral, and the door and windows of the Priests' House. Beyond these, and dominating them, rose the high roof of the Theatre Royal. We were close enough to hear sometimes the shouts and clapping of hands; and I remember the dreadful noise at, I think, the destruction of Nineveh, in the play of 'Sardanapalus'. Charlie had been taken to see it, probably on its first night, and then gave us so graphic a description of its excitement and terror, that for the rest of the week of its performance in the theatre, when the sound of the yells and crashes in the final scene shook the quiet of the darkened nursery, I held my breath in fear. Different indeed was the Sunday sound of the organ and choir in the pro-Cathedral, especially on the Sunday of the week when the Carl Rosa Opera Company were performing in the theatre, for members of it used on that day to sing in the choir. In this way came perhaps some of my earliest musical thrills, when Handel's 'Hallelujah Chorus' rang out in, to me, an unaccustomed glory of sound, across the lane and the backgreen, and in at the nursery windows, tremendous above the low thunder of the organ.

About the roof of the Theatre Royal there comes to me a clear and startling memory. One Saturday morning, when I was about five years old, in coming in from our morning walk with Ann, the nursery door was opened, and we stood suddenly aghast, staring at the familiar room lit up by a strange and terrifying crimson glow. Louis and I rushed to the window, crying out at the sight of the leaping flames and columns of thick smoke rising from the theatre roof. I remember the excited interest of everyone, and the exclamations of Ann and the other maids as the roof fell in with a crash: my father's uneasiness as the window-panes grew hot: the coming in of a fireman to see that all was safe: and the restless night that followed that day of alarms, with the noise of engines and the crackle of fire lasting well into the night: the shouts in the street, and then the dawn breaking with the acrid smell of burnt and smouldering ruins.

There was an aspect of this theatre fire that filled the minds of those about me, and which therefore impressed itself deeply on my mind. Charlie and I had been in the theatre the very night before the fire, watching the Pantomime from the stage box, and had been taken at the end behind the scenes by Mr. and Mrs. Wyndham, and had gazed, thrilled and wondering, up into the dark spaces of ropes and pulleys and huge canvas. And the next day all these were smoking ruins. According to everyone, Charlie and I had a marvellous escape. Indeed Aunt Louisa, who thought theatres were wicked places, was convinced that it was only by a special mercy of Providence that we had not been burnt alive with the theatre.

Eleanor Sillar (1870-?)

Cable Car Days

What created greater consternation in our young minds during those first few weeks in Auld Reekie than the cable-cars that, not so very long before, had displaced the horse-trams? Those vehicles, it would seem, were already obsolete at the time of their installation. Yet, this fair city had to tolerate them for about twenty years. On the level and uphill, they could travel no faster than the cable, underground. This, to our immense delight, was not as swiftly as we could run, and gave us a sense of superiority in at least one sphere in our new environment. But we could not compete with them when they rattled downhill, under gravity, unlawfully free of the cable. What with the taking off and the putting on of the gripper wheel at every terminus, what with the eternal changing of cables everywhere *en route* by the winding and rewinding of that primitive, purring arrangement, municipal transport in the Scottish Capital was incredibly slow. When a cable snapped, as so often happened, the entire life of the city seemed at a standstill. In course of time, a breakdown gang lingered wearily from the tramway depôt at Tollcross to locate the trouble – no easy matter – and rectify it. When two cables failed at the same time, the city assumed an aspect of semi-paralysis. Something resembling naval manœuvres, with squadrons of miniature vessels anchored immovably in straight lines, now ensued in the herculean effort to lever at least some of the vehicles on to such sections of the system as were still functioning. Eventually, the citizens adopted the line of least irritation: they developed the habit of walking. No one in a hurry sat on in an Edinburgh tramcar when anything delayed it for more than a few seconds. At the first hint of a stoppage, one readily recognized which passengers were residents and which were strangers. The latter sat on in vain hope: the former, inured by long experience, and without a symptom of surprise or impatience, rose and proceeded to their respective destinations on foot. Taxi-cabs were still a novelty in Auld Reekie, so that the more *élite* moved from place to place by horse-cab – by the old growler – unless they were in a position to hire a motor vehicle from an undertaker's. The approach of summer, however, brought fleets of hansom-cabs from winter storage. These now appeared with a freshness imparted by a thorough spring-cleaning and the liberal use of fresh paint, and were in great demand among American tourists.

Those old cable-cars of ours were eminently safe. They simply could not have left the metals if they had wanted to, unless fore and aft gripper had snapped simultaneously, which was as unlikely as anything in the world. You may well imagine that, with a system so admirably designed to prevent recklessness in driving – a system so rigorously opposed to anything that might rob our thoroughfares of their age-long decorum – street accidents were exceedingly rare. Our tramways became the subject of music-hall jokes throughout the realm. And, when the minimum fare was raised to twopence for a distance one could cover on foot in a few minutes, Glasgow, our rival in matters municipal, derived much satisfaction from her electrical system, with its minimum halfpenny fare. But, if the City Fathers, through lack of foresight, had to retain this antiquated mode of transport, sorely trying our patience for more years than we like to remember, it ultimately brought us the well-earned compensation of one of the speediest and most luxurious tramway systems in the country.

Alasdair Alpin MacGregor (1889-1970)

Talking with Five Thousand People in Edinburgh

This extraordinarily powerful poem by Hugh MacDiarmid (Christopher Murray Grieve) first appeared in Poetry Scotland No. 2 in 1945. It displays all those characteristics which have marked out MacDiarmid as a world class literary figure with its powerful polemicism and accomplished lyricism.

Talking with five thousand people in Edinburgh yesterday
I was appalled at their lack of love for each other,
At their lack of ecstasy at the astounding miracle
Of being alive in the flesh and together with one another,
And amazed that men and women each superficially so different
Should be so obviously the product of the same temperament,
Dyed in the same vat to a uniform hue.
In each the mood, the atmosphere, the peculiar nature
Of the tension produced, all the intangibles in fact,
Were almost identical – the same unresolved discords,
The same sultry hates, the same murderous impulses
Below the surface of decorous lives, the same
Hopeless struggle against an evil no one dares name
– The same growing understanding that the substitute names
They use for it are wide of the mark, that the name must be
  spoken,
That it will be impossible soon not to speak it out plump and
  plain,
The whole five thousand of them, as with a single voice.
But yesterday I listened to the mutual criticisms,
The sneers, the belittlings, the cynical acceptances,
Misunderstandings, indifferences, looking down their noses,
Pursing their mouths, giving meaning looks, till I saw all these
  people
As specialists in hates and frustrations, students of helpless rages,
Articulators of inarticulate loathings, and suddenly understood
That the trouble was no one knew where the centre lay
Of the system of discontent in which they were pent,
All emotionally suspended and dubious
(Saying all sorts of things with the single exception
Of what they ought to be saying – what they needed to say;
Their powers of speech all hopelessly misapplied)
Because their talk evaded, deserted, their real theme.

They expressed themselves in despairs, doubts, grumblings and fears.
None of them had yet made clear contact with the sources of his or her power.
They were all fascinated by their hatred of something – but of what?
The passion of that nameless hatred got itself partially expressed
By seizing on this or that – on anything – in lieu of its true object.
These were occasions for the rages but not the causes.
Edinburgh produces and sustains agonising tensions of life
– Edinburgh, a blinded giant who has yet to learn
What the motive spirit behind his abilities really is.

So that as I spoke with these five thousand people
Each of us was more or less lost
In the midst of the events so powerfully presented.
All who should help to open the way for true expression
– The teachers, the ministers, the writers – are living like maggots
On dead words in an advanced state of decomposition,
Big words that died over twenty years ago
– For most of the important words were killed in the First World War –
And Edinburgh has not given birth to new words yet
In which it can say anything worth saying, make anything but animal noises.
Edinburgh – But Edinburgh is no worse than anywhere else;
All the big centres of mankind are like thunder-clouds to-day
Forming part of the horrific structure of a storm
That fills the whole sky – but ere long
Will disappear like the fabric of a dream.

Perhaps Edinburgh's terrible inability to speak out,
Edinburgh's silence with regard to all it should be saying,
Is but the hush that precedes the thunder,
The liberating detonation so oppressively imminent now?
For what are its people standing in their own light,
Denying life infinitely more abundant,
Preferring darkness to light, and death to life?
Edinburgh is capable here and now of a human life
As illimitably greater than any it has yet known,
As any human being's is to the lowest order of animal existence.

All they need to do is to lift up their hearts
And conceive nobler conditions of life, acquire
The feelings which will give forms to such a life, and at once
The necessary organs of these will appear,
Just as life at first put out arms and legs.
All they need to do is to be true to themselves
And not like some foolish woman who cries
There's thunder in the air and stuffs her ears with cotton wool
And goes to bed and hides herself under the blankets
Afraid of the thunder and lightning – the bridegroom who
  enters in.

There is no one really alive in Edinburgh yet.
They are all living on the tiniest fraction
Of the life they could easily have,
Like people in great houses who prefer
To live in their cellars and keep all the rest sealed up.

There is nothing to prevent them except themselves
Having all that the mind of man can know
Or the heart of man conceive.

Total strangers to all the events
Taking place around and in and through them.
No one with either the scientific training
Or the courage and desire to learn
What is going on beneath the surface of life.

Few, if any, of life's collisions here
Are on the purely individual plane.
There is no general scheme behind it,
No real general purpose,
No genuine fighting spirit.
Is there no one to fight this decline of honour,
This hypocrisy, meanness, and boredom?

Let the demagogues denounce me, and betray me too
As Burns was betrayed and Bakunin and Maclean;
Serve me as Utin served Marx, with vile slanders to expel
Bakunin and James Guillaume. *Veritas odium parit.*
Friends, you know. I am guilty of it. Let it rest.
At the worst, *in magnis et voluisse sat est.*

I stand to my position, do what I can,
And will never be turned into a 'strong, silenced man,'
For I am corn and not chaff, and will neither
Be blown away by the wind, nor burst with the flail,
  But will abide them both
  And in the end prevail.

For I am like Zamyatin. I must be a Bolshevik
Before the Revolution, but I'll cease to be one quick
When Communism comes to rule the roost,
For real literature can exist only where it's produced
By madmen, hermits, heretics,
Dreamers, rebels, sceptics,
– And such a door of utterance has been given to me
As none may close whosoever they be.

Let a look at Edinburgh be called
Just an educational film then
Such as we see any day on the screen.
'The Abortion,' say, or 'Why Does It Rain?'
Or 'How Silk Stockings Are Made,' or, finally,
'What Is the Difference Between A Man and A Beaver?'

It's far too late in the day
  For a fellow like this
Trying to organise a conspiracy of feelings
  In Edinburgh of all places.

Let us fall in with the wishes of Authority,
Hush to treasonable rubbish like 'The Red Flag';
Let us study – and in the end be content to be
Each of us no better than a carted stag.

Hugh MacDiarmid/C. M. Grieve (1892-1978)

The Lamplighter

From his boyhood home in Edinburgh's Heriot Row the young Stevenson would watch the lamplighter on his nightly round. It was to be a strong, recurring image.

My tea is nearly ready, and the sun has left the sky;
It's time to take the window to see Leerie going by;
For every night at tea-time and before your take your seat,
With lantern and with ladder he comes posting up the street.

Now Tom would be a driver and Maria go to sea,
And my papa's a banker and as rich as he can be;
But I, when I am stronger and can choose what I'm to do,
O Leerie, I'll go round at night and light the lamps with you.

For we are very lucky, with a lamp before the door,
And Leerie stops to light it as he lights so many more;
And O! before you hurry by with ladder and with light,
O Leerie, see a little child and nod to him tonight.

Robert Louis Stevenson (1850-94)

A View from Calton Hill

An ice age glacier carved this footstool
To crag and tail formation, pimpled now
With small observatories squinting
Through sodium-stained night skies
I look the other way, observe the town

There stood the house where Robert Burns
Over a dish of tea paid illicit court
To Clarinda, such a genteel perfidy
And he to romp and carouse with scullions
Later in the noisome howffs of Canongate

Below a highway roars where once
The whores silently bawled their wares
Pimps flickered darkly, drunk seamen
Fought in the polyglot street and the Law
Looked on bemused as keepers in a zoo

Across the chasm where a Georgian square
Was toppled, once shabby but dignified
Like a bereft duchess down on her luck
A lump of hound-patrolled Chicago
Now blocks a view of hills and home

Tower blocks gather on city fringes
Wait till numbers increase before advancing
Already their spies the cranes have alighted
Are selecting morsels of the living town
We are taught not to complain of progress

And behind those towers loom shadows
Are they the shadows of unbuilt towers
Rank upon rank of them advancing
Like a wall, a tidal wave of shadows
Is it the Ice again, so soon?

Stanley Roger Green (1929-)

CHAPTER 3

GLASGOW

I Belong to Glasgow (Chorus)

Will Fyffe, born in Dundee, became one of the most accomplished and best loved pantomime comedians of his day.

I belong to Glasgow
Dear Old Glasgow town!
But what's the matter with Glasgow?
For it's going round and round.
I'm only a common old working chap,
As anyone can see,
But when I get a couple of drinks on a Saturday,
Glasgow belongs to me.

Will Fyffe (1885-1947)

You Lived in Glasgow

You lived in Glasgow many years ago.
I do not find your breath in the air.
It was, I think, in the long-skirted thirties
when idle men stood at every corner
chewing their fag-ends of a failed culture.
Now I sit here in George Square
where the War Memorial's yellow sword glows bright
and the white stone lions mouth at bus and car.
A maxi-skirted girl strolls slowly by.
I turn and look. It might be you. But no.
Around me there's a 1970 sky.

Everywhere there are statues. Stone remains.
The mottled flesh is transient. On those trams,
invisible now but to the mind, you bore
your groceries home to the 1930 slums.
'There was such warmth,' you said. The gaslight hums
and large caped shadows tremble on the stair.
Now everything is brighter. Pale ghosts walk
among the spindly chairs, the birchen trees.

In lights of fiercer voltage you are less
visible than when in winter you
walked, a black figure, through the gaslight blue.

The past's an experience that we cannot share.
Flat-capped Glaswegians and the Music Hall.
Apples and oranges on an open stall.
A day in the country. And the sparkling Clyde
splashing its local sewage at the wall.
This April day shakes memories in a shade
opening and shutting like a parasol.
There is no site for the unshifting dead.
You're buried elsewhere though your flickering soul
is a constant tenant of my tenement.

You were happier here than anywhere, you said.
Such fine good neighbours helping when your child
almost died of croup. Those pleasant Wildes
removed with the fallen rubble have now gone
in the building programme which renews each stone.
I stand in a cleaner city, better fed,
in my diced coat, brown hat, my paler hands
leafing a copy of the latest book.
Dear ghosts, I love you, haunting sunlit winds,
dear happy dented ghosts, dear prodigal folk.

I left you, Glasgow, at the age of two
and so you are my birthplace just the same.
Divided city of the green and blue
I look for her in you, my constant aim
to find a ghost within a close who speaks
in Highland Gaelic.
                    The bulldozer breaks
raw bricks to powder. Boyish workmen hang
like sailors in tall rigging. Buildings sail
into the future. The old songs you sang
fade in their pop songs, scale on dizzying scale.

Iain Crichton Smith (1928-   )

Trial Trip

Leslie Pagan, whose yard is faced with imminent closure in the depression of the thirties, takes his last ship down the Clyde and reflects bitterly on the collapse of hopes and dreams for bosses and workers alike.

The *Estramadura* went down the river on the Wednesday afternoon, and Leslie Pagan travelled with her.

He was busy and preoccupied while the tugs moved her from the basin in their fussily efficient way. She was still his own, and the more precious for being the last he had in that kind. His heart was in his mouth when her cruiser-stern cleared the pierhead with only a foot to spare. He was haunted by daft fears that this winch would not function and that bollard fail to hold the pull of the tow-ropes. The extinction of a series of lights on the promenade deck at one moment gave him the panic notion that the dynamos had broken down. Knowing well that the apprehension was excessive, he was haunted by a sense of the fallibility of the intricate and interdependent mechanisms of the ship; her security, the thousands of pounds of value she represented, resting perhaps on an abraded inch of insulation on a mile or so of electric cable.

As soon, however, as she was fair in mid-channel, her head downstream and her beautiful light hull towering over the riverside buildings, he suddenly resigned his creation to chance and the skill of the pilot. At another time he would have been fretfully active until her anchor-chain rattled over the Tail of the Bank, dodging now into the engine-room, now up steel ladders to where the steering-gear churned forward and back again with its own queer air of independence, and then hurrying to the bridge and the battery of telltale lights up there. But now he did nothing, keeping in a mood of uneasy detachment out of the way of busy men in overalls. He found a corner for himself on A deck, well forward below the navigating bridge, and in that retired position stood for a long time – watching, as it were, the last creation of his own hands pass forever beyond him.

It was in a sense a procession that he witnessed, the high, tragic pageant of the Clyde. Yard after yard passed by, the berths empty, the grass growing about the sinking keel-blocks. He remembered how, in the brave days, there would be scores of ships ready for the launching along this reach, their sterns hanging over the tide, and how the men at work on them on high stagings would turn from the job and tug off their caps and cheer the new ship setting out to sea. And now only the gaunt, dumb poles and groups of men, workless, watching in silence the mocking passage of the vessel. It was bitter to know that they knew – that almost every man among them was an artist in one of the arts that go to the building of a ship; that every feature of the *Estramadura* would come under an expert and loving scrutiny, that her passing would remind them of the joy of work and tell them how many among them would never work again. It appalled Leslie Pagan that not a cheer came from those watching groups.

It was a tragedy beyond economics. It was not that so many thousands of homes lacked bread and butter. It was that a tradition, a skill, a glory, a passion, was visibly in decay and all the acquired and inherited loveliness of artistry rotting along the banks of the stream.

Into himself he counted and named the yards they passed. The number and variety stirred him to wonder, now that he had ceased to take them for granted. His mental eye moving backwards up the river, he saw the historic place at Govan, Henderson's of Meadowside at the mouth of the Kelvin, and the long stretch of Fairfield on the southern bank opposite. There came Stephen's of Linthouse next, and Clydeholm facing it across the narrow, yellow ditch of the ship-channel. From thence down river the range along the northern bank was almost continuous for miles – Connell, Inglis, Blythswood, and the rest: so many that he could hardly remember their order. He was distracted for a moment to professionalism by the lean grey forms of destroyers building for a foreign Power in the sheds of a yard that had dramatically deserted Thames for Clyde. Then he lost himself again in the grim majesty of the parade. There came John Brown's, stretching along half a mile of waterfront at Clydebank, the monstrous red hull of Number 534 looming in its abandonment like a monument to the glory departed; as if shipbuilding man had tried to do too much and had been defeated by the mightiness of his own conception. Then came, seeming to point the moral, the vast desolation of Beardmore's at Dalmuir, cradle of the mightiest battleships and now a scrapheap, empty and silent forever, the great gantry over the basin proclaiming stagnation and an end.

Even where the Clyde opened out above Erskine, with the

Kilpatricks green and sweet above the river on the one hand and the wooded, fat lands of Renfrewshire stretching to the escarpment of Misty Law on the other, the sight of a legend – FOR SALE – painted large on the walls of an empty shed reminded him with the effect of a blow that Napier and Miller's were gone, shut down, finished, the name never to appear again on a brass plate below the bridge of a good ship. And he suddenly remembered that there lay on his desk at the office a notice of sale of the plant at Bow, Maclachlan's on the Cart by Paisley. His world seemed visibly to be crumbling. Already he had been appalled by the emptiness of Lobnitz's and Simons's at Renfrew, and the sense of desolation, of present catastrophe, closed the more oppressively upon him.

As they rounded the bend by Bowling, passing close under the wooded crags of Auchentorlie on the one hand and, as on a Dutch canal, past the flats of Erskine on the other, his eye was taken by the scene ahead. The jagged, noble range of the Cowal hills made a purple barrier against the glow of the westering winter sun. Now he was lost for a space in wonder that this cradle and home of ships enjoyed a setting so lovely. Through the gap of the Vale of Leven he could see the high peak of Ben Lomond, and his fancy ranged up those desolate, distant slopes. But then the dome of Dumbarton Rock, the westernmost of the chain strung across the neck of Scotland, brought him to think of the mean town at its base, and of Denny's yard in the crook of the Leven behind it, and of the lovely, fast, small ships they could build, and of the coming of the turbine. And another yard there, Macmillan's, derelict.

Past Dumbarton, the river opening to the Firth, the scene took on an even more immediate grandeur. The sands of the Pillar Bank were showing in golden streaks through the falling tide. The peninsula of Ardmore was a pretty tuft of greenery thrust out towards the channel. Dead ahead lay the mouth of the Gareloch, backed by the jagged peaks on the western side of Loch Long. A man could almost feel the freshness of the open sea coming to meet him over the miles of island, hill and loch; and Leslie Pagan marked how the fresher and larger waves slapped against the sides of the *Estramadura* and could almost imagine that the ship responded with quiver and curtsey to their invitation.

That openness of the river below the derelict timber ponds of Langbank, however, is deceptive; for still the channel must run round the end of the bank and close into the Renfrewshire shore.

There are miles of waste space there over the shallows, and Glasgow is more than twenty miles away before a ship of size has more than a few feet of water between her keel and the bottom. Port Glasgow and Greenock look across miles of sand and sea to the Highland hills, but the yards there must launch their ships into narrow waters; so that the man who had built the *Estramadura,* scanning the shores, saw thereabouts an even thicker crowding of berths than he had marked on the upper reaches.

It was another roster of great names, older, more redolent even than those that had become namely about Glasgow with the deepening of the Clyde. Ferguson's, Duncan's, Murdoch's, Russell's, Hamilton's . . . . Even he could not be sure that he had them right; there had been so many changes. Out on Garvel Point, under the old marooned Scots mansion-house, stood Brown's – the 'Siberia' of the artisan's lingo. There came Scott's East Yard – was it not once Steele's, where the clippers were built? There came the Greenock and Grangemouth, once the artisan's 'Klondike'. Then Scott's Mid Yard; then Caird's, the last of the lot – closed down. It was queer to see how Newark Castle survived in its pink grace and antiquity among the stocks and gantries.

Here history went mad – the history of the countryside and the history of shipbuilding in fantastic confusion. Here they had moved a sixteenth century church stone by stone that a yard might be extended, and with it carted away the poor bones of a poet's love. This town of Greenock, sprawling over the foothills of Renfrewshire, had had its heart torn out to make room for ships. It was as if a race had worshipped grim gods of the sea. And now the tide had turned back. Greenock's heart lay bare and bleeding – for the sake of a yard that had never cradled a ship since strangers, afire with the fever of wartime, took it and played with it and dropped it. Never again, in any calculation of which the human mind was capable, would the Clyde be what it had been.

George Blake (1893-1961)

A Small and Great City

From his vantage point in Ruchill Park, Laidlaw looked out over the city. He could see so much of it from here and still it baffled him. 'What is this place?' he thought.

A small and great city, his mind answered. A city with its face against the wind. That made it grimace. But did it have to be so hard? Sometimes it felt so hard. Well, that was some wind and it had never stopped blowing. Even when this place was the second city of the British Empire, affluence had never softened it because the wealth of the few had become the poverty of the many. The many had survived, however harshly, and made the spirit of the place theirs. Having survived affluence, they could survive anything. Now that the money was tight, they hardly noticed the difference. If you had it, all you did was spend it. The money had always been tight. Tell us something we don't know. That was Glasgow. It was a place so kind it would batter cruelty into the ground. And what circumstances kept giving it was cruelty. No wonder he loved it. It danced among its own debris. When Glasgow gave up, the world could call it a day.

Standing so high, Laidlaw felt the bleakness of summer on his face and understood a small truth. Even the climate here offered no favours. Standing at a bus-stop, you talked out the side of your mouth, in case your lips got chapped. Maybe that was why the West of Scotland was where people put the head on one another – it was too cold to take your hands out your pockets. But it did have compensations.

Laidlaw had a happy image of the first man out after the nuclear holocaust being a Glaswegian. He would straighten up and look around. He would dust himself down with that flickering gesture of the hands and, once he had got the strontium off the good suit, he would look up. The palms would be open.

'Hey,' he would say. 'Gonny gi'es a wee brek here? What was that about? Ye fell oot wi' us or what? That was a liberty. Just you behave.'

Then he would walk off with that Glaswegian walk, in which the shoulders don't move separately but the whole torso is carried as one, as stiff as a shield. And he would be muttering to himself, 'Must be a coupla bottles of something still intact.'

William McIlvanney (1936-)

Greensleeves

An old woman alone in a Glasgow tower block has little left save her memories of happier times. With this sensitively drawn cameo Alan Spence presents a devastating indictment of a misconceived housing policy which has blighted the lives of so many in the city.

The ice-cream van it was with its harsh metallic jangle. She could only just recognize the tune for what it had once been. Not that coarse parody, stilted and mechanical, a tin brashness, a gaudiness of noise. But somewhere in it, all but lost, was an echo of something old. Still to be heard through all that distortion. The faintest of memories of times long past. She heard and she remembered. The tune was called Greensleeves.

She must have learned it first at school. So many years. Half a century and more. But further back than that it went, all sadness and grace, all minstrels and knights and ladies in high towers, imprisoned.

And this was a tower high enough. Twenty-two storeys of concrete and glass. Boxes on boxes, and hers right at the top. Half way to heaven as the young man next door would say. People on the lift were always saying things like that. Whoever was nearest the door would press the buttons for everyone, repeating the numbers like a bingo-caller. Legs eleven they would say, or Lucky for some, thirteen. Like a language all of its own. For her floor it would be Top of the House, or All the twos, or sometimes Two little ducks. That was the one she liked best, though she thought a two was more like a swan. Two little swans. Swans were like the tune again, the way it used to be. Played on a flute, bending and gliding. Curve of the swan's neck, dipping to meet its own reflection. Ripples on an old pond. Swansong.

At first she'd been terrified of the lifts, the rickety way they clanked and jarred from floor to floor. But gradually she'd become used to it although sometimes the fear came back, especially if she was alone. The lift would creak and shudder its way up and up and she would feel the emptiness below her, increasing as she got further from the ground, suspended, supportless, a sheer black drop into nothing at all.

But the lifts were about the only place she ever saw her neighbours. It was like passing through a strange town and just catching glimpses of the people who lived there. Descending or rising through layer after layer, and every layer a few more lives she would never know. Sometimes people were friendly, but there were times too when nobody would utter a word, all lost in themselves. Strange the atmosphere when nobody spoke, every one staring straight ahead or looking down at their feet, anything rather than catch another's eye. Sometimes it was just surliness, like the young man from the seventeenth floor with his neat suit and his newspaper and his rolled umbrella. He never seemed to talk to anybody. Others she thought were just shy, like the little apprentice from the ninth. More often though, the people who didn't talk just seemed too tired or preoccupied to make the effort, coming home deadened and tense after a day's work. Then at other times it was all bustle, people babbling away, children chattering and crowding on with footballs or scooters or bikes. Sometimes it was nice at weekends, people coming home in the evening, glad for the moment to be free. She liked it then, everybody was happier, more relaxed, more ready to talk and joke and laugh. But the lift would gradually empty towards the top and by the time it reached her floor she was usually alone again. Sometimes at the weekends though it became a bit chaotic, and the lifts were always breaking down because too many people would crowd on at once. And there was always sure to be somebody loud and drunk. At times it could be really disgusting, with people being sick or even using the lifts as toilets. And then the poor caretaker would have to clean up the mess. Only the other day the big Highlander from the fourteenth had caught somebody at that.

A young boy it had been.

'Staunin therr bold as ye like,' he'd said, 'pishin in the coarner! So ah took um bi the scruff a the neck an rubbed is bloody nose in it! Told um if they acted lik wee dugs they'd get treated like them. Dirty wee tikes!'

She'd thought that was a bit cruel and maybe a bit coarse as well, but she couldn't help laughing with the others. The Highlander was an ex-policeman. A fine big man she thought. She could imagine how angry he must have been at the boy. The lifts were always marked with their slogans, strange symbols, their own names, the names of their gangs. The Highlander called them cave-paintings, said the boys were animals. The slogans, scraped and painted, were spreading to other parts of the building. Even downstairs, right outside the caretaker's office, where the sign said No Ball Games No Loitering, the walls had been daubed and sprayed. But at least it wasn't as bad yet as other blocks she'd heard about. According to the papers and the television, some of them were already on the way to being slums. She'd even heard people on the bus talking about these blocks here as if they were slums. Two women it had been, sitting just behind her.

'And I mean,' one had said, 'you should see some of the children, running about wild. Like wee savages. And as for some of the language!'

'Mind you,' the other had said, 'you can't really expect anything else. They're all just shifted out from Partick and Govan, and all these dirty old tenements are just falling to bits. It's not as if they've ever known anything better.'

She thought of her own home over in Ibrox. Near enough to Govan, but nowhere near to being slums. A decent red sandstone block, clean and solid and old, with tiles in the close and polished wooden banister-rails and stained-glass windows on every landing. The one on her landing had the head and shoulders of a young knight or squire, panels of twining flowers on either side, yellow, red and green, and up above patterns of red and blue squares. The whole close was always quiet, and the daylight that filtered through the windows was tinted and softened by the coloured glass. The back court itself, when seen through windows like these, was a bright painted garden, a landscape tinted and framed.

That was how she liked to remember it. Like another age. The stillness of a summer afternoon. It had been a fine building. Even the storm of a few years back hadn't damaged it at all. But the area was due for redevelopment, so down it had to come to make way for a supermarket or a wider road or another block of flats.

One afternoon, a month or two after she'd moved, she'd been back in Ibrox to go to a jumble-sale. When she'd passed by they were pulling the building down, grey rain drizzling on the wasteground where half a street had been. She'd stood and watched as the workmen heaped spars of wood on a bonfire and bulldozers and lorries cleared away the rubble. The ground had shaken, a terrible rumble and crash as another wall crumbled and fell in a cloud of choking yellow dust. The dust cleared and the building stood, laid open like a doll's house, and there where the second storey had been was one wall of her home, old layers of wallpaper peeling, tattered edges flapping in the wind. And where the fireplace had been was the back of a blackened hearth and a broken chimney and a line of soot left by every fire she'd ever burned. And the whole ruin flickered and wavered in the haze of the workmen's bonfire, crackling and hissing and spitting in the rain.

Alan Spence (1949-)

THE SLAB BOYS

The scene is the Slab Room at A. F. Stobo & Co. (Carpet Manufacturers) of Elderslie, near Paisley, where the colours are mixed by Spanky and Phil. It is the late fifties and Phil's Maw has just been 'taken away' . . .

PHIL: She wasn't all that bad either . . . not for her, that is. All she done was run up the street with her hair on fire and dive through the Co-operative windows . . .

SPANKY: Thought that was normal down your way?

PHIL: Yeh . . . but that's mostly the drink.

SPANKY: How long'll she be in this time?

PHIL: Usual six weeks, I expect. First week tied to a rubber mattress, next five wired up to a generator.

SPANKY: That's shocking.

PHIL: That's when we get in to see her. Never knew us the last time. Kept looking at my old man and saying 'Bless me, Father, for I have sinned.' 'Course, he's hopeless . . . thinks it's like diphtheria or something. 'The doctors is doing their best, Annie . . . you'll be home soon. You taking that medicine they give you?' Medicine? Forty bennies crushed up in their cornflakes before they frogmarch them down to the 'Relaxation Classes', then it's back up to Cell Block Eleven for a kitbag-ful of capsules that gets them bleary-eyed enough for a chat with the consultant psychiatrist.

SPANKY: Not much of a holiday, is it?

PHIL: Did I ever tell you about that convalescent home my Maw and me went to? At the seaside . . . West Kilbride . . .

SPANKY: Don't think so . . .

PHIL: I was about eleven at the time. Got took out of school to go with her . . . on the train. Some holiday. Place was choc-a-bloc with invalids . . . headcases soaking up the Clyde breeze before getting pitched back into the hurly-burly of everyday life . . . Old-age pensioners, their skulls full of mush . . . single guys in their forties in too-short trousers and intellects to match . . . Middle-aged women in ankle socks roaming about looking for a letter box to stick their postcards through. Abject bloody misery, it was. Dark-brown waxcloth you could see your face in . . . bathroom mirrors you couldn't. Lights out at half seven . . . no wireless, no comics, no nothing. Compulsory hymn-singing for everybody including the bed-ridden. Towels that tore the skin off your bum when you had a bath. Steamed fish on Sundays for a special treat . . .

SPANKY: Bleagh . . .

PHIL: The one highlight was a doll of about nineteen or twenty . . . There we all were sitting in our deck chairs in the sun-lounge . . . curtains drawn . . . listening for the starch wearing out on the Matron's top lip . . . when this doll appears at the door, takes a coupla hops into the room, then turns this cartwheel right down the middle of the two rows of deckchairs . . . lands on her pins . . . daraaaaa! Brilliant! I started to laugh and got a skelp on the nut. The Matron was beeling . . .

SPANKY: About the skelp?

PHIL: About the doll's cartwheel, stupid. Two old dears had to get carried up to their rooms with palpitations and a guy with a lavvy brush moustache wet himself. It was the highspot of the holiday.

SPANKY: What was it got into her?

PHIL: Who knows? Maybe she woke up that morning and seen her face in the waxcloth . . . remembered something . . . 'Christ, I'm alive!' Everybody hated her after that.

SPANKY: Did you have much bother when they took your Maw away last night?

PHIL: No . . . they gave her a jag to knock her out.

John Byrne (1940-)

Glasgow Kisses

These kisses are of a rather more romantic nature than those alluded to today in the expression 'the Glasgow kiss'.

Kiss'd yestreen, and kiss'd yestreen,
Up the Gallowgate, down the Green:
I've woo'd wi' lords, and woo'd wi' lairds,
I've mool'd wi' carles and mell'd wi' cairds,
I've kiss'd wi' priests – 'twas done i' the dark,
Twice in my gown and thrice in my sark;
But priest, nor lord, nor loon can gie
Sic kindly kisses as he gave me.

Anonymous

George Square

George Square
idleness
an island
children splashing
in a sea of pigeons
pigeons strutting
pigeon-toed.

And we
city dwellers
sitting
separate
close together.
City dwellers
we only know
nature captive –
zoos and gardens
Latin-tagged.
We know no earth
or roots.
We see no slow

season shift
but sudden summer
blaze a concrete day
and catch us unawares.

We can find no sense
in traffic lights'
continual change of emphasis.

Nature captive:
this is a city
nature's barred.
But the flowers
bound and bedded
bloom
incurable as cancer
and as for fat old ladies'
flowery
summer dresses
my god, they really are
a riot.

Liz Lochead (1947-)

The Butchers of Glasgow

The butchers of Glasgow have all got their pride
But they'll tell you that Willie's the prince
For Willie the butcher he slaughtered his wife
And he sold her for mutton and mince

It's a terrible story to have to be telt
And a terrible thing to be done
For what kind of man is it slaughters his wife
And sells her a shilling a pun

For lifting his knife and ending her life
And hanging her high like a sheep
You widnae object but you widnae expect
He wid sell the poor woman so cheap

But the Gallowgate folk were delighted
It didnae cause them any tears
They swore that Willie's wife Mary
Was the best meat he'd sold them for years

Matt McGinn (1928-75)

Sweet Saturday Night

This is a delightful account of a bus journey home one Saturday night in 1937.

Sweet Saturday night,
When the week's work is done.
Old Song

You cannot afford to be fastidious in your choice of transport when you are twelve miles or more from Glasgow and it is late on a Saturday night. So long as the vehicle you board appears to be capable of sustained motion you must step as hopefully into a tumbril as an Elijah's chariot.

Yet having made your bed, you may at least look around you with disdain or dismay before you lie on it. And as I groped my way to a seat in the 'bus that had come rattling over the cobbles I was filled with misgivings about the pleasures of travel during the next forty minutes. The 'bus was a museum piece, so old that it should have been preceded by a man carrying a flag. It was a tumbril indeed. And from what I could make out of my travelling companions they were as fine a set of malefactors as ever rode to the gibbet. But that was a first impression. The mingling odours of cigarette smoke, fish and chips, and warm bodies dull one's perceptions of the essential nobility of man. In such an atmosphere a squadron of archangels might well convey an impression of unbounded rascality. There were no wings or shining armour among my fellow-passengers.

Nor was that all. The deplorable conclusions inspired by the foul air were heightened by the presence of a man playing an accordion to which most of the company were singing with spirit. The normal decorum of the Scot and his traditional liking for whisky often lead one to attribute public displays of hilarity to the bottle. So that I feared for the moment that I was in the presence not merely of rascals but of drunken rascals. The inference proved to be unjust, for although there might have been a dram or two spread thin among the company, they were sober, and with one exception, admirable men indulging, as is fitting on a Saturday night, a natural merriment.

The exception was a negroid young man who sat in a front seat near the accordion player, by this time identified as Charlie. It appeared to be a matter of principle with Charlie that he should play any piece that was called for, but his personal preferences were clearly for familiar Scottish airs and particularly for strathspeys in which he revealed a remarkable virtuosity. I am no connoisseur of the accordion. It is not everybody's instrument, yet it appears to me that its music is heard to perfection in a 'bus. They say of cheese that it digests everything but itself. So with the 'bus. Its noise and rattle mellow all noises but its own. The accordion tends to gustiness, yet this defect and others inherent either in the instrument or the performer are flattened out by the grinding of gears and the rumbling of protesting machinery, so that the resulting music is not only tolerable but pleasant.

But the negroid young man had a voice that was proof against all mellowing, he sang so high and he sang so shrill. His was the authentic voice of Saturday night, the ear-splitting falsetto that fastens on sentimental waltz tunes and overrides the air in a fury of misshapen harmony. It is heard in all the quarters where the common people crowd to take their pleasures. It may rise no higher than a husky croon, or it may have the power and penetration of a ship's siren. It is fed on fish suppers, hot peas and vinegar in Italian ice-cream shops, and cheap seats at the cinema, and its mournful or strident howling expresses a world of unrealised sentiment.

The negroid young man howled as if his heart would break. The song of his own choosing, was "When you played the organ and I sang 'The Rosary.' " He sprawled out on his seat, his legs stretched wide apart, his thumbs in the armholes of his waistcoat, his head flung back, and his eyes tight closed in an ecstasy of pleasure as his heart warmed to the commonplaces of the vulgar tune.

Louder and shriller he sang until the music of the accordion and the sturdy bellowings of two passengers at the rear of the 'bus made no more impression than the murmur of bees. At last it ended in a delirious scream from the negroid young man, who held an awful top note till the veins in his neck swelled and the colour of his face turned to an apoplectic purple. Then like a punctured balloon he collapsed, and rattling windows and rumbling machinery were heard once more sweet as summer rain.

'We'll hae nae mair o' that.'

The speaker was a mild little man with a shrivelled face and pathetic monkey eyes. But for all his seeming meekness his voice recorded stern disapproval of the negroid young man and his dreadful song.

'Johnnie,' he said, 'Johnnie, will ye sing ma favourite, "The Bonnie Lass o' Ballochmyle"?'

But Johnnie paid no heed. He was absorbed in the happy rhythm of quadrilles; and balancing himself in the narrow space between two seats, pantomimed the "paddy bash and bow to partners." His elbows were squeezed into his sides and his leg of mutton hands thrust out from his hips. He threw back his head, stuck out his chest, assumed the half-anxious, half-vacuous smile of the earnest dancer, and seemed to flow across the floor of the 'bus to meet his partner, and then to retreat again with his head and shoulders now drooping. Two waggles of his hips, an upward thrust of his hands, a triumphant 'hooch!' and the pantomime ended suddenly as the lurching 'bus threw him off his balance and tumbled him in a heap on his seat.

The mild little man called out again for 'The Bonnie Lass,' but Johnnie shook his head dourly.

'Aw, Johnnie, please, ma favourite.' The little man was so plaintive and insistent that it seemed another refusal must make him burst into dismal weeping. Johnnie yielded with little grace, and as Charlie and the accordion conducted some preliminary investigations into the vagaries of the tune, the negroid young man spat with venomous contempt. But the little man was justified in his importunity, for Johnnie, middle-aged and moon-faced with a large and wanton mouth, sang with the tenderness and sweetness of a young lover, and benign contentment oozed from the little man. The song carried us through the mean and crowded streets until it ended as the 'bus lurched heavily round the corner by Duke Street prison.

'We're hame,' said Charlie, who had not spoken a word since I joined the 'bus forty minutes earlier, and as he began to pack his accordion into its case we all grew self-conscious, a little uneasy at our cheerful abandon. The atmosphere reeked of cigarette smoke, fish and chips, and warm bodies, and I longed for the refreshment of a hot bath. As we stepped from the 'bus the rain fell cold and dismal.

R.N. Biles (1937)

The Streets of Glasgow

In his novel The Albannach, *first published in 1932, Fionn Mac Colla makes plain his aversion to Glasgow through the feelings and experiences of his hero, Murdo, down from the Highlands at the University. In his distaste for the City, Mac Colla has much in common with Muir and his hero of* Poor Tom *(1932).*

It was in that room that Murdo was happiest all that term. It was long that the streets affected him in a curious and unpleasant way. He was from the region of great hills and wide moors where he had been accustomed to walk about leisurely revolving his thoughts in a world entirely his own, except when one would pass him as leisurely as himself. In the part he came from people had a way of their own of going about things. You could tell by looking at a man whether he was abroad on an affair of importance or merely for pleasure or on some ordinary routine business of life in those parts. If it was the last – taking peat from the hill or seaweed from the shore or provisions from the town – a man would be taking his time to it and looking around him. On the other hand if you saw a man, and haste on him to get to a place, you knew at once he had a very good reason for it – that there was illness, maybe, before or behind him – and without asking questions you did what you could to speed him on his way, even if it was only to give him the middle of the road.

In the streets there was no time for leisure or for thought. The crowds that seemed to be forever rushing here and there prevented anything but a rapid and bewildering flicker of impressions that, because they could not at once be arranged and assimilated, produced a sort of giddiness. It had been weeks before Murdo began to realise that these hurrying, scurrying folks were probably rushing to nothing more pressing than their tea.

After a time, however, he fell into the ways of the city. He would rush along to a corner and wait there for a car, with haste on him to be out of that place and going somewhere else. He would walk smartly along the streets, dodging in and out among the crowd, hurrying with a great air of purpose to get to nowhere in particular. He would even upon occasion knock against people and glare at them as they used to do at him, then hurry on feeling as genuinely annoyed as if he had really been going somewhere and they had hindered him.

And all the time he was falling into the bustling city ways he was feeling pleased with himself in some way, as if he was progressing well, getting free of his rustic slowness and coming abreast of the times.

When he went to Glasgow first what most of all made him conscious of himself in the streets was the young women. They would mince along in their smart dresses cut so as to reveal their calves and suggest the rest of their bodies, swaying their hips and generally carrying themselves as if they well knew every man in the street desired them. If one of them looked at you it was usually with an arch glance, as if to say: 'I know you would give absolutely *anything* to sleep with me, you poor animal, but I am ineffably above all that sort of thing. It merely amuses me.' He had always understood such was the feeling of most women about the thing, and when a girl looked at him like that, as not infrequently happened, he at once concluded the glance was critical and hurried past, very conscious of himself, feeling he had been detected in an act of gross discourtesy if he had not desired her or in a kind of vulgar dogginess if perchance he had. By the end of the term, however, for long periods together he even failed to notice the young women at all and would walk through a whole street of them with a calmness and indifference that was new and surprising and that he found very pleasant when at times the extent of it had come home to him. This indifference was partly no doubt the result of familiarity; and partly he knew it was something else.

Fionn Mac Colla (1906-75)

Nevertheless Jean's action was to her only another proof of the corrupting influence of Glasgow. In her heart she blamed Glasgow for all the misfortunes that had happened since they had come south, though she did not say this for fear of being laughed at. Yet it was inconceivable to her that had they all stayed in the surroundings she knew and trusted, Mansie should have taken Tom's girl. It was simply the portion of the corruption of Glasgow allotted to them, their private share of the corruption that was visible in the troubled, dirty atmosphere, the filth and confusion of the streets, the cynical frankness, hitherto unknown to her, with which people here talked of their privatest affairs, their fathers and mothers, sisters and brothers. She could not understand them or their ways, and she grew shy of talking about Tom and Mansie even to Jean, and especially after Jean joined the I.L.P. For with that Jean had identified herself with Glasgow; she had become by deliberate choice a Glasgow girl, and – who could tell? – perhaps she would no longer even understand. And when one evening Mrs. Manson found Robert Blatchford's *Britain for the British* in a drawer in Mansie's bedroom, it seemed to her that she no longer understood her family and that Glasgow had taken them and made them almost as strange as itself.

But worse was her fear of all the machinery, machinery she did not understand, and with which Tom was so unavoidably associated. Indeed Tom had now more accidents than ever; his hands were perpetually in bandages. He had always been reckless; he was now indifferent as well; but what exposed him most of all to accidents was the fact that, feeling shut out from everything, he felt shut out too from the very work he was doing every day, and so never penetrated within it to that security which work itself seems to give. He never reached that almost trance-like abstraction which we envy in the workman bowed over his bench, enclosed in his task as in a private Eden where time no longer exists, so remote and calm that even a child will become quiet and hesitate to speak to him. Tom remained outside, and this made him irritated with his tools, and in his irritation he began to treat them disrespectfully, began indeed to acquire an impatient scorn for machinery wherever he encountered it. Nothing, however, punishes disrespect more promptly and ruthlessly than machinery, and when Tom was brought home late one Saturday night with his head bandaged and his blue serge suit covered with mud, it was because he had treated a tramcar with insufficient deference. He had been drinking; yet while descending the stairs to get off he had provocatively kept one hand in his trouser pocket, using only the other as a support. When, after what seemed a long time, he found himself lying in dirt and water in the street with a crowd of strange people round him, he naturally enough felt cold and miserable, for it was the middle of November; but he also felt a little frightened. These people standing round meant well, he could see that; yet he was helplessly exposed to them like an exhibit, and the overpowering stream of kindness that they poured down on him was like a threat and filled him with sudden panic; he felt as though he had been lynched in some strange way, lovingly and tenderly lynched by the assembled Y.M.C.A.

Edwin Muir (1887-1959)

The Glasgow Underground

I know a lot of folk go fancy places at the Fair
They like to sail on steamers or to hurtle through the air
But I've a favourite route that goes to many ports of call
Although unless you looked you'd never notice it at all

Chorus:
There's Partick Cross and Cessnock,
Hillheid and Merkland Street
George's Cross and Govan Cross
Where a' the people meet
West Street, Shields Road
The train goes round and round
Oh it's lovely going your holidays
On the Glasgow underground.

Clifford Hanley (1922-)

Point of Departure

James Cameron spent much of his early working life in Scotland. He invested British Journalism with a quality of writing rarely emulated. His principles were often at odds with the Establishment and the newspaper proprietors for whom he worked, but his integrity and feeling for what was morally right characterised his unique talent. This is an extract from his autobiography.

About this time the publishing company decided to transfer me from Dundee to Glasgow. I was greatly torn about this, because while I was badly worried at the prospect of leaving the only two people who meant anything to me, Elma and my father, I felt by now so confined and exasperated by Dundee that I would have gone almost anywhere to escape it. In my case I had no particular choice, and so I moved southward again, and started work on the *Sunday Post* in Port Dundas Road, just below the Cowcaddens. There I remained for some five years, passing my days in the pursuit of journalism the confused character of which must have been unusual even then, and would be totally and wildly impossible today.

In those days there was no tangible demarcation line between the functional processes in the editorial department of a provincial newspaper of this kind. Between the sub-editor and the reportorial staff no such schism or tribal difference existed as exists today, since everybody on the newspaper was both alternately, or even sometimes simultaneously. Much of my time was occupied in writing articles of a character almost excruciatingly homely and domestic, treating of the more trivial sort of family or social incident in a style, which I soon bitterly found came fairly easily to me, that somehow combined the facetious and the didactic, the worldly-wise and the innocent; an assemblage of recognizably nudging clichés that was defined in our literary terms as 'couthy'. Few essays before or since can have been as deadly, but the technique was not hard to master, and to this day I detect in myself sinister atavistic regressions into this appalling sly cosiness of style. This work was – in conformance with our editorial policy of refusing any employee the dignity of individuality – not signed, a fact which causes me great relief today; for the purposes of these compositions I would assume the character of A Feckless Housewife, A Henpecked Husband, Wee Wully, The Saftest o' the Family, Always a Wallflower, A Bairn Without a Name, and kindred archetypes of the ridiculous, eccentric, or pathetic. Everything had to be written in paragraphs one sentence long, and as far as possible in what was held to be the homely idiom of the Scottish working class, which is to say a costive coyness larded with apostrophes and Doricisms which bore as much likeness to the demotic speech of the Gorbals, say, as it did to Greek. Considerable value was placed on what were known as 'human stories', which by definition concerned animals. To this end I would be obliged to write under the title of Percy the Poodle, or An Unloved Alley-cat. In this character I authored some work so truly horrible that it met with heartfelt acclaim. From time to time I ghosted in serial form the life-stories of eminent boxers or released murderers or minor domestic functionaries of the Royal Household, all of whom, varied as their activities had presumably been, recounted their Exclusive Stories through me in a style uniformly homely, moving, gripping and couthy. It is true that in this way I came into contact with people and aspects of life that might otherwise have passed me by – for a time I became oddly involved in the activities of the professional boxing industry, in the wild macabre days of Benny Lynch, and a reluctant interest in that sad sport has never quite left me. I acted as journalistic amanuensis to an eerie creep who was contributing a series called 'Secrets of the Mayfair Vice Rings', who conscientiously established his bona-fides by attempting to seduce me on the top deck of a green tram. At intervals I would be despatched, at the conclusion of some especially repellent murder trial – and there seem to me to have been in those days about one a month – to call upon some distracted or avaricious mother up a close in Lanark or Motherwell and guide her hand through an article entitled 'Why My Boy Should Not Be Hanged'. Between these endeavours and my consistent *oeuvre* of canny suburban humour a kind of balance was maintained. I learned to do almost anything after a fashion. and nothing well. I was paid six pounds a week.

The great day was Saturday. This, being press day for our Sunday paper, was for me a regular climax of variety, a professional routine that would be quite unimaginable today. It must be remembered that our organization was not only a non-union shop, but designedly and even militantly so. Only many years later did a fairly close association with my own Union reveal to me the outrages and heresies I had innocently committed long before against every sacred canon of organized labour. At the time it merely seemed to me that I was somewhat overworked. The principle was thus: early in the morning I would repair to the office to be informed what event or happening of the day would provide the most fruitful material for a 'nice wee middle'. It could be anything from a rugby international at Murrayfield to the opening of the General Assembly of the Church of Scotland; there were occasions when I did both at once. I would then attend this affair, return to the office and describe it in the kind of flippant and oblique style that was catalogued as 'light reading'. I would then sub-edit the copy – which, since it was my own story, entailed only the insertion of a few stylistic indications to the printer. While this prose was being set in type, I would then produce pen and ink and a pad and make two drawings in illustration of the theme, one of the dimensions of a double-column line block and the other of a single.

By the time I could send these along to the process department the galley-proofs of the nice wee middle were ready to be proof-read; I proof-read them. I then wrote a couple of winsome little captions for the pictures.

The afternoon was now wearing on; by and by it was time to move over to the printing department, where it was my duty to make up the page on the stone. At this point my departure from all the tenets and doctrine of reasonable union practice moved from the unorthodox to the incredible. It is a cardinal and fundamental law in the whole mystery of newspaper production that print is print and editorial is editorial, and the twain shall meet only through a ritual of intermediary communication as rigid as it is inviolable. On the one hand is the concept, the assemblage of notions or phrases or information definable perhaps as Journalism; on the other hand is the material and tangible expression of these ideas represented by innumerable little slabs of linotype metal ranged in long rectangles, which are type. The Editorial produces the source material; it can be good or bad or indifferent, either inspirational and deathless or meaningless gibberish as far as the printer is concerned; but the physical technique and expertise of actually transferring this nebulous stuff into communicable shape is the concern of the printer alone, and no alien hand must interfere. This is an ancient and proper canon, accepted everywhere – except, to be sure, where I worked in those peculiar days. When it was decided where in the page to place my nice wee middle, and where to dispose the accompanying blocks, the man on the stone would tell me: 'Away and fetch us over thon galleys, son', and I would then trot off and bring back the columns of type to be laid in the forme, full of dread lest I should blunder or stumble and drop the lot on the floor in an inextricable scatter of pied type. If this sounds a trifling or even incomprehensible act to occasion so much retrospective awe I can only say that nowhere else could it have happened; to have the editorial stone-sub manhandling type in this cavalier way can only be likened to a village priest casually calling up some passing Freemason plumber to read the Mass for him while he has a quiet jar in the vestry.

The nice wee middle having been disposed of, with an appropriate heading composed in the vernacular and rounded off, if humanly possible, with an exclamation-mark, to point up the exquisite allusiveness of its humour, the hour came to take my place on the subs' table with my six colleagues. They ranged from Mr James Borthwick the editor to everyone who happened at the time to be engaged on nothing else, including a curiously witty and cryptic casual with a club-foot, whom one saw at no other time, and whose talent and career, amounting almost to a vocation, was such an encyclopaedic and personal acquaintance with every police station-sergeant in Glasgow that he could elicit on the phone the most informative details of every affray, rape, or grievous bodily harm occurring within the city limits almost before the incident had been completed. He was by far the busiest of our little crew. Throughout the night his voice provided a running obligato to our scratching pencils as he sat in his corner with the telephone wedged between ear and shoulder – he had a special cavity, or socket, embedded in the region of his clavicle with which nature had equipped him for the purposes of conducting telephone interviews while his hands were busy writing, or rolling cigarettes, or drinking cups of tea. 'Ay, Jock boy, good, good; to the effusion o' blood, eh; that's no' bad at all. Four fellas to this one lassie up the close-mouth; fine, fine. Fish-shop afire up by Bridgton; good, good – no fatal casualties, eh; pity, never mind, there's time enough; we can take fatalities up to around midnight; do your best, lad; try and get me a wee slashing in the Gorbals; it's a thin night for the town edition.'

James Cameron (1911-1984)

CHAPTER 4

THE LOWLANDS

The Monks of Melrose

The monks o' Melrose made guid kail,
  On Fridays when they fasted;
Nor wanted they guid beef and ale
  As lang's their neighbour's lasted!

Traditional

Ayrshire and Galloway

This old rhyme points out what each of the three districts of Ayrshire, and the neighbouring territory of Galloway, were remarkable for producing in greatest perfection. The mountainous province of Carrick produced robust men; the rich plains of Kyle reared the famous breed of cattle now generally termed the Ayrshire breed; and Cunningham was a good arable district. The hills of Galloway afford pasture to an abundance of sheep.

Carrick for a man,
  Kyle for a cow,
Cunningham for corn and bere,
  And Galloway for woo'.

Traditional

Tintock

Tintock Tap is one of the most conspicuous hills in a part of Lanarkshire which is in general rather flat.

On Tintock-tap there is a mist,
And in that mist there is a kist,
And in the kist there is a caup,
And in the caup there is a drap;
Tak up the caup, drink aff the drap,
And set the caup on Tintock-tap.

Traditional

Selkirk in the Days of Bonaparte

The foisting of prisoners upon a reluctant civil population is not a twentieth century invention. . .

Selkirk in the time of the French prisoners was a small place of two thousand inhabitants or less, the houses nearly all picturesquely thatched, very few roofed with slate as at present. It must have been matter of no small difficulty in such a community suitably to house a sudden influx of strangers. Indeed there *was* very great difficulty, until it was discovered that the Frenchmen were to pay for their accommodation, and then the difficulty vanished. But it would be hard at the present day to find in Selkirk lodgings of any sort at the rate (2s. 6d. a week) which then satisfied owners of houses.

The following is the French prisoner's description of Selkirk: "The town is encircled by beautiful hills on all sides; in the centre it had a large square adorned with a fountain; a very fine bridge crossed the Ettrick. An ordinary-looking building belonging to the National Church and a much larger one owned by the Presbyterians, or rather the sect known by the name of Anti-Burghers, who had for their pastor an excellent and venerable man named Lawson, were the only two buildings in Selkirk worthy of notice."

The hills are still beautiful; perhaps, owing to extensive tree planting, more beautiful now than then; still within a step of Selkirk is the purple heather, and the heartsease and blue-bell a-swing in the summer breeze; still on every side the view lies wide and glorious. And even in the winter, when snow first wrapped them in its winding sheet, one can gaze, and repeat with heartfelt and perfect sincerity:

> "By Yarrow's stream still let me stray,
> Though none should guide my feeble way;
> Still feel the breeze down Ettrick break,
> Although it chill my wither'd cheek."

It must have been a dull, uneventful, depressing life, that of the prisoners in Selkirk, more especially in those months between October and March, when darkness comes early and the days are chill and grey. What news they got was chiefly of fresh disasters to their country's arms in Spain, and the rejoicing of the townsfolk over Wellington's victories was of necessity exceedingly bitter to the Frenchmen. It was execrable taste on the part of the inhabitants of Selkirk thus to show their joy, says the writer of the Reminiscences – "indelicate," he calls it. But the chances are that they were chiefly mannerless schoolboys who thus behaved. I fear he looked for more than poor fallen human nature is prepared to give, if he expected the townspeople entirely to suppress their pleasure. Many a heart in Selkirk was then following with dire anxiety the movements of our Army in the Peninsula, dreading the news that any hour might bring of mishap or death to son, brother, or friend; every soul in the place took the profoundest interest in the welfare of those men who had gone from their little community "to fecht the Frainch" and, however desirable it might be that the feelings of prisoners should not be lacerated, it seems too much to expect that the townsfolk should go apart in secret places in order to express, without offence, the joy they must feel when those they loved were covering themselves with glory.

Provided that no one was ill-mannered enough to jeer at or to taunt the prisoners, I hardly think they had a right to complain, more especially as they themselves had already sinned in respect of rejoicing openly over victory. On a certain occasion they heard of a great French success in Russia. Two prisoners concealed themselves and were locked up in the church one Sunday after evening service; about midnight these men admitted their comrades, and together they roused sleeping Selkirk by a terrific joy-peal of bells. Honours were easy between the two nations, I think. Both acted under strong feeling; those were strenuous days, and feeling naturally ran high. . .

Except on this occasion of the bell-ringing, and one other, when the French officers with some difficulty had induced certain of the townsfolk to drink to the health of the Emperor, and to shout '*Vive l'Empereur,*' friendly relations were unbroken. But the latter unpleasantness at one time had threatened to ripen into a very ugly affair. Bloodshed was narrowly averted. Friendship, however, was restored, and the prisoners continued to make the best of their situation. They obtained a billiard table from Edinburgh; they started a café, they opened a theatre, with an excellent orchestra of twenty-five performers "superior to all those to which the echoes of our Scottish residence had ever till then resounded."

This theatre was established in a barn which then belonged to the writer's grandfather. Frescoes on the walls, which had been painted by the prisoners, were still fairly fresh in colour though hopelessly obscure as to design, when the writer saw them in his early boyhood.

In connection with the time when Peace was proclaimed and the prisoners were being sent back to France, it is pleasant to have to record an incident greatly to the credit of Selkirk. The pockets of the Frenchmen were naturally, in their situation, not very well filled; indeed, amongst the hundred and ninety they could raise no more than £60, a sum not near sufficient to provide transport to the sea-port of Berwick for the entire party. They resolved, therefore, to march on foot, using what money they had to hire carriages for the few among them who were in bad health. After an excited night (spent by most of the ex-prisoners in the Market-place, where they shouted and sang till daylight, like a pack of schoolboys), just as they were preparing to set out on their long tramp to Berwick, "an altogether unexpected and pleasant sight met our view," writes M. Doisy. "Vehicles of all kinds came pouring in by the streets converging on the centre of the town, carriages, gigs, tilburys, carts, and a few saddle-horses, all of which had been sent by the inhabitants of the surrounding parts to convey us free of expense as far as Kelso, about half-way to Berwick. This delicate attention had been so well calculated, and so neatly accomplished, that we could not do otherwise than avail ourselves of it with many thanks. We therefore separated from our Selkirk friends without carrying away on the one part or the other any particle of grudge that might previously have existed between us."

Similar good feeling, however, appears to have been very general between the French prisoners and the people of the many Border towns where the former were quartered – though it was almost too much to expect that no unpleasantnesses should ever occur, when we remember how great a bogie the Emperor Napoleon then was to the majority of British people, and how to hate the French was looked on as almost a virtue. "Bless us, and save us, *and keep the French from us*," was a common form of invocation, then and later. Persons more ignorant or prejudiced than their neighbours were sure, sooner or later, to overstep the mark, and bring disgrace on their nation by boorish or brutal conduct to the defenceless prisoners, Thus, at Jedburgh for instance, not only did schoolboys sometimes jeer at and stone the Frenchmen, but one bitter old man, who no doubt thought that in hating the French he was only carrying out a manifest duty, actually pointed his gun at, and threatened to shoot, a prisoner whom he found outside the mile limit. A very regrettable incident occurred, too, in the same town during rejoicings over a great British victory. An effigy of the Emperor, mounted on a donkey, was paraded by torchlight through the streets and was then publicly burned, in full view of the deeply-pained French officers. Whatever the faults of the Emperor, he was at least adored by his army, and such instances of brutal ill-manners were bound to lead to bad blood and to reprisals.

Amongst themselves, the prisoners do not seem to have been quarrelsome, nor were duels common – for which fact, of course, the lack of suitable weapons may probably have been responsible. There was, however, a duel at Lauder between two of the prisoners quartered in that town, and one cannot help thinking that it must have suggested to Stevenson the duel in "St. Ives," between prisoners in Edinburgh Castle. In Stevenson's novel, they fought with the separated blades of scissors, securely lashed to sticks. At Lauder, they used the blades of razors secured in similar fashion. But, whereas in "St. Ives" the result was the death of one combatant, in the real duel at Lauder no greater harm came of it than slashed faces. It might be bloody enough, a duel with razor-blades, but it could not be very dangerous, except to the tips of noses.

Andrew and John Lang (1913)

Kelso Horse Show

Morning discovers it, sprawled in a loop the river
swings itself through the meadow on. Already
horse-boxes, floats and cars have runnelled the edge
of the field to a slush of muddy grass. A steady
straggle of people thickens the booths and the ring.
April neighs coldness. White clouds scud
last winter off the skies. The show-ground shakes
to life as buyers, catalogued with hunches, thud

in cautious canters, swerved by the boundary hedge.
Ponies nudge stakes, or rub a child's hand,
soft as their noses. Shouldering knotted halters
the sellers wait their turn behind the stand
where the auctioneer patters, hoarse with loss or profit.
Hunters and hacks parade reluctant paces,
plodding a clomped-up circle. The bidding sways
among five hands, then swings between two faces –
a fighting man whom enemy winds have leathered
smooth as a saddle; and in from the lean hills,
a Border farmer – both of them aware
their urge for satisfaction is the will's
ability to knock down for a song
whatever each has sent his heart upon,
though couldn't care for less as soon as got.
Down goes the Colonel's arrogance; down, down,
before a folly richer than his own.
Hard on the hunter's hooves, a gelding bears
reflections of so many hopeful selves
that most must be unbridled small despairs.
But sold or bought, the time and the place are the horses;
the sweet smell of their sweat, the strung hay
they munch their breath on, the patient stable darkness
rippling their flanks, commotions the livelong day
till it breaks away from its minute-by-minute grazing,
from Countified calls and bawdy Irish curses;
an image riding its own reality
to a sense of recognition no one rehearses;
and for all the human dressage, the play of purses,
something out of the past in me rejoices.

Maurice Lindsay (1918-)

A Galloway Fox Hunt

The Bongill clipping, a red-letter day for the shepherds of the glen, was drawing near. Sandy, the Caldons herd, was too happy to think of going to bed. In an hour or two he must start to climb the mountains in order to be on the top of Curleywee by daybreak. He was overjoyed because, after a long courtship, Nan o' the Buchan had that evening promised to marry him. In the gloaming, accompanied by his dog, he sauntered to the foot of Maldenoch, on the side nearest Loch Trool.

A light was burning in Buchan farm-house when he began to breast the hill. Here and there other lights indicated the sites of many little farms and crofts into which the glen was divided. Away to the north-west the faint glow of sunset lingered above the rugged outline of the mountains. Being in no hurry, he zig-zagged up the mountain-side. Choosing always the easiest point of attack, he soon stood under the beetling crag which crowns Maldenoch. All the lights, save that in Buchan farm-house, were now out, and Sandy knew that Nan was busy working, so that she might be free on the morrow to go up to Bongill and assist Mrs. MacMillan in preparing refreshments for the shepherds. The sky had become overclouded, and there was a cold wind blowing. Sandy resolved to shelter under the crag; he drew his collie close beside him, and wrapped his plaid around both. But the light in the Buchan kept him awake and thinking of Nan. At last the light disappeared, and in a few moments Sandy was asleep.

But the shepherd was too anxious about his work to sleep long; in an hour or so he awoke to find the stars shining brightly overhead. He rose hurriedly, and feeling chilled, he kept his dog trotting till he reached the Jerrold Whup. From that peak he learned that the Bongill folk were already astir. He noticed that the shepherds were making for the top of Curleywee, the point where they must commence 'gathering' the sheep for the clipping. Along the ridge of Lamachan the comparative levelness and smoothness of the ground enabled the shepherd to maintain a steady, swinging pace. The eerie sighing of the Shiel Jaw floated up to him as he plodded on in the darkness, and as he passed above the Clints o' Gaharn a loud 'whee-o-o-o' told him that the the keen ear of an eagle had heard the unwonted sound of footsteps on the mountain-top. At the first faint gleam of dawn he was able to locate the narrow neck which joins High Bennan-brack and Curleywee. It was not yet daylight when he stoutly assailed the last 'whup' – the crown of Curleywee. He lay down upon his plaid to await the hour which had been agreed on for 'gathering' the hill.

Sandy's thoughts of Nan at last constrained him to rise to his knees and outpour his gratitude to Heaven. Far away he could hear the barking of dogs. He raised his head, but remembered that the other herds and their dogs would already be out upon the hills. No sooner had he resumed his devotions than from the crest of the hill there came a loud 'Harkaway! halloo! halloo!' and, looking up, he saw Alan M'Callum, the fox-hunter.

'Halloa,' said Alan, 'what the deil are ye daein' here on yer han's and knees at this time o' the mornin'?'

Sandy was both nettled and taken aback at the intrusion, but, rising, he replied, 'Oh, I was jist like the Culsharg whaups – stickin' my neb in the grun' to keep mysel' frae bein' blawn aff the tap.' The loud baying of dogs interrupted further explanation, and Sandy changed the subject. 'What gars ye come here huntin' and frichtening the sheep sae late in the year?' he asked.

'Oh,' replied Alan, 'Auchenleck has been losin' sae mony lambs that he asked me to hunt the foxes oot frae Lamachan.' Watching eagerly the trail of the hounds, the hunter added, 'The vixen has ta'en them oot ower Lamachan, an' I fear she'll reach the big scree on Maldenoch afore they catch up on her.' Soon, however, the hounds doubled back. 'Gran', man,' cried Alan, 'but I doot she'll win to the Fox Rock' – the allusion being to a place where a hound tried to follow a fox on to a 'dass,' and, falling over a cliff, was killed.

The sun, rising brightly over Curleywee, revealed the little red fox gliding along the mountain-side, and making for the Fox Rock on the Breesha, with the hounds in hot pursuit. 'The game's up,' said Alan, 'we could never get her oot o' yon scree, though we howkit for a thoosan' years.' But, to his surprise, the fox suddenly headed away from the clints and straight for Curleywee.

'Dod, man,' said Alan, 'that's the best hunt I ha'e seen for mony a day.' On came the hunt. 'That beats a'!' he exclaimed. 'It's The Horner's dog that's leading the hounds.'

The vixen crept round the steep side of the mountain, and still maintained her lead. She swerved under the precipice, right beneath the spot where Alan and Sandy lay concealed. Alan saw that she must pass between two rocks only a yard apart. As the streak of red-and-white flashed through, he raised his gun and fired. The hind legs of the fox swerved outward, and Alan thought that he had killed her. He rose and watched breathlessly, but out from the far side of the big rock emerged the fox – showing just for a moment before she disappeared behind a jutting crag. Alan fired again, but the fox sped on, apparently unhurt. The hunt was now seen to full advantage. Easily traced by the white tip of her tail, she glided up the gully towards the Clints o' Gaharn, near the Loup o' the Laggan, with the hounds in full cry.

'Tally-ho! Tally-ho! Forward, forward!' cried Alan, as, streaming along the mountain-ridge, were seen the huntsmen – a mixed company of landlords, farmers, shepherds, gamekeepers, footmen, and, most striking of all, big Andra Kennedy, The Horner, wearing his usual headgear – a tile hat! But the sight which attracted Sandy was more uncommon. An anaemic footman, carrying a luncheon-basket, came up. Sandy pointed downward to the Breesha, which was wreathed in a cloud of mist, and asked, 'Saw ye ever ocht like that aboot Lunnon?' Distinctly reflected upon the cloud could be seen the shadow of the hounds at the heels of the fox. The Cockney footman, turning languidly away from the wonderful sight, inquired merely, 'When we get round that cornah, shall we be in sight of 'ome?'

The loud baying of hounds seemed to betoken a 'kill.' But a speck of red, hard pressed by The Horner's dog, appeared up the scree that leads to the Loup o' Laggan; the rest of the pack was following lower down. The vixen made a frantic effort to clear the steep clint at the head of the scree, but did not reach the crest, and, falling, was pounced on by The Horner's dog. She bit viciously, escaped, and sprang again at the clint. The dog sprang after her.

Just as the pack approached the top of the scree and made the merry music the huntsman loves to hear, Andra Kennedy, who had been lying in wait on the top of the clint, saw Alan taking aim, and perceiving the danger his dog, Yerra, was in – for it was Yerra that led the hunt – jumped to his feet, leaped in front of Yerra and, flourishing his tile hat, uttered a loud 'awowch' that echoed through the glen.

The fox dodged through the pack and, skirting the scree, reached a strong 'yird,' from which the huntsman knew it was impossible to unearth her. Alan, the handsome huntsman, stood sharply outlined against the dawn on the northern spur of Curleywee. Flinging down his gun, he exclaimed savagely, 'Curse Kennedy and his dog. The vixen has beaten us efter a'!'

Andrew McCormick (1932-)

The Border Warrior Knight

From The Lay of the Last Minstrel, *a graphic portrayal of the tough, uncompromising warrior knight of the Borders.*

A stark moss-trooping Scott was he,
As e'er couch'd Border lance by knee:
Through Solway sands, through Tarras moss,
Blindfold, he knew the paths to cross;
By wily turns, by desperate bounds,
Had baffled Percy's best blood-hounds;
In Eske, or Liddel, fords were none,
But he would ride them, one by one;
Alike to him was time or tide,
December's snow, or July's pride;
Alike to him was tide or time,
Moonless midnight, or matin prime;
Steady of heart, and stout of hand,
As ever drove prey from Cumberland;
Five times outlawed had he been,
By England's King, and Scotland's Queen.

Sir Walter Scott (1771-1832)

In Search of Scotland

First published in 1927, H. V. Morton's In Search of Scotland *remains, for me, a classic: a book which is as fresh today as ever. This first extract recounts a meeting in the Borders.*

I was sitting on a stone in the grass beside the broken north aisle of Melrose Abbey. Birds were singing; and I had just drunk a glass of beer with a bow-legged man who told me endless, and probably apocryphal, stories of the Duke of Buccleuch's hounds. If I was thinking of anything it was that Melrose is the most beautiful of Border towns. It must have improved since Walter Scott's time, because he states that Kelso is the most beautiful, if not the most romantic, place on the Borderland. I cannot think that anyone would prefer Kelso to Melrose. Melrose is just as Scottish as Kelso is French.

I became aware of a strange scratch and rustle on the other side of the wall. Some one was trying to walk along the narrow ledge and turn the corner without falling off. Then – such strange things do occasionally happen to the traveller – a remarkably long, slim leg in a brown silk stocking appeared round the corner of the wall and felt blindly for a foothold. Lower and lower it felt, revealing itself with the generosity of authentic beauty.

My intention, which was to spring forward helpfully and guide the foot to a stone, was arrested by the sight of a narrow tartan garter. The next instant a girl with very blue eyes was pulling her skirt down over her knees.

'My!' she said, 'you bet I wouldn't have done that fool thing if I had known there was an audience.'

'Boston!' I said to myself.

I assured her that I had been fast asleep. American girls of this type go round the world in ecstatic troops attended sometimes by a slightly older girl even more lovely than her charges. I looked round for the rest of the college.

'I guess you haven't see a guide-book lying around?'

'No,' I replied, hastily making a search among the daisies.

'Darn it!' she said. 'I've come back for it. I want to read about the Heart.'

'Bruce's heart?'

'Sure.'

'Shall I tell you?'

'Why, certainly, if you know the story.'

'Have a cigarette?'

'Well, yes, I guess I will.'

I told the story, which, I suppose, every Scottish school child must know, for it seems to possess every sign of being the Scottish equivalent of England's story of Alfred and the cakes. When Bruce was dying he ordered that they should cut his heart from his body, place it in a casket, and take it on a pilgrimage to the Holy Land. The Douglas took it, but, being a good Scotsman, got into a fight in Spain, where he was slain in a battle with the Moors. The heart of the Bruce, denied greater sanctuary, was brought home and buried before the high altar of Melrose Abbey.

'I think it is a perfectly horrible story,' said the girl. 'Those old boys did some awful things with themselves alive or dead.'

She smoked reflectively.

'I suppose it's true?'

'In 1920, I am told on excellent authority, the Office of Works, discovered, during excavations here, a casket containing a heart. It was said to be Bruce's heart. Then some one found that it was not buried in the right place, so they concluded that it must have been the heart of a monk.'

'You don't say so!' she said, which is American for our equally idiotic 'Not really!'

I looked at her critically as she sat with her superb legs crossed, flicking cigarette ash on the daisies. She was a perfect flower of the New World. All this was to her improbable and unreal. She was slightly contemptuous. It was rather stimulating. Most American girls of her age are generally so eager to absorb the history of a new country that their brains are frequently a chamber of horrors in which Edward the Conqueror and William the Confessor chase one another through labyrinths of wild inaccuracy. This brain was beautifully free from history.

'Do you like Scotland?'

'No, I like Paris.'

I wanted to ask her why she wore tartan garters, but at this point a sallow American wearing horn spectacles came round the corner and said:

'So there you are! Ma and I have been bawling the place down.'

'Hallo, Daddy! I've been learning things.'

Her father was one of those middle-aged Americans with eyes of steel and a heart full of queer nooks and crannies of emotion. As soon as I saw him I knew that he was embarked on one of those sentimental journeys which happen to all successful Americans. I do not know whether Polish Americans, German Americans, Czecho-Slovakian Americans, Italian Americans, or all the other kind of Americans, are to be discovered pervading the churchyards of Europe with an air of wistful uncertainty; but I do know that every American with English, Scottish, or Irish blood in him comes back at some time to find his roots. They drift about unlikely towns and villages like prosperous ghouls, poring over old parish registers with expectant fingers, and standing for a long time before half-obliterated tombstones. This, I think, is the most lovable trait in the character of the American.

Scotland was, to this man, a tremendous romance. I was inclined to think that his daughter's diffidence was a barrier which she had erected as a protection against his enthusiasm. In level tones, like a strong man sawing a gigantic tree, he spoke to me shyly of seeing Scotland for the first time, of finding all kinds of memories awakening in him – memories of his father and, more dimly, of his grandfather. And as he talked his steely eyes softened and belied the matter-of-factness of his words.

'We came from Perth in the 'forties, I guess,' he said. His eyes kindled. 'We are a sept of the Clan Macdonald.'

'A nice bright tartan,' I said, with a glance at the girl.

'Beast!' she said quickly.

'But, I guess,' his voice sawed on, 'there are none of our family here now; but I do remember my father said that my grandfather was buried in Perth. It is just fine to be here at last.'

He smiled. I liked him. It was a pity he could not have left his women in Paris. Somewhere deep down in him his Scots blood was stirring, puzzling him a lot, I think. I wondered how many of these wanderers really find their roots or know them when they see them.

H.V. Morton (1892-1979)

Border Keeps

The policy of the Scots deterred them from erecting upon the Borders buildings of such extent and strength, as, being once taken by the foe, would have been capable of receiving a permanent garrison. To themselves the woods and hills of their country were pointed out by the Great Bruce as their safest bulwarks; and the maxim of the Douglases, that "it was better to hear the lark sing than the mouse cheep," was adopted by every Border chief. For these combined reasons the residence of the chieftain was commonly a large square battlemented tower, called a *keep,* or *peel,* placed on a precipice, or on the banks of a torrent, and, if the ground would permit, surrounded by a moat. In short, the situation of a Border house, surrounded by woods, and rendered almost inaccessible by torrents, by rocks, or by morasses, sufficiently indicated the pursuits and apprehensions of its inhabitants.

No wonder, therefore, that James V, on approaching the castle of Lochwood, the ancient seat of the Johnstones, is said to have exclaimed, "that he who built it must have been a knave in his heart." An outer wall, with some slight fortifications, served as a protection for the castle at night. The walls of the fortresses were of immense thickness, and they could easily be defended against any small force; more especially as, the rooms being vaulted, each storey formed a separate lodgment, capable of being held out for a considerable time. On such occasions, the usual mode adopted by the assailants, was to expel the inhabitants by setting fire to wet straw in the lower apartments. But the Border chieftains seldom choose to abide in person a siege of this nature. The common people resided in paltry huts, about the safety of which they were little anxious, as they contained nothing of value. On the approach of a superior force, they unthatched them, to prevent their being burned, and then abandoned them to the foe. Their only treasures were a fleet and active horse, with the ornaments which their rapine had procured for the females of their family, of whose gay appearance the Borderers were vain.

Sir Walter Scott (1771-1832)

The New Tay Bridge

The new Tay Railway Bridge of this poem blew down, of course, on December 28, 1879, demonstrating that MacGonagall was as imprescient a lyricist as he was bad.

Beautiful new railway bridge of the silvery Tay,
With your strong brick piers and buttresses in so grand array;
And your thirteen central girders, which seems to my eye,
Strong enough all windy storms to defy.

And as I gaze upon thee my heart feels gay,
Because thou art the greatest railway bridge of the present day;
And can be seen for miles away,
From north, south, east, or west, of the Tay,
On a beautiful and clear sunshiny day,
And ought to make the hearts of the *Mars* boys feel gay;
Because thine equal nowhere can be seen,
Only near by Dundee and the bonnie Magdalen Green.

Beautiful new railway bridge of the silvery Tay,
With your beautiful side screens along your railway;
Which will be a great protection on a windy day,
So as the railway carriages won't be blown away;
And ought to cheer the hearts of the passengers night and day,
As they are conveyed along thy beautiful railway.
And towering above the silvery Tay,
Spanning the beautiful river from shore to shore;
Upwards of two miles and more,
Which is most wonderful to be seen –
Near by Dundee and the bonnie Magdalen Green.

Thy structure, to my eye, seems strong and grand,
And the workmanship most skilfully planned;
And I hope the designers, Messrs. Barlow & Arrol, will prosper
for many a day,
For erecting thee across the beautiful Tay.
And I think nobody need have the least dismay,
To cross o'er thee by night or day;
Because thy strength is visible to be seen –
Near by Dundee and the bonnie Magdalen Green

Beautiful new railway bridge of the silvery Tay,
I wish you success for many a year and day,
And I hope thousands of people will come from far away,
Both high and low, without delay,
From the north, south, east and the west,
Because as a railway bridge thou art the best;
Thou standest unequalled to be seen –
Near by Dundee and the bonnie Magdalen Green.

And for beauty thou art most lovely to be seen,
As the train crosses o'er thee with her cloud of steam
And you look well painted with the colour of marone,
And to find thy equal there is none;
Which, without fear of contradiction, I venture to say,
Because you are the longest railway bridge of the present day;
That now crosses o'er a tidal river stream,
And the most handsome to be seen –
Near by Dundee and the bonnie Magdalen Green.

The New Yorkers boast about their Brooklyn Bridge,
But in comparison to thee it seems like a midge,
Because thou spannest the silvery Tay,
A mile and more longer I venture to say;
Besides the railways carriages are pulled across by a rope,
Therefore Brooklyn Bridge cannot with thee cope;
And as you have been opened on the 20th day of June,
I hope Her Majesty Queen Victoria will visit thee very soon;
Because thou art worthy of a visit from Duke, Lord, or Queen,
And strong and securely built, which is most worthy to be seen –
Near by Dundee and the bonnie Magdalen Green.

William McGonagall (1825-1902)

Blue Bonnets over The Border

March, march, Ettrick and Teviotdale,
Why the deil dinna ye march forward in order?
March, march, Eskdale and Liddesdale,
All the Blue Bonnets are bound for the Border.
Many a banner spread,
Flutters above your head,
Many a crest that is famous in story,
Mount and make ready then,
Sons of the mountain glen,
Fight for the Queen and the old Scottish glory!

Come from the hills where the hirsels are grazing,
Come from the glen of the buck and the roe;
Come to the crag where the beacon is blazing,
Come with the buckler, the lance and the bow.
Trumpets are sounding,
War-steeds are bounding,
Stand to your arms then, and march in good order,
England shall many a day
Tell of the bloody fray,
When the Blue Bonnets came over the Border!

Sir Walter Scott (1771-1832)

CHAPTER 5

THE HIGHLANDS AND ISLANDS

I went to Scotland and found nothing there that looks like Scotland.

Arthur Freed, defending studio production of the film Brigadoon, *1950s.*

The Real Gaels

And so the Highlanders, the real Gaels of Scotland, though much reduced in numbers, continue to exist as a lively and enlivening element in the Scottish scene. It is the Higland heritage that Scotland still puts most prominently into the shop window devoted to Scottish tradition. The bagpipes, the kilt, the tartan, the Celtic fluency of speech – you may find all these and other Gaelic things all over Scotland, but their origin was in the Highlands. Scotland would indeed be a dull country if you removed from it all the few genuine pure Gaels left in the Highlands and Islands. Without the Highland traditions and heritage, however, even as they exist in the Lowlands and in the great towns Scotland would just not be Scotland; it would be unthinkable.

Moray McLaren (1901-71)

A Highland Dwelling

A graphic description of the poverty extant in the Highlands some thirty years after the '45.

It was a delightful day. Lochness, and the road upon the side of it, shaded with birch trees, and the hills above it, pleased us much. The scene was as sequestered and agreeably wild as could be desired, and for a time engrossed all our attention.

To see Dr. Johnson in any new situation is always an interesting object to me; and, as I saw him now for the first time on horseback, jaunting about at his ease in quest of pleasure and novelty, the very different occupations of his former laborious life, his admirable productions, his *London,* his *Rambler,* &c. &c.

immediately presented themselves to my mind, and the contrast made a strong impression on my imagination.

When we had advanced a good way by the side of Lochness, I perceived a little hut, with an old-looking woman at the door of it. I thought here might be a scene that would amuse Dr. Johnson; so I mentioned it to him. 'Let's go in,' said he. We dismounted, and we and our guides entered the hut. It was a wretched little hovel of earth only, I think, and for a window had only a small hole, which was stopped with a piece of turf, that was taken out occasionally to let in light. In the middle of the room or space which we entered, was a fire of peat, the smoke going out at a hole in the roof. She had a pot upon it, with goat's flesh, boiling. There was at one end under the same roof, but divided by a kind of partition made of wattles, a pen or fold in which we saw a good many kids.

Dr. Johnson was curious to know where she slept. I asked one of the guides, who questioned her in Erse. She answered with a tone of emotion, saying, (as he told us,) she was afraid we wanted to go to bed to her. This *coquetry,* or whatever it may be called, of so wretched a being, was truly ludicrous. Dr. Johnson and I afterwards were merry upon it. I said, it was he who alarmed the poor woman's virtue – 'No, sir, (said he,) she'll say, 'there came a wicked young fellow, a wild dog, who I believe would have ravished me, had there not been with him a grave old gentleman, who repressed him: but when he gets out of the sight of his tutor, I'll warrant you he'll spare no woman he meets, young or old.' – 'No, sir, (I replied,) she'll say, 'There was a terrible ruffian who would have forced me, had it not been for a civil decent young man who, I take it, was an angel sent from heaven to protect me.'

Dr. Johnson would not hurt her delicacy, by insisting on 'seeing her bed-chamber,' like *Archer* in the *Beaux Stratagem.* But my curiosity was more ardent; I lighted a piece of paper, and went into the place where the bed was. There was a little partition of wicker, rather more neatly done than that for the fold, and close by the wall was a kind of bedstead of wood with heath upon it by way of bed; at the foot of which I saw some sort of blankets or covering rolled up in a heap. The woman's name was Fraser; so was her husband's. He was a man of eighty. Mr. Fraser of Balnain allows him to live in this hut, and keep sixty goats, for taking care of his woods, where he then was. They had five children, the eldest only thirteen. Two were gone to Inverness to buy meal; the rest were looking after the goats. This contented family had four stacks of barley, twenty-four sheaves in each. They had a few fowls. We were informed that they lived all the spring without meal, upon milk and curds and whey alone. What they get for their goats, kids, and fowls, maintains them during the rest of the year.

She asked us to sit down and take a dram. I saw one chair. She said she was as happy as any woman in Scotland. She could hardly speak any English except a few detached words. Dr. Johnson was pleased at seeing, for the first time, such a state of human life. She asked for snuff. It is her luxury, and she uses a great deal. We had none; but gave her sixpence a piece. She then brought out her whisky bottle. I tasted it; as did Joseph and our guides: so I gave her sixpence more. She sent us away with many prayers in Erse.

James Boswell (1740-95)

Shores

If we were in Talisker on the shore
where the great white mouth
opens between two hard jaws
Rubha nan Clach and the Bioda Ruadh,
I would stand beside the sea
re-newing love in my spirit
while the ocean was filling
Talisker bay forever:
I would stand there on the bareness of the shore
until Prishal bowed his stallion head.

And if we were together
on Calgary shore in Mull,
between Scotland and Tiree,
between the world and eternity,
I would stay there till doom
measuring sand, grain by grain,
and in Uist, on the shore of Homhsta

in presence of that wide solitude,
I would wait there for ever,
for the sea draining drop by drop.

And if I were on the shore of Moidart
with you, for whom my care is new,
I would put up in a synthesis of love for you
the ocean and the sand, drop and grain.
And if we were on Mol Stenscholl Staffin
when the unhappy surging sea dragged
the boulders and threw them over us,
I would build the rampart wall
against an alien eternity grinding.

Sorley MacLean (1911-)

The Herring Fishers

The hard life of the herring fishers of the east coast of Scotland, personally experienced by Christian Watt (see page 137), also forms the theme of Neil Gunn's novel The Silver Darlings, *which so skilfully captures for the reader the lives of the Highland fishermen of Caithness.*

And then the incident happened.

Dunster had been luckier than many places on the rocky coasts of that northern sea in so far as loss of life was concerned. Hardly a season passed without its storms and alarms, but actual tragedy had been rare. Perhaps Henry and Finn had set a high standard of daring against the weather, and though there was little overt rivalry among boats, yet no skipper liked hanging about the shore when another was at sea, not unless his weather judgement had been proved in the past and was respected. However that may be, several boats were at sea in the dawn of a darkling April morning, when an easterly gale sprang up. Henry and Finn had been a little uneasy, because the sea had a nasty 'lift' in it; there had been a 'carry' on the sky they did not like, and they could smell bad weather about. But in the winter-spring fishing particularly, such an uneasiness was not unusual, and did little more than keep the eye lifting and the ear alert.

They were about to start hauling a great line with its hundred hooks on snoods a fathom apart when they saw and heard the wind coming. Such an onset occurred frequently enough to have found a common form of description in the mouths of the fishermen: 'A lump of wind struck us'. The lump now struck them with a sweeping flattening violence, and Finn and another threw themselves on the loosely stowed canvas. Henry's face was into the weather. 'It's coming, boys!' he cried, when he had assured himself of what was behind the lump.

They were about five miles from Dunster, and Henry's decision to leave the line and make for home was immediate. Over the blackened water, scuds of drift were racing. With a peak of sail to give steering way Henry ran his *White Heather* dead before it. The uneasy sea began to rise with great rapidity. But they were not frightened of the sea; what sat in Henry's mind was fear of the shore, where in no time the rollers would be breaking. There was no harbour, no breakwater, nothing but the open beach and the stony river mouth. And apart from that crescent of beach, with some deathly skerries beyond its southern horn, there was nothing but gaunt cliff, whose base far as the eye could reach was already white spume. That the tide was low was an added anxiety.

They could see the other boats making for home. None of them had been so far out as the *White Heather,* and already several were approaching the bay, and three more, a little to the south'ard, were fighting hard against the drift for the wind was a little north of east. Two of them should make it, but the third, some distance behind, would have all she could do to keep off the skerries. Yes, it would be touch and go with her!

The crew felt exhilarated. Already in their bodies was the fight with the beach, the leaping overboard, the gripping of the gunnel, the heave upward of the bow to keep the bottom planking from getting stove in. To save the boat each in risking his life would know a high thrill. For the boat was more than all, it was their challenge to the sea, arousing in them not thought of risk but an exalted courage. And Henry was there, jealous of his seamanship, anxious in the moment of test that he should acquit himself creditably before his fellows.

Finn glanced back at him. Henry's thin face was set calm, but its lines held as in a faint fixed smile, the irony that was characteristic of him. Somehow this touched Finn with the emotion of comradeship and he glanced away – and saw well to the west and fairly low in to the rocks the heaving darkness of a small boat. He cried out and pointed. They all looked and their faces quickened, for they knew on the instant that that boat was doomed.

'It's Daniel Bannerman,' cried Henry. . .

At that moment Roddie had been working unceasingly on Duncan's body for thirty minutes. After five minutes, no-one could believe that any life was left in the body. Roddie lifted his own head, working patiently at the same time. 'Donnie, change that hand,' he said; and Donnie at once forgot the hurt of the lashing 'No!' Una took the other hand, because Finn was wet through and now, after the exhausting effort of the rock, could hardly keep his teeth from chittering as he lay on the ground. Others made a wind-break, and in a deep half-circle the crowd stood looking and waiting. Then they saw Duncan's mother do a thing that silently and strangely moved them all. Anticipating Roddie's order to chafe the feet, she stripped the boots off and the two pairs of thick socks, and then with a curious whimper, she unfastened her bodice and placed the cold lifeless feet between her deep breasts, and covered them over with the bodice, and pressed them inward, while the tears flowed down her face and she murmured, 'My boy! my own boy!'

At the end of twenty minutes, which seemed to everyone a much longer time, they were satisfied there was no hope. Heads were shaken. Folk felt that Roddie's patience was being overdone. This was a refusal to recognize death, a taking away from its dread dignity. The slow incessant handling of the poor lifeless body . . . it was time Roddie gave up.

But Roddie did not give up, and no one dared to suggest to him to do so, for though patience could dwell in this man as in a stone, there could at the same moment be in him the explosive lash.

Then Finn gave up hope, and he saw that Una had no hope left either. The hands were limp and cold, the hands of the dead. He had never seen her as he saw her now, all the movement of her mind, its emotions, its courage, its fear; the sudden access in which she pressed the hand against her face, against her neck, and then continued to chafe it upward as Roddie had told her.

'You'd better go home, Finn,' said Roddie, looking at him.

'No,' answered Finn lightly, and clenched his hands and

gritted his teeth to keep the idiotic trembling within bounds. At that moment he encountered Una's eyes and they looked at him directly, knowing him, and he was aware of a movement within him, profound as tragedy, as death, before her eyes fell to their task.

Then hope went from Roddie – not, after the first few minutes, that it had been very strong. But the curious automatism that his mind could achieve in certain situations, when time became obliterated in endurance, decided to keep him going for still a little while. But conscious hope now left him, and if the father of Duncan had told him to desist, he would have done so.

Only the mother had any hope left, and it was hardly hope so much as a blind surging effort to give warmth back to the cold body. She nursed the feet against her breast as if she were giving them suck of her heart's blood. She lay on her side, curved inward towards them, and the father who had to endure this strange sight, got held as in a trance, for he knew the warmth of life there was in this woman, and how as a woman she was the great fighter of death.

And then it was, when hope was going to sink away from her also, that she roused herself against death, and called from the deeps of her spirit to her son, pouring her life into him, and for answer she felt a pressure of the cold feet against her breasts, and she gave a great cry to her far-wandering son, guiding him back to her.

Roddie saw the slow tremor pass over the body, the lips part, and the head reach forward a little in a motion of vomit.

'Dear God, he's living!' he said, in a harsh voice of wonder.

Neil M. Gunn (1891-1973)

Surprises at Stornoway

James Hogg, otherwise known as the Ettrick Shepherd, made a tour of the Highlands and Western Isles between 1802 and 1804. Fortunately, many of his experiences were chronicled in letters to Sir Walter Scott. This letter of Sunday, June 26, 1803, recounts some memorable experiences in the Western Isles at Stornoway.

Barvas
Sunday 26th June

Dear Sir, – We at length entered the harbour of Stornoway, and about seven o'clock in the evening cast anchor within a very short space of the houses, having been exactly sixty hours on the passage, a distance of scarcely so many miles.

As soon as I arrived, I went to the head inn, held by Mr. Creighton, a silly, despicable man, but privileged in having an excellent wife. During the whole of that evening I could not walk without taking hold of everything that came in my way, impressed with an idea that all things were in motion. I was very unfortunate in not meeting with the people to whom I was recommended here. I had a letter for Mr. Chapman at Seaforth Lodge, but he was absent in Uig, parting some land, and Mrs. Chapman being in a poor state of health, I never presented myself. I had a letter to Mr. Donald Macdonald, and another to Mr. Robertson, both of Stornoway, and in whose company I spent some time; but the one was obliged to go from home in the packet, and the other did not come home until the last day that I was there.

I wandered about the town and neighbouring country for three days, sometimes in a company with one, and sometimes with another. There is a Captain Marshall, from the neighbourhood of Fochabers, lodging in the same house with me, a sober, sensible man, with whom I was very happy.

I was indeed greatly surprised at meeting with such a large and populous town in such a remote and distant country. It was but the preceding week that I ever heard of it, and yet it is quite unrivalled in all the west of Scotland north of the Clyde, either in population, trade, or commerce. I was informed by Mr. Robison, comptroller of the Customs, that, according to the last survey, which was then newly taken, the town and suburbs contained nearly seventeen hundred souls. Mr. Macdonald, to whom I mentioned this, doubted its containing so many, but was certain that there were above a thousand.

There is one full half of the town composed of as elegant houses, with even more genteel inhabitants, than are generally to be met with in the towns of North Britain which depend solely on the fishing and trade. The principal and modern part of the town stands on a small point of land stretching into the harbour in the form of a T, and as you advance back from the shore the houses grow gradually worse. The poor people have a part by themselves, on a rising ground to the north-east of the town, and though all composed of the meanest huts it is laid out in streets and rows as regularly as a camp. The houses on the shore to the eastward and those at the head of the bay are of the medium sort. It hath an excellent harbour, and is much ornamented by the vicinity of Seaforth Lodge, which stands on a rising ground overlooking the town and harbour. The town is much incommoded by the want of streets or pavements. Even the most elegant houses facing the harbour, saving a small road close by the wall, have only the rough sea shore to pass and repass on, which being composed of rough stones, which fly from the foot, grinding on one another, forms a most uncomfortable footpath.

As the peculiarities observable in the modes and customs of the inhabitants are applicable to the whole island, I shall note a few of them on taking leave of it. I shall only observe here, that the well directed and attended schools, the enlightened heads, and enlarged ideas of a great number of the people of Stornoway bid fair to sow the seeds of emulation, and consequently of improvement in that remote country. It is a general complaint through all the Long Island that the poorer sort are much addicted to pilfering. I persuaded myself that I saw a striking evidence to the contrary in the inhabitants of this town. During the daytime there were thousands of white fish spread on the shores, drying on the sand. When night came they were gathered and built up in large heaps, and loosely covered with some coarse cloth, and when the sun grew warm next day were again spread. Now, my dear Sir, I'll wager you durst not have exposed your fish in such a manner at Edinburgh, for as fine a place as it is.

Although the island is not noted for riots, I had no very favourable specimen of their absolute command over their passions. On the very night of my arrival a desperate affray took place in the room adjoining to that in which I slept. Several respectable men, the collector, and one of the Bailiffs, were engaged in it. It was fought with great spirit and monstrous vociferation. Desperate wounds were given and received, the door was split in pieces, and twice some of the party entered my chamber. I was overpowered with sleep, having got none at sea, and minded them very little, but was informed of all by Mr. Marshall. A ship's captain, in particular, wrought terrible devastation. He ran foul of the table, although considerably to the windward, which he rendered a perfect wreck, sending all its precious cargo of crystal, china, etc. to the bottom, and attacked his opponents with such fury and resolution that he soon laid most of them sprawling on the deck. Some of the combatants being next day confined to their beds, summonses were issued, and a prosecution commenced, but the parties being very nearly connected a treaty was set on foot, and the preliminaries signed before I left Stornoway.

James Hogg (1770-1835)

Hebridean Alarms: An Inspector Calls

It may well have been a Hebridean who coined the phrase: 'When the Good Lord made time, he made plenty of it.' And if it was, why not? But the chestnut has been hung round his neck to imply that the islander will not willingly do today what can be put off till tomorrow, and I am certainly not living proof to the contrary. But, in those boyhood days about which I'm writing, it was difficult, if not pointless, to cultivate a sense of urgency when life was governed by time and tide, by season and weather, and by communication and transport. Every stick of wood and every sheet of corrugated iron and every piece of ancillary hardware from shelf brackets to nails had to be imported – invariably from Glasgow or from Greenock, because it was from there that the venerable coasters *The Dunara Castle* and *The Hebrides* sailed on their Odysseys round the myriad islands of the west coast with us at the tail end. Certain shops and firms in those faraway places had near monopolies of our community's trade by virtue of the fact that they could interpret the islanders' needs as expressed in rough sketches and fractured English, and acted on them as expeditiously as the schedules of the two ships allowed. Some of those firms won themselves trust and loyalty which were to help swell their prestige and their profits for decades, and their names became part of the vernacular. For years I had to pause and think whether Peter Fisher was the Galilean apostle or the Glasgow supplier of paints and wallpapers.

But it mattered not how efficient the suppliers, their deliveries were still governed by the schedules of *The Dunara* and *The Heb*, and their schedules, in turn, were governed by the tide and weather because, in those days, they had to unload at some very exposed rough jetties or even ferry their cargoes ashore in dribs and drabs by rowing boat. It could well be a month before an order despatched from our village was finally delivered, and it could well be that when it was delivered the weather had turned so stormy that only an idiot would attempt to manoeuvre a six-foot sheet of plywood or corrugated iron; or else the materials would appear on the very first day of a spell of dry weather which had to be seized upon for the cutting of the peat or the shearing of the sheep – whichever chore was seasonal at the time.

These were factors not always appreciated by the bureaucrats in Edinburgh whose morning coffees and afternoon teas arrived on their desks at the pre-ordained times regardless of whether or not *The Dunara Castle* was being held up in Castlebay for nine days by a force ten gale. And so, when the days were sufficiently lengthened and the salmon were deemed to be running well in the Outer Islands, the men from the Board tore themselves away from their offices and their wives and set out on their pilgrimages to check on the progress being made by the new crofters on the new land which had been bestowed upon them.

While the men from Edinburgh may not have understood the problems governing the tempo of island life, the men of the islands understood the official mentality fine.

As soon as news came that an inspection was imminent all the proper seasonal work was temporarily abandoned, and work on the new houses was resumed with vigour even if it meant stripping off some sarking or corrugated iron that had already been laid, and going through the motions of nailing it back on again. By whatever means, every man jack in the village was busy as the government's hired car jolted its way down the road, stopping here and there to justify its journey. Since a tour of the crofting communities was a coveted "perk" for the office-bound officials, they came round in strict rotas so that, in fact, the same pair never came on successive occasions, making it extremely difficult for one delegation to decide whether or how much advance had been made on what had been seen by the previous one. The crofters, who could modulate the fluency of their English as the occasion demanded, were always cautiously reassuring. And, at the end of the inspection, they always wished the officials 'a nice holiday'. At which the men from the Board flashed uncertain little white smiles and continued their journey towards the hotel where, I am sure, they coined new aphorisms on the theme of God making plenty of time.

Finlay J. Macdonald (1925-)

Whisky Galore

Peat-stacks became a little larger than they usually were at this time of the year. Ricks suggested that the cattle had eaten less hay than usual this winter. Loose floorboards were nailed down. Corks bobbed about in waters where hitherto none had bobbed. Turf recently disturbed was trodden level again as carefully as on a golf-course. In one household only was there anything in the nature of a panic. This was at the post-office where Joseph Macroon would not be back from Edinburgh until the *Island Queen* brought him over from Obaig next day. The news that a strange motor-boat with the Exciseman, the Constable, and an officer in uniform was headed for Kiltod from Snorvig struck Peggy and Kate Anne with dismay.

'*A Mhuire, Mhuire,* what will we do if they come here?' Peggy asked tremulously. 'They'll put my father in prison if they find all that whisky in the shed.'

'Don't be saying such a thing, *a Pheigi,*' her sister adjured her. 'They mustn't be finding it. Where's Kenny?'

'Och, Kenny!' Peggy scoffed. 'It would just be a fine excitement for Kenny if his father was taken away to prison.'

'What will we do then?' Kate Anne asked in much agitation.

Peggy took her father's decrepit spy-glass and went outside the shop to watch the hostile boat.

'He's looking terribly fierce,' she said to her sister.

'Who is?'

'The Constable. *A Mhuire mhàthair,* just as black as a crow. And there's a soldier with him right enough. The other will be the Exciseman from Nobost. They're just coming straight for us.'

'There's Kenny down by the quay,' said Kate Anne. 'Kenny!' she cried. '*A Choinnich!*'

But their younger brother paid no attention. He was absorbed in watching the approach of the *Pearl*.

'Will they be taking us away with them if they find all that whisky?' Kate Anne asked.

'Och, I don't know what they'll be doing,' said Peggy almost in despair.

'Will I run up to the Chapel House and ask Father James what we'd better do?' Kate Anne suggested as a last hope.

'Father James will be thinking about his own whisky,' her sister replied. 'He'll just be laughing at us. Och, there's only one thing we can do. We must just empty it all away.'

'What will himself be saying when he comes back from Edinburgh and finds all his whisky gone?' Kate Anne asked.

'Don't be daft, Kate Anne. If he comes back from Edinburgh and finds us gone and his whisky too, what will he be saying then at all?'

'Where would we be gone to?'

'To prison. Where else?'

'To prison? Us?' Kate Anne gasped. '*A Dhia,* Peggy, come on and pour it all away before they get here.'

At this moment the decrepit spy-glass, which only Joseph Macroon himself knew how to nurse, collapsed in Peggy's hands, and without waiting to see which direction the hostile boat was taking, she led the way at a run toward her father's big shed at the back in which the lumber of years was stored.

'We'll never get all these bottles out before they catch us,' Kate Anne declared when they pulled away the tarpaulin from the pile of cases.

'We'll try anyway,' said Peggy resolutely. 'Maybe they won't be coming here first. Get a hammer and a chisel and don't be standing there like a dummy. I'm sure it's me that will be glad when I'm married. Going off to Edinburgh like that and leaving us here with all this whisky! Wait you till my father comes back tomorrow and see what I'll be telling him.'

As fast as the girls could pull them out of the cases they opened the bottles and poured out the liquid gold on the floor of the shed. Highland Hope and Highland Heart, Tartan Milk and Tartan Perfection, Stag's Breath and Stalker's Joy, yes, even Stalker's Joy, which Joseph had finally decided was the brand he liked best of all and of which he had collected a dozen bottles for his own consumption, all were blended ruthlessly upon the earthen floor of the big shed for only the air to taste.

'*A Mhuire, Mhuire,* I feel quite funny, Kate Anne,' said Peggy when nothing remained of the contents of at least a couple of hundred bottles of whisky except the heady fumes.

'I'm just going round inside my head like a top,' her sister declared. . .

The return of Joseph Macroon from Edinburgh, where he had not succeeded in persuading the Department of Agriculture to support his notion of applying for a licence to sell spirituous liquor at Kiltod, was less happy that Tuesday than the return of Major Quiblick to Nobost.

As soon as the *Morning Star* brought him across from the *Island Queen* he went to his shed, having heard on the pier of the activity on Little Todday the previous day. He opened the door. He sniffed the air. He muttered something under his breath. He darted forward and pulled away the tarpaulin. He gazed at the hillock of empty bottles. He groaned. He took from his head the ceremonious bowler he had been wearing to keep his end up in Edinburgh. He flung it down on the whisky-soaked earthen floor, and hurried away to his own room at the back of the shop.

'A Pheigi! A Chatriona! A Choinnich!' he cried. *'Cà bheil sibh? Thigibh an so! Thigibh! Thigibh! A Dhia nan Gràs, cà bheil sibh?'*

'What's the matter, father?' Peggy asked coming in from the post-office. 'Kenny's away back to Snorvig for the mail. And Kate Anne's away with him.'

'My whisky! Who's after throwing away all my whisky?'

'Kate Anne and I were afraid the Constable was coming here. They were all over the island yesterday and everybody was hiding away their Minnie as hard as they could be.'

'*A Dhia*, then why weren't the two of you hiding it?' the stricken father moaned.

'How could we be hiding all those cases?' Peggy asked indignantly. 'Kate Anne and me nearly killed ourselves opening them and emptying out the bottles. I don't know how many there were.'

'Eighteen cases,' Joseph groaned. 'Two hundred and sixteen bottles, and twelve of them Stalker's Joy, the best of all. Daughters? *Ochòin mo thruaighe!* They're just a misery and a burden to a man.'

King Lear himself was speaking.

Compton Mackenzie (1883-1972)

Travel in The Highlands

Henry Cockburn was born in the Parliament Close of Old Edinburgh in 1779 and after education at the High School and the University of Edinburgh he was called to the Scottish Bar in 1800. In 1834 he was made, as Lord Cockburn, a judge of the Court of Session and, in 1837, a Lord of Justiciary. His shrewd and perceptive Journal of his years as a Circuit judge (1837-54) provide us with some unique insights into social life around Scotland.

Musing along in the carriage to-day, I thought I had better try to recall some of the features of our ancient Circuits, which time has effaced. I have known Scotland. Circuitously, for above forty years. Many curious recollections arise on looking back on such a travelled road. The shades of many old lords, famous barristers, notorious provosts, sonorous macers, formal clerks, odd culprits, and queer witnesses reappear. But like wayside objects that we cast behind us on a journey, they cannot all be retained, and many must be let die. Some things, however, may be worth preserving.

Those who are born to railroads, or even to modern mail-coaches can scarcely be made to understand how we, of the previous age, got on. The state of the roads may be judged of from two or three facts. There was no bridge over the Tay at Dunkeld, or over the Spey at Fochabers, or over the Findhorn at Forres, nothing but wretched, pierless ferries, let to poor cottars, who rowed, or hauled, or pushed a crazy boat across, or more commonly got their wives to do it. There used to be no mail-coach north of Aberdeen, till, I think, after the battle of Waterloo. It consisted of a sort of chaise, drawn by two horses, and held three persons, two of them placed as usual in a chaise, and the third stuck into a kind of sentry-box opposite, with his back to the horses, and, of course, there were no front windows. To reach Inverness by the mail thirty or even twenty-five years ago took only about nine hours short of the time required to get to London. If the direct Highland road was preferred, then there was neither public conveyance nor post-horses. It was necessary to take the same horses all the way from Perth, and then the journey occupied three entire days from Perth and four from Edinburgh. I once came from Inverness to Perth with the Justice-Clerk, Charles Hope, who was always very kind to me, and used to take me about with him; and our days' work, with his four horses, were these: The first day we got to Kinrara, where we dined with the famous, clever, agreeable, profligate old Duchess of Gordon, who gathered all the neighbours within many miles for a ball. The second day brought us, towards its close, to Dalnacardoch; the third to Perth. Of course we had to rest and feed the steeds every stage. Even the public coach, when set agoing, delighted the lieges by making them sleep only two nights by the way. They could only reach Perth (the Queensferry very bad) the first day. Starting next morning at five, Pitmain was accomplished about nine at night, and Inverness appeared on the evening of the third day. The ark of a vehicle was generally moved by three horses, but for the stage between Dalnacardoch and Dalwhinnie it had four, and sometimes it had only two; and no set ever escaped with a single.

It was not just so bad on other Circuits, but it was bad enough. Dumfries and Ayr were both unattainable in one day; and Inveraray was out of the world. Even Glasgow was a good day's work; and hence the inns next it, and next Edinburgh, were excellent, for Scotch inns of that day, and were generally crowded every night. The fact is incredible now – but it is a fact – that there were few hostels more resorted to by newly married pairs than those of Midcalder, Uphall, Holytown, Noblehouse, and Blackshiels. These now mean ruins were then bowers of Hymen. It was not distances or bad roads that were the obstacles to progress, so much as the want of horses.

Henry Cockburn (1779-1854)

Highland Women

The young women of the mountains of Scotland are, in general, remarkably clean, when compared with our peasants. There is a charm in the arrangement of their hair, and an ease and grace in their manner of holding their head. Their short petticoat, commonly of a deep colour, shows off the whiteness of their legs, which are admirably shaped, though large and vigorous. They have the beauty of strength.

Charles Nodier (1780-1844)

The Kilt

The common habit of the ordinary Highlander is far from being acceptable to the eye . . . this dress is called the *quelt*; and, for the most part, they wear the petticoat so very short, that in a windy day, going up a hill, or stooping, the indecency of it is plainly discovered.

Edward Burt (d. 1755)

Highland Hospitality

When beginning to descend the hill towards Loch Lomond we overtook two girls, who told us we could not cross the ferry till evening, for the boat was gone with a number of people to Church. One of the girls was exceedingly beautiful; and the figures of both of them, in grey plaids falling to their feet, their faces only being uncovered, excited our attention before we spoke to them: but they answered us so sweetly that we were quite delighted. At the same time they stared at us with an innocent look of wonder. I think I never heard the English language sound more sweetly than from the mouth of the elder of these girls, while she stood at the gate answering our inquiries, her face flushed with the rain; her pronunciation was clear and distinct, without difficulty, yet slow, like that of a foreign speech. . . We were glad to be housed, with our feet on a warm hearth-stone: and our attendants were so active and good-humoured, that it was pleasant to have to desire them to do anything. The younger was a delicate and unhealthy-looking girl: but there was an uncommon meekness in her countenance, with an air of premature intelligence, which is often seen in sickly young persons. The other moved with unusual activity, which was hastened very delicately by a certain hesitation in her looks when she spoke, being able to understand us but imperfectly. They were both exceedingly desirous to get me what I wanted to make me comfortable. I was to have a gown and petticoat of the mistress's: so they turned out her whole wardrobe upon the parlour floor talking Erse to one another and laughing all the time. It was long before they could decide which of the gowns I was to have: they chose at last, no doubt thinking it was the best, a light-coloured sprigged cotton, with long sleeves, and they both laughed when I was putting it on with the blue linsey petticoat; and one or the other, or both together, helped me to dress, repeating at least half a dozen times, 'You never had on the like of that before.' They held a consultation of several minutes over a pair of coarse woollen stockings, gabbling Erse as fast as their tongues could move, and looking as if uncertain what to do: at last, with great diffidence they offered them to me adding, as before, that I have never worn 'the like of them.'

The hospitality we had met on this our first entrance into the Highlands and on this day, the innocent merriment of the girls with their kindness to us, and the beautiful figure and face of the elder, comes to my mind whenever I think of the ferry house and waterfall of Loch Lomond, and I never think of the two girls but the whole image of that romantic spot is before me, a living image, as it will be to my dying day.

Dorothy Wordsworth (1771-1855)

A Highland Community

The little Highland community in which Kenn lived was typical of what might be found anywhere round the northern and western shores of Scotland: the river coming down out of the wooded glen or strath into the little harbour; the sloping croft lands, with their small cultivated fields; the croft houses here and there, with an odd one on a far ridge against the sky; the school, the post office, and the old church, where the houses herded loosely into a township; and inland the moors lifting to blue mountains.

On flat ground by the harbour were the cottages of most of the regular fishermen, but many of the crofters also took part in the fishing seasons, for wealth was unknown amongst them, and poverty had to be outwitted by all the means in their power. Sea-fishing and crofting were the only two occupations of the people, and however the rewards of their labour varied from season to season they were never greatly dissimilar over a whole year or over ten years. Thus in the course of centuries there had developed a communal feeling so genuine that the folk themselves never thought about it. They rejoiced and quarrelled, loved and fought, on a basis of social equality. Even the big farm was absent and so there were no bothies and farm servants, and none of the children that went to school had a father who thought of someone above him as 'the master'. The solitary exception was the laird's farm. It was run by a grieve and had a bothy where two ploughmen from a southern county lived. These ploughmen always referred to the grieve as 'the maister', and this provoked a certain laughing astonishment amongst the children of that place, for the grieve was a cross-grained wizened little man and when he found boys playing about his stackyard or around the steading, he would shout at them in a high-pitched voice. They would vanish as if the devil were after them, and when they had got together again they would mimic him and double up with mirth.

The laird was a being apart, who visited his mansion house only at intervals. He did not belong to them and they never thought about him; for even their rents were collected by a factor who came for the purpose from his lawyer's office in the county town. The people had an instinctive fear of this factor, and always assumed their best dress and manners when they went before him to pay their dues. Sometimes they had not the money to pay and then, after the mother and father had had a long miserable morning together, the father would set out to the hateful meeting. There was nothing in the world, no hardship, no danger, he feared half as much as having to admit that he could not pay his full rent. His legs would feel weak under the burden of shame as he went his way. 'I would rather,' said Davy, 'have the seas breaking in white smoke over me with nowhere to run for.'

Accordingly the laird and his factor were outside the daily run of their lives altogether, and the only real touch with this curious menace or tyranny of the mansion house was found in the gamekeepers.

Neil M. Gunn (1891-1973)

The Stallion Man

From infancy onwards, we crofter children grew up surrounded by quadrupedal sex and it is a miracle of instinct that we didn't accept quadrupedal modes as the norm instead of having to await enlightenment from *Playboy* and the *Kama Sutra.* We had seen the bull and the ram, the dog and the cat, set about their business purposefully after minimal skirmishing. But our aristocratic stallion – and for all I know this may be an effetism of aristocracy at all levels – had to be helped. After a bit of sniffing and snorting around an impatient mare, the stallion would wait for the man to take him by one of the front fetlocks and encourage him upwards. Only then would the animal languidly release from his body something which, for all the world, resembled the black concertina hose which comes out of the back of a modern tumble-drier, and this the stallion man had to guide into the appropriate channel. It can't have been the most enlightening of professional duties although veterinary surgeons have to do worse, but it didn't deserve the opprobrium which accrued to the poor Stallion Man. He was the object of jibes and innuendous jokes to his face and behind his back, and, to this day there is no greater Gaelic insult to hurl at a toady or someone who performs another's menial jobs than to call him a 'cock boy'. But that year's cock boy was to gain for himself a moment of glory, and a dinner before which, for once, he wasn't made to wash his hands.

Gillespie and I had had a hey-day, sawing and drilling and nailing together pieces of wood into models of our imaginings, and we had begun to tire of the whole thing while we still had ten fingers apiece. Just as we were thinking of trailing off in search of some other adventure I spotted the box of matches which my father had forgetfully left on the new hearth. And his comments about having tested the chimney flashed back to me. It was obvious from the charred remains of shavings at the base of the chimney pipe that they were the very stuff that he had used, and there were still mounds of them around. Between us, it took only a few minutes to make a sizeable heap and, after several broken matches, we had it ablaze. Had we left it at that things mightn't have got out of hand, but our triumph went to our heads when we looked up and saw, spiralling from the chimney top, shapely puffs of creamy white smoke that would have sealed the election of half a hundred Popes. We decided to compound our success by heaping on to the burning shavings all the constructions that we had nailed together during the previous hour, and soon we had a roaring bonfire that would have roasted an ox – and might conceivably have roasted us had the Stallion Man not arrived at the gate as the wooden frame-work of the gable-end began to catch fire.

It must have been the first time that the Stallion Man moved quickly in his life. He whipped the huge felt horse cloth off the horse's back, rushed into the house, threw us out bodily and unceremoniously, and, like a man possessed, began to smother the flames. The situation was under control by the time my father arrived on the scene, gasping for breath and ashen faced, after a burst across the hill from Barabel's such as he had probably not indulged in since he had gone over the top at the Battle of Arras.

'Thank God you're all right', he said, looking at Gillespie and myself. 'And as for you', he went on turning to the Stallion Man, 'it was Fate that sent you the way.'

The Stallion Man appeared not to hear him.

'This is as tattered as a whore's hole,' he grumbled, thrusting his raw, scorched fist through the middle of the singed horse cloth, and I noticed the muscle in my father's jaw twitch as his eyes flicked in the direction of Gillespie and myself. 'The Board's going to have something to say about this!'

He was wrong. By the time he left the schoolhouse, cleaned and salved and with a good meal in him, the stallion's broad back was draped in a folded suit-length of Harris Tweed which had been ordered for Sir Thomas Lipton who was an occasional visitor to Harris on one or other of his yachts. As it turned out, the ripening years wouldn't have allowed Sir Thomas much wear out of the tweed anyway, but when the cock boy came round the island next he was sporting a suit that would have graced a game-keeper while the stallion seemed perfectly happy in a traditional horse cloth with the Government's seal still crisp on it.

I don't know what quiet persuasion my father had used on my mother but, apart from the first flurry of nervous anxiety, she never referred to the near catastrophe again. Father mentioned it once during the evening. While my mother was putting the baby to bed he looked at me for a long time over the bowl of his pipe, which had a habit of tilting ceiling-wards when he was in quizzical mood, and then said, 'I don't believe in giving rows for things which won't happen again anyway, but I'd give a lot to know what you'll be up to next.' Obviously I was in no position to hazard a guess myself, but before the silence became embarrassing my mother came through from the bedroom having remembered that she hadn't heard what had befallen Wee Barabel who had been tangentially involved in it all.

Apparently the whole problem had been there for my father to see and to solve as soon as he reached her little hovel. On the night before last a couple of the hillside lads – 'the bloods' as they were called – had crept up while she was asleep and stuffed her one and only window with turf. And she had spent thirty-six hours in bed waiting for the dawn, puzzled only by the fact that her bladder was making her reach for the pot more often than usual. It was while he was letting in the light and trying to comfort Barabel for the lost day in her life that father had noticed the smoke and flames rising from the roadside down below.

'Boys!' said my mother, as she was to say so often in the future, 'I'm afraid it's worse they get as they get older.' And that reminded her that it was time for me to be in bed. I was conscious of the fact that she was even more solicitous than usual as she tucked me into bed, whispering so as not to waken the baby.

'You close your eyes and go to sleep now; you've had quite a day of it!' She kissed me and crossed over to close the curtains against the light of the setting sun.

'Look mammy', I said, sitting up and holding up the old woollen bedspread which come down through a couple of generations, 'this coverlet is as tattered as a whore's hole.'

She jerked as if someone had hit her in the rib-cage. Her mouth opened, but she decided to say nothing. And she walked quickly from the bedroom leaving the curtains half drawn. I lay back on the pillow confirmed in my suspicion that I had found a new phrase worth hoarding for future use.

Finlay J. Macdonald (1925-)

ORKNEY

The Orkney Islands are such an interesting little community that they deserve a longer description than I have given to the places I stopped at in the Highlands; also I know them much better, having been brought up in them, and can speak of them with more confidence. They are far less spectacular than the Western Highlands, and the tourist in search of the immediately picturesque will find little to repay him in them. He will find no attempt, either, to entertain him; and I have heard of holiday-makers hopefully going to Orkney and after two days of appalled disillusion taking the boat back to Aberdeen or Leith, and proceeding straight to Dunoon or Blackpool. He will find a group of little islands, some quite flat, some hilly, all of them almost treeless, and all remarkably well and efficiently cultivated. He will also find a population of small farmers and crofters, naturally gentle and courteous in manners, but independent too, and almost all of them moderately prosperous. If he goes there in the middle of June, the long light, which never fades at that time of the year, but ebbs and ebbs until, before one can tell how, morning is there again, will charm and tease him; he will lose his sleep for a few nights and be discontented during the day, and feel that he is not quite in the real world. If he has an eye for such things, he will be delighted by the spectacle of the quickly changing skies and the clearness and brightness of all the colours. But he will not come to know much about the place unless he lives there for quite a long time, habituating himself to the rhythm of the life, and training himself to be pleased with bareness and simplicity in all things.

Edwin Muir (1887-1959)

Death of a Community

George Mackay Brown's novel Greenvoe *provides us with a vivid and enduring picture of the life and death of a remote community. Although, for the purposes of the story, Greenvoe happens to be an Orkney community, the universality of the message is plain for all to see.*

The cone of Korsfea was shorn off. The lock of Warston was drained; red-throated divers and eiders and swans had to seek other waters. Hellya was probed and tunnelled to the roots.

The operation began one day when a gang of a dozen men with enormous baggage landed on the pier from the *Skua*. The strangers pitched tents in the field beyond Bella Budge's. A score of men crossed over from Hrossey the following day, and occupied the tents. All that week the *Skua* ferried more and more workers across; within a week they outnumbered the island people. Their vivid faces were everywhere in the island. Their feet beat on the roads with a different rhythm. Consignments of picks and shovels arrived. A first wooden hut was erected in a field under Korsfea; after a fortnight a few clerks occupied it.

Joseph Evie and William Scorradale achieved wealth in one wild month. The new inhabitants of Hellya had to be fed and refreshed like other men. At the end of every day Bill Scorradale secreted sheaves of banknotes in his mattress. The workmen trudged into the village every nightfall. Queer Irish quarrels broke out in the bar one week-end. Bill Scorradale didn't care. Let them fight. Tolerantly he rubbed his hands on his shiny apron. The longed-for harvest had come. He sweated up from the cellar with bottles a score of times a day. Ivan Westray assisted him behind the bar for two pounds a night.

Mrs. Olive Evie stood behind her counter and could have sold her Fair Isle jerseys – suddenly raised in price to seven guineas – over and over again, and her melons and her tins of corn-beef and herring. The labouring work, which seemed to be taking place where the pasture of The Glebe met the heather of Korsfea, made the navvies very hungry; also they were paid high wages. Mrs. Olive Evie sent her retail prices rocketing. Mr. Joseph Evie was in the town most of the time; he was said to be finalising plans for the future of Greenvoe and its inhabitants.

Ivan Westray shuttled back and fore between the town and the island all day, week after week. He raised his fare from fifteen shillings to a pound per crossing, then to twenty-five shillings. Nobody queried it. Men with drawing-boards and theodolites and briefcases crossed over to the island; security officers with Alsatian dogs; clerks, cooks, cable-men, crane-drivers, pier-builders, more and still more labourers. Ivan Westray would cross over in the morning with bunches of picks and shovels piled here and there about the *Skua* – in the afternoon with a watchman's hut lashed to the cabin roof – in the evening with a sextet of cement-mixers.

The temporary camp was uprooted. The labourers moved into huts adjacent to the work-site. A wooden town sprang up overnight, with cook-house, laboratory, laundry, canteens, sick bay, offices, a hall, a detention centre. The Irishmen began to beat out a hard black ribbon between the pier and the site. Work started on a perimeter fence.

The island began to be full of noises – a roar and a clangour from morning to night. A thin shifting veil of dust hung between the island and the sun. The sea birds made wider and wider circuits about the cliffs. Rabbits dug new warrens at the very edge of the crags.

A phrase – 'black star' – was uttered by one of the engineers over pints in Scorradale's one Friday night. It went from mouth to mouth in the following days, whispered, as if it was a piece of magic, a very secret codeword. Even the villagers used it – to them it stood for the new music that had taken possession of Hellya. In fact there was nothing mysterious about it. 'Operation Black Star' – that was how the word was openly described in advertisements for workers that appeared in *The Orcadian* and in the window of Mr. Joseph Evie's store.

After six weeks of pile-driving and crane-swinging, the pier got a temporary wooden extension. After that larger boats could approach and tie up. Great cargoes of cement were unloaded, lorries, more hut sections, cranes, bulldozers, transformers.

What exactly was happening up there between the Glebe and Korsfea? It was impossible for any villager or islander to find out – the almost completed fence was too well guarded by men and dogs and barbed wire – but it seemed, from things the labourers said in drink, that a system of tunnels was being dug into the heart of the island, five of them in all (said Jock MacIntosh the foreman from Glasgow) radiating out from one central underground chamber. So it was indeed a kind of black star that was being burned and blasted under the roots of Korsfea and Ernefea and The Knap. What it was for, of course none of the navvies could say. It could be for oil or silver, though they didn't think so. All that mattered to them was that they were being paid large wages, with plenty of overtime and bonuses. The beer in their new canteen up at the site was passable, and there was bingo twice a week and a film show every Friday evening. It could be some kind of atomic work, they could not say. . . *See us six more pints of heavy, Scorrie.*

George Mackay Brown (1921-)

In Bloody Orkney

This bloody town's a bloody cuss –
No bloody trains, no bloody bus,
And no one cares for bloody us,
In bloody Orkney

The bloody roads are bloody bad,
The bloody folks are bloody mad,
They'd make the brightest bloody sad
In bloody Orkney. . . .

Everything's so bloody dear,
A bloody bob for bloody beer,
And is it good, – no bloody fear,
In bloody Orkney. . . .

No bloody sport, no bloody games,
No bloody fun; the bloody dames
Won't even give their bloody names,
In bloody Orkney.

Best bloody place is bloody bed,
With bloody ice on bloody head,
You might as well be bloody dead,
In bloody Orkney.

Captain Hamish Blair, attrib. c. 1940

A Shetland Lullaby

Hushy-ba my curry ting,
Cuddle close to mammie,
Cuddle close and hear me sing,
Peerie mootie lammie.
Glancin' goold and siller shells,
Fae da mermaid's dwellin';
Bonnie flo'ers fae fairy dells,
Past a' mortal tellin';
Wha' oh wha' sall get but de,
Hert o' my hert, life o' me.

Saftly, saftly, humin grey,
Owre da sea is creepin',
An' it's nedder nicht nor day,
Wakin' time nor sleepin';

But da waves upo' da shore
Whisper still my lammie,
Doun da lum, an' troo da door;
Cuddle close to mammie.
Cosier da couldna be–
Hert o' my life, life o' me.

Bonnie blue een blinkin' fast,
Peerie mootie lammie;
Sleep has taen de noo at last,
Cuddlin' close to mammie.
Blissens be attendin' de,
Happy be dy wakin',
For wir ain comes fae da sea,
Whin da day is breakin'.
Daybreak, licht o' hame is he–
Hert o' my life, life o' me.

Anonymous

blissens: *blessings*
een: *eyes*
humin: *gloaming, twilight*
mootie: *very small*
siller: *silver*
curry: *dear*
goold: *gold*
lum: *chimney*
peerie: *small*
wir: *our*

To a Midge

If the Scottish Tourist Board could banish the rain and the midge from the Highlands – preferably simultaneously – then the tourists would multiply overnight.

Wee strippit irritating beastie
Wha daurs o me to mak a feastie
An finds the juice o me sae tasty,
Ye can digest;
Ye needna crawl awa sae hasty
Ablow ma vest!

I hae a bottle here o lotion,
A sticky, smelly kind o potion,
That's guaranteed tae cause commotion
Tae midge or flee;
I'll sort ye fir yir wicked notion
O bitin me!

Curse on yir clan! I'm dune wi jokin;
For chreech ye dinna gie a docken;
So now a smokin fire I'm stokin
Wi breckans green–
Aye, deil! yons fairly got ye chokin,
An bleared yir een!

Let TOWERISTS seek from every nation
This land's romantic desolation;
Thou MIDGE will give them irritation
Beyond all ills:
At dusk they'll dance with desperation
On muirs and hills.

Eilidh Nisbet

CHAPTER 6

THE GRANITE CITY AND THE GOLDEN HAIRST

The Granite City

Lewis Grassic Gibbon (James Leslie Mitchell) was born of peasant folk at Seggett in the parish of Auchterless, Aberdeenshire, in 1901. In a tragically short life of thirty-four years he wrote some of the finest literature to come out of the north-east of Scotland – an area far from bereft of extraordinarily fine writers. Above all, it was Mitchell's roots in the soil and the landscape and his grasp of conversational style and speech patterns which lend such authenticity to his writings. He has frequently been imitated or used as a model but never surpassed and remains the master of north-east prose.

Bleakness, not meanness or jollity, is the keynote to Aberdonian character, not so much lack of the graces or graciousness of existence as lack of colour in either of these. And this is almost inevitable for anyone passing his nights and days in The Silver City by the Sea. It is comparable to passing one's existence in a refrigerator. Aberdeen is built, largely and incredibly, of one of the most enduring and indestructible and appalling building-materials in use on our planet – grey granite.

It has a flinty shine when new – a grey glimmer like a morning North Sea, a cold steeliness that chills the heart. Even with weathering it acquires no gracious softness, it is merely starkly grim and uncompromising. The architect may plan and build as he will with this material – with its variant, white granite, he may rear the curvetting spires and swooping curlecues and looping whirlimagigs of Marischal College – and not escape that sense of one calamitously in jail. Not only are there no furbelows possible in this architecture, there is amid it, continually, the uneasy sense that you may not rest here, you may not lounge, you cannot stand still and watch the world go by. . . .

Lewis Grassic Gibbon (1901-35)

The Land: Autumn

At noon I crossed a field off which the last of the stooks had been lifted and led captive away, the gaping stubble heads pushed through the cricks of clay, the long bouts of the binder wound and wheeled around the park, where the foreman had driven his team three weeks before. And each of those minute stubble stalks grew from seed that men had handled and winnowed and selected and ploughed and harrowed the earth to receive, and sown and tended and watched come up in the rains of Springs and the hot Summer suns – each and all of these – and out and beyond their kindred trillions in the other parks, up to the biggings of Upperhill there, and south through all the chave of the Howe to the black lands that start by Brechin and roll down the coast till they come to the richness of Lothian and the orchards of Blairgowrie. . . . This is our power, this the wonder of humankind, our one great victory over nature and time. Three million years hence our descendants out on some tremendous furrowing of the Galaxy, with the Great Bear yoked to The Plough and the wastes of space their fields, will remember this little planet, if at all, for the men who conquered the land and wrung sustenance from it by stealth and shrewdness and a savage and surly endurance. Nothing else at all may endure in those overhuman memories: I do not think there is anything else I want to endure.

The ricks loom tall and white in the moonlight about their yellow bosses: folk are loosening the heavy horses from the carts and leading them tramp, tramp across the cobbles of the close: with a scrape and clatter by the water-trough and a silence and then the sound of a slavering long, enjoyable long suction: I feel thirst in sympathy with that equine delight of cool, good water in a parched mouth and throat. Then a light blinks through the cobwebs of the stable, an impatient voice says *Wissh!* and harvest is over.

Quiet enough here, because the very young and irresponsible are not here. But elsewhere, nights like this, up and down the great agricultural belts of Scotland, in and about the yards and the ricks, there is still some relic of the ancient fun at the last ingathering of the sheaves – still a genial clowning and drinking and a staring at the moon, and slow, steady childes swinging away to the bothies, their hands deep down in their pouches, their boots striking fire from the cobbles; still maids to wait their lads in the lee of the new-built stacks, and be cuddled and warm and happy against brown, dank chests, and be kissed into wonder on the world, and taste the goodness of the night and the Autumn's end. . . . Before the Winter comes.

Lewis Grassic Gibbon (1901-35)

So that was the harvest madness that came on Chris, mild enough it had been, she fell fast asleep in the middle of it. But it scored her mind as a long drill scores the crumbling sods of a brown, still May, it left neither pleasure nor pain, but she'd know that track all the days of her life, and its dark, long sweep across the long waiting field. Binder and reaper clattered and wheeped through the brittle weather that held the Howe, soon the weather might break and the stooking was far behind in Blawearie. But Will would have nothing to do with night-time work, he laughed in John Guthrie's face at the mention of it and jumped on his bicycle and rode for Drumlithie evening on evening. Father would wander out by the biggins and stare at the parks and then come glinting into the house and glower at Chris, *Get off to your bed when you've milked the kye;* and she made little protest at that, she was tired enough at the end of a day to nearly sleep in the straw of the byre.

But one night she didn't dare sleep, for up in the room he'd shared with mother she heard John Guthrie get out of bed and go slow padding about in his stocking soles, like a great cat padding there, a beast that sniffed and planned and smelled at the night. And once he came soft down the cowering creak of the stairs and stopped by her door, and she held her breath, near sick with fright, though what was there to be feared of? And she heard his breath come quick and gasping, and the shuffle of his hand on the sneck of the door; and then that stopped, he must have gone up or down, the house was quiet, but she didn't dare sleep again till Will came clattering home in the still, small hours.

For the harvest madness was out in Kinraddie if Chris had been quick to master hers. And though a lad and a quean might think their ongoings known to none but themselves, they'd soon be sore mistaken, you might hide with your lass on the top of Ben Nevis and have your bit pleasure there, but ten to one when you got up to go home there'd be Mistress Munro or some claik of her kidney, near sniggering herself daft with delight at your shame.

First it was Sarah Sinclair and the foreman at Upperhill, Ewan Tavendale he was, that the speak rose round: they'd been seen coming out of the larch wood above the Upperhill, that wood where the daftie had trapped Maggie Jean, and what had they been doing there on their lone? It was Alec Mutch of Bridge End that met them, him taking a dander over the moor to the smithy with a broken binder-blade for mending. The two hardly saw him at first, Miss Sinclair's face was an unco sight, raddled with blushing it was like the leg of a tuberculous rabbit when you skinned the beast, Ewan slouched along at her side, hang-dog he looked as though it was his mother he'd bedded with, said Alec, and maybe that's how it had felt. Alec cried a *Good night!* to the pair, they near jumped out of their skins, and went on with the story to the smithy beyond the moor. And from there you may well be sure it went through Kinraddie fast enough, the smith could tell lies faster than he could shoe horses; and he was fell champion at that.

Truth or no, Chae Strachan got hold of the story and went over to Upperhill to see Ewan Tavendale and ask in a friendly way what he meant to do about Sarah, his sister-in-law, the daft old trollop. And maybe he'd have settled things canty and fine but that he came on Ewan at the wrong bit minute, he was sitting outside the bothy door with the rest of the bothy billies; and when Chae came up there rose a bit snigger, that fair roused Chae, he stopped bang in front of them and asked what the hell they were laughing at? And Sam Gourlay said *Little, damned little,* looking Chae from head to foot; and Ewan said he felt more in the way of weeping than laughing at such a sight, and he spoke in a slow, impudent way that fair roused Chae's dander to the boiling point.

So, being a fell impatient man, and skilly with his hands, he took Sam Gourlay a clout in the lug that couped him down in the stour and then before you could wink he and Ewan were at it, ding-dong, like a pair of tinks, all round the Upperhill close; and Upprums came running in his leggings, the creature, fair scandalized, but he got a shove in the guts that couped him right down in the greip where once his son Jock had been so mischieved; and that was the end of *his* interfering. In a minute or so it was plain that Ewan, fight though he might, was like to have the worst of the sett, he was no match for that madman Chae. So the rest of the bothy lads up and went for Chae; and when he got back to Peesie's Knapp he'd hardly a stitch on his back. But Ewan, the coarse, dour brute, had a cut in the face that stopped *his* mouth for a while, and a black eye big enough to sole the boots on Cuddiestoun's meikle feet, folk said.

Lewis Grassic Gibbon (1901-35)

THE HOWE O' THE MEARNS

Laddie, my lad, when ye gang at the tail o' the plough
An' the days draw in,
When the burnin' yellow's awa' that was aince a-lowe
On the braes o' whin,
Do ye mind o' me that's deaved wi' the wearyfu' south
An' its puir concairns,
While the weepies fade on the knowes at the river's mouth
In the Howe o' the Mearns?

There was nae twa lads frae the Grampians doon to the Tay
That could best us twa;
At bothie or dance, or the field on a fitba' day
We could sort them a';
An' at courtin'-time when the stars keeked doon on the glen
An' its theek o' fairns,
It was you an' me got the pick o' the basket then
In the Howe o' the Mearns.

London is fine, an' for ilk o' the lasses at hame
There'll be saxty here,
But the springtime comes an' the hairst – an' it's aye the same
Through the changefu' year.
Oh, a lad thinks lang o' hame ere he thinks his fill
As his breid he airns–
An' they're threshin' noo at the white fairm up on the hill
In the Howe o' the Mearns.

Gin I mind mysel' an' toil for the lave o' my days
While I've een to see,
When I'm auld an' dune wi' the fash o' their English ways
I'll come hame to dee;
For the lad dreams aye o' the prize that the man'll get,
But he lives an' lairns,
An' it's far far ayont him still – but it's farther yet
To the Howe o' the Mearns.

Laddie, my lad, when the hair is white on your pow
An' the wark's put past,

When your hand's ower auld an' heavy to haud the plough
I'll win hame at last,
An' we'll bide our time on the knowes whaur the broom stands
braw
An' we played as bairns,
Till the last lang gloamin' shall creep on us bath an' fa'
On the Howe o' the Mearns.

Violet Jacob (1863-1946)

best, beat. *sort,* beat. *theek,* thatch. *ilk,* each.
breid, bread. *lave,* rest. *fash,* worry. *knowes,* knolls. *Howe,* a shallow valley.

Aikey Brae

David Toulmin is the pen name of John Reid who lives in retirement in Aberdeen after over forty years as a farm servant in rural Aberdeenshire. His formal education ended on his fourteenth birthday and he began work the following day as a 'fee'd loon' for £6 10s. per half year. Gradually, he discovered he had a remarkable ability to express, through the medium of the short story the hard, rough life of the farm worker. This short story, taken from his first collection published in 1972, describes a rare day off from the farm.

In the old days down in the How o' Buchan hoeing and haymaking were always associated with Aikey Fair. If you were finished with the hyow and well forrit with the hay you had a good chance of a day off for Aikey. The seasons were late in those days, because the working methods were more primitive, but if you had the hay in the 'trump (trampled) cole' that was good enough, for there it could remain until the start o' hairst, maturing in the sun, when you could build it into rucks on dewy mornings, or when the weather was too damp for harvesting.

But of course the peats were another snag, and it was an awful punishment having to rickle peats on Aikey Day, when most other folks were away at the fair, so you did your damntest to have the peats all set up on their ends to dry before Aikey. Aikey Fair was considered a general holiday, and apart from term and market days, and a day off at the New Year, it was about the only holiday you would get.

Wednesday was the recognised day of the Fair, the first Wednesday after the nineteenth of July, but if your boss wasn't a kirk elder you could jump on your bike and take a run up on the Sunday before then, when the fun really started, and if you didn't care a damn you went in any case, but sometimes it was frowned upon in those days.

Aikey used to be a horse-fair, when all the lads would be there with their horses for the market, their manes rolled and their tails tied up with coloured segs, standing in rows like patient cavalry, waiting a buyer. They must have missed a lot of the fun these lads, standing all day with a horse on a lead; sometimes without a bite of dinner, unless the dealer gave them a tip and the cottar lads spent most of it on a sweetie for the bairns.

But that there was fun at Aikey in those days there is no doubt; even though you didn't have much to spend, your money went a long way compared with nowadays. For one thing a bicycle was cheaper to park than a car, and if you wanted to save a sixpence on that you could throw your bike into a hedge at Old Deer and walk up the hill for nothing. There used to be acres of bicycles parked at Aikey, and 'Old Briggie', the farmer of Bridge-end said it was the best paying field he had, though he never planted anything in it but bicycles, and that but once a year, while it lay in grass perennially.

But if you had a new bike it was safe with 'Briggie,' because he stood there and watched them all day. You gave him your tanner and licked a label and stuck it on your saddle and put your bike in a stall, and he gave you the other half of the ticket so that you'd know your new Raleigh or your Hercules from the hundreds of others that stood in long rows beside it. And if you didn't take the trouble to scrape 'Briggie's' label off your saddle folks would know for weeks to come that you had been to Aikey Fair.

And gaen the kitchie-deem was with you you paid for her bike as well, especially if she gave you one of those bewitching smiles that have a sweetness in youth that last you till your old age. Some lads had got the length of a motor-bike and were taking their quines on the back pillion, so maybe you were lucky that this quine had come along with you, because most of them were looking for lads with motor-bikes, to take them away to dances and such like. But you didn't care much for hooching and dancing, and maybe the quine just liked your company, so you took her by the hand up the brae and set her down among the heather bells, and you thought she was the finest picture in all the fair.

There was a kind of sparkle in her soft eyes that was maybe worth more than diamonds, especially if you didn't care much for money, and a velvet gloss on her hair as it tumbled about in the sun glint, with maybe a bit coloured ribbon in it, tryin' to beguile a daft gowk like yourself that had been looking all the week at a mare's tail tied up with segs.

She had a straw hat with a red band and a checked tweed coat, but as it was a stifling day these lay beside her on the heather; and there she sat with bare arms in a print frock, net stockings and brown brogue shoes, her smiling lips reminding you of a combed honey and a scent about her like carnations, shy and blushing as a sunrise.

You must have looked an awful gowk yourself sitting there in your best blue suit and an open collar white sark you had borrowed from the third horseman; hand-sewn brown shoes that were far too dear but suited your vanity, even a watch-chain across your waistcoat and your hair oiled and parted in the middle; your Bogie-roll left at home in your kist and smoking a long-stemmed Sunday pipe filled with scented tobacco.

Ah well, when you'd had your fill of looking at the quine and listening to the music of her laugh, and maybe stealing a kiss on the sly, you'd take her hand again and you'd dander down to the fair to see the sights and maybe listen to the pipe bands. She was quiet like your quine and didn't have much to say, and you liked her all the better for this, so she took her coat on her arm and her hat in her hand and down the brae you'd go, the soft wind playing with her hair and her voice a timid whisper.

But you couldn't hear each other speaking for the din of the carnival, the hurdy-gurdy organ on the chair-o-planes grinding out 'That Ole Black Mammy o' Mine,' and the chairs loaded with screaming quines swinging out over your heads. But you soon discovered that your quine wouldn't go on any of the whirligigs; she wasn't going to have her legs swinging out in the air above the gaping crowds, she was far too shy for that, so you took her to see the Death Riders on their Wall of Death, clinging to their motor-bikes like flies in a jar, screaming up nearly to the rim of the giant barrel when they were at full speed, their tyres nearly touching your toes where you stared down at them from the railing. Three motor-bikes were on the wall at one time, with a game bit quine on the pillion of one of them, flying round and round like a bool in a brose caup, the roar of their engines like to deafen you and the speed of their machines shaking the wooden structure under your feet, while all the time you were feart that they flew over the top of the wall. But eventually, when they felt you'd had your money's worth they snorted down their bikes and descended to the grass circle, when everybody threw down pennies to the riders, because it was said that no insurance company would take them on at such a risk. This was above your admission money, and maybe it was just a gimmick, but you felt it was worth it and you threw your meck with the others, maybe a tanner if you felt big hearted.

So you came down the steps from the tower of death and went and had a bit keek at one of Cleopatra's handmaidens who had been in a trance for two-thousand years, though you would have liked to pinch her in the right places to make sure. But you wondered how they had managed to feed the creature all these years, and a lot of other things that entered your head as you looked at her under her silken veil. She was the colour of faded lilies; smooth as wax, cold as death, not a tremble on her eyelids, and her breathing wouldn't have stirred a feather. She was the picture of a living corpse, if such a thing could be.

In another tent a pirate-looking lad was throwing knives at a quine nearly naked, just missing her fair skin by the breadth of your finger nail. But you couldn't spend all your penny-fee on the side shows; on the penny arcades, the spinning wheel, the fortune-tellers, the fat woman or the midget, on the ghost train or the coconut shies, the shooting galleries or the Chep-Johns, so after a squint at yourselves in the contorting mirrors you'd buy an ice-cream cone for yourself and one for your quine. And you'd listen for a while to the evangelists preaching repentance to the sinners, reminding the ill-gotten creatures that the Kingdom of God was at hand, or that the end of the world was in sight, with all the fire and brimstone, till they had your quine nearly frightened to death, listening to all that stite, for you knew fine it wasn't the way religion should be taught, so you took her away.

When you'd finished licking your cone you took a swing with the mallet to see if you could ring the bell at the top of the pole, but for all the fencing posts and sheep-stakes you had driven into the yird you couldn't manage it, and maybe it served you right for trying to show off in front of the quine. But you was a fair hand at ruggin' the swingle tree so you would have a pull at the handle on the brass box, where a clock registered your stupid might; but you didn't make much of that either, and you wasn't going to rive at the thing or you ruptured yourself.

You had just got your breath back when who should appear but the old shepherd from Scrapehard, where your father was cottared, the first time you had seen the man without a crook, or his dogs at heel, Rip and Fanny, and he was fair taken with your quine and said he would tell your mither he had seen you with a lass at Aikey Fair. Not that you cared a damn for this but you were a bit bashful with the quine and didn't want to be seen by more folk of your acquaintance than you could help, so you went away up the hill again, out of the steer, for if you want to meet folks you haven't seen for half-a-century go to Aikey Fair, and if they aren't dead you are almost certain to find them on the brae.

You didn't care much for drink but you'd buy a bottle of ginger-beer and a packet of Abernethy biscuits and you'd have a bit picnic up on the hillside, away from the noise and the sweat, where there was peace and quiet, and you could look at the beauty of your quine against the pine trees and the pale summer sky.

So after your ale and biscuits you took this bit slip of a quine up to see the Druids' Circle on the summit of Aikey Brae, where it overlooks Crichie and the lands of Pitfour and Aden, Saplinbrae and Bruxie, and you explain to the quine what you know about the Druids and their weird circles of standing stones that are thousands of years old, and you tell her that under certain circumstances, peculiar to the Druids, she might have been slaughtered on the alter stone as a sacrifice to the Sun God, while the Druid priests stood around chanting in their white robes and smearing her blood on the stones.

The blood-thirsty creatures must have had a gie chauve to get these monoliths dragged up the hill at Aikey and hoisted on their ends in geometrical formation, for the mathematicians would have us believe that their formation has something to do with astronomy, or the measuring of time, like a sundial, because the Druids set their stones to catch the noon-day shadows in the same position in most of their circles, and if that be so the Druid circles were the first clocks in existence, long before the sand-glass.

So you are fair engrossed with the Druid creatures and their blood rites and orgies and the quine thinks that you must be daft or something to be so taken up with a circle of lintel stones that could have been set up on their ends for the nowt to scratch their hides on. Maybe some day she'd learn to share your thoughts, but in the meantime she chides you for tearing her fine net stockings on the whins and briars that grew on the hillside.

Oh aye, she'd heard about the Pict creatures being converted by that Saint Drostan chiel that had landed at Aberdour, there had been a picture about it in her school book; and there was that kirk in Auld Deer that had been biggit in his name. Abody kent aboot that. Did you think she was a dunce? So you tells her about the Monks of Deer and the ancient Book of Deir they had written in Gaelic about religion; written out by in yon rickle of stones that used to be the grand Abbey of Deer, before the laird of Pitfour carted most of it away to build his steadings. She said you should have been a minister or something, and not just a farming chiel, and you laughed at this and said that you wasn't a bit religious, it was just that you liked to know the history of the place. But you couldn't help telling her that she was standing on one of the most sacred spots in all Scotland, what you might call the cradle of our religion, where the Pagan and the Saint have left their mark.

And you told the quine about the Holy Fair that the Monks had started for the relief of the poor and the upkeep of their Abbey; the Holy Day which became a local hol(i)day and was the real beginning of the Fair but was named after the tink who fell into the Ugie with his pack or got soaked in the rain and spread his trinkets to dry on the Brae. And the folks on their way to Old Deer bought all the trock that Aikey had spread out in the blink of sun between the thunder pelts. So Old Aikey came back again next year on the same day with a huge pack on his back, almost all that he could stagger with, and he spread it out on the heather and the passers-by bought every knick-knack that he had. Then the old fool went away and got drunk and told all the other hawkers about the folks at Old Deer that were daft about strings of beads and silk scarfs and brooches and such like, so the next year a great birn of tinks came to Aikey's Brae and some of them sold their shelts to the farming chiels and that was the start of the horse market. Syne the gypsies came with their caravans and their fortune-tellers and their travelling clowns and before long you had a real jamboree on the hillside.

You wasn't sure how it got started on the Sunday, but maybe it was because the tinks came at the week-end to get their stalls up for the Wednesday, and when there were so many ill-mannered creatures standing about watching they might as well sell them something, so they got yoked on the Sunday.

Now that there were motor cars folk came from far and wide to Aikey. The railway folk had even started running trains on a Sunday for the Fair, and they had built a halt anent the Abbey of Deer to let the heathens walk up to the steer that was on the hill. They said it was to accommodate the clergy that wanted to visit the old abbey once in a while, and you wouldn't deny that there were some creatures in long black frock-coats that came off the train on a Sunday, and you supposed that they were Monks though they minded you on Hoodie-craws that went trooping over the field to the ruin of an abbey, where a bit brig had been erected to let them over the Ugie. And you thought they were there for a benediction until they whips out their fishing-rods from under their frocks and hardly leaves a trout or salmon in the Ugie for a common body. And they pokes and bores around this cairn of an abbey till you thinks they have taken up residence in the place, reading great screeds of poetry and chanting out loud until you are fair deaved and feart to go near the place in the dark. They nearly put you off poaching these unearthly creatures and you could say that there was hardly any need for a Water Baillie while they were moaning around in the woods.

And here was Jamie Sutherland scrubbing the herring scales off his motor-lorries and fitting them out with forms for seats and a tarpaulin cover for a hood, tearing out and into Peterheid with passengers for the Fair, though mostly on the Wednesday for fear of offending the fisher folk. The smell of herring and petrol made them an exciting experience and next day you could see the same lorries back at the pier with their herring barrels. They said that Jamie Sutherland bought his first Clydesdale at Aikey Fair, and that next year he went up with one horse and came back with seven.

And yon Sandy Burnett from Mintlaw, him that left the ploo at Lunderton and went and bought a bus to drive folks to Aikey, and look at him now with three or four of them on the road, and likely to get more of them as every Aikey goes by.

But you had blethered long enough about Aikey, so you took the quine by the hand and went linking down the brae to the fair again. Hunger had taken the quine, and as you were a bit jaded yourself you went into a tent for your tea. A lot of people were leaving the fairground, so you went and got your bicycles out of "Briggie's" park, but the road was fair jammed with folk and you had to walk nearly all the way to Old Deer, where the drunks were stitering about in front of the Aden Arms Hotel, and a lad was nearly feart to go by lest they pull your quine off the bicycle.

Next day you'd get all the banter from the other lads for taking the deem away to Aikey, and they'd tease the quine about it too at dinner time; but you didn't care a damn, and neither did she, for something had sprung up between you which made you sacred to each other, whatever they said, and a wink on the sly was a bond of understanding, until such time as you had the chance to seal it with a kiss, in glad remembrance of Aikey Brae.

David Toulmin (1913-)

Fun on the Green

This passage is taken from Jessie Kesson's autobiographical novel The White Bird Passes. *Janie is a small girl living in the slums of a Scottish town in the 1920s (in actual fact, Elgin). Her father has long disappeared and her mother is a prostitute. Her world is one of street games, poverty and gossip, the Cruelty Man, crude vice and clamorous vitality. The Lane, where she lives, and The Green, where she plays, are the limits of Janie's world.*

The Green was as much part of the Lane as the communal pump in the causeway. If you weren't in the Lane you were "down at the Green". There was no third alternative. Even if there had been, you would have been out of your mind to have chosen it in preference to the Green.

The summer through, the Green's chair-o-planes, whirling high, blistered with colour and blared with music. The Devil's Own Din was how the sedate residents of Hill Terrace described it in a protest to the Lord Provost and Town Council, but to the Laners who were the true lovers of the Green it was music.

It was *If you were the only Girl in the World* sung in a frenzied, birling chorus by the angels and cherubs painted on the awnings of the chair-o-planes; it was the voices of spielers imploring, hectoring you into seeing The Strongest Man in The World, as crowned heads of Europe were privileged to see him, and You that wasn't a crowned head of any place at all, what in the Name were you standing waiting for, when you could walk right in. A tanner a time. And the best tanner's worth you'd ever be likely to see this side of heaven, that is if you were ever likely to get there at all.

It was thin men at coconut stalls wheedling you into three balls for tuppence, and a prize every time.

It was the show's women in bright head-scarves shouting to each other from the steps of their caravans about their washing and their children; of how liver had been ninepence at Auchnasheen last week, but would be less by the time they got to Auchnashelach. Auchnasheen and Auchnashelach, Udale Bay and Duirinish. The bright, far-sounding names of places drifting up through streamers and balloons as bright and remote as themselves.

It was the sound of a smack on a child's bare bottom and a rising scream of protest.

It was all noise gathered into the chair-o-planes in the centre, held there, and flung over and outwards in a singing crescendo of adoration:

> O, O, how I love you,
> How I love you,
> My dearest Swanee.

The Green had its own social scale. Lord John Sanger's circus was the cream of its aristocracy. When the circus arrived, the chair-o-planes, the Strong Man, the coconut stalls, withdrew from the centre of the Green and huddled themselves away in a more remote direction, like younger sons knowing their proper place but still dependent.

When winter came and the last circus elephant had trumpeted its way to the station, and the show's last caravan rumbled along the North Road, leaving only faded, brown circles on the Green's grass to prove that they had ever been there at all, the tinkers, the third and last grade of the Green's society, took over.

The show they put on was less spectacular than that of their forerunners. Their caravans were still horse-drawn, shaped like wagons and made of green canvas. Their tents were small and brown. But the tinkers also had the magical facility of rolling far-sounding places round their tongues.

Aikey Fair, "Where the ale cost only tuppence and a tanner bocht a gill." Raffan Market, its horse sales with brown, furtive tinkers "wheezing gajes for jowldie" – taking country men for suckers. Blairgowrie, the great trek southwards to the berry picking, and "I'll show ye the road and the miles to Dundee, Janie." Still southwards but nearer home, to the farming lands up Donside way, "There's no place like Aberdeenshire, Janie, and no folk so fine as them that bide by Don."

And, though Janie had never been beyond the Lane, through her own imagination and through close companionship with Beulah, the Green's oldest tinker, she knew their ways and their meeting places almost as well as she knew the Lane.

Jessie Kesson (1916-)

At the Feeing Market

In Aberdeenshire the feeing market is both a time of celebration and of business: farm labourers gather in search of employment and the whole event adopts a social dimension of great significance.

The earliest thing that Nancy could recall was the feeing market on a sunny day, the heavy-faced farm-hands and farmers, the servant lasses in their Sunday-best, and the constant jerk-jerk upon her arm as her mother pulled her through the throng. There was one wonder after another all packed together in the market square – rows of stands covered with painted candy and wooden-headed dolls that clapped round brass hands when you pressed upon their breasts; a clown, with a terrifying, wide, bloody smile, shouting creakily:

"Come and see, come and see,
A horse's head where its tail should be."

A dwarf with a bucket and a monster brush scrubbing an elephant – sight after sight, each more amazing than all that went before; but nothing so entrancing as the tall gold-skinned gentleman, far more elegant than the laird, even upon an Easter

Sunday, who stood upon a platform, calling in purling cadence the magic of "Jujah, the One and Only Instantaneous Painkiller. Step up, ladies and gentlemen, only one shilling a bottle."

Between his tapered fingers, covered with rings of gold, he held delicately a small bottle. Nancy marvelled at his hands; their blue-white palms were many shades lighter than their brownish-yellow backs, and the finger-nails were like none that she had ever seen, but strangely purple, as if the blood beneath were trapped and gasping for breath. Chains of gold crossed and recrossed his double-breasted waistcoat, and pendent from them hung many large-pronged human teeth. His trousers were a lively blue, traced with a fine white line, giving a jaunty note which balanced the dignity of his black frock coat and tall silk hat, poised at a breathless angle on his close-curled head. At intervals he would sing melodiously:

"If you've pains in the back,
TRY JUJAH!
Or a bilious attack,
TRY JUJAH!
If you've measles, or the dropsy,
Or the chronic pipsy-wopsy,
Try the inky pinky medicine,
JUJAH!

Then he would woo the yokels to step up with their aches and pains and prove the wonder of "Jujah, the One and Only."

"One drop applied to the spot and all pain vanishes; any lady or gentleman here with an aching tooth step this way."

The crowd began pushing a young farm-hand with a swollen face toward the platform.

"This way, this way. Now, my pretty gentleman, where is the tooth? – Ah, one moment, one moment, please. One drop of the marvellous painkiller upon the spot and all pain vanishes. Watch the face, ladies and gentlemen. See the pain disappear."

With incredible ease he whipped the tooth out and held it aloft, crying:

"Not an instant of pain – see the happy smile upon his face."

Prompted by the swarthy one's persuasive eloquence, the victim smiled sheepishly and spat a red mouthful upon the platform. He was turning away, but the honeyed voice coaxed again. Obeying it, he reluctantly handed over a shilling, took a bottle of the 'One and Only' and lumbered down to his hooting companions.

'Pains in the back, arms or ribs, this way, this way, please!'

The hand gripping Nancy's slackened; she found herself alone in the crowd, and saw her yellow-haired mother mounting the platform beside the medicine-man.

Watching their meeting, an emotion blind of understanding but vivid as pain shot through her. Something was meant by that glow in the dark face that bent upon her mother's; something terrifying was meant by the glamour in her mother's face as she looked back at him. This was all that Nancy knew, but she knew it to her very core, and in her fear screamed her mother's name.

But these two were set apart and deaf to any cry but the cry that clamoured in their blood.

What followed had faded from the child's mind. But that moment, shaken with fear and jealousy and desolation, would never fade. She came to know later that her mother had gone away with the medicine-man, but this news was only an echo of what she already knew. She had seen it with her eyes and felt it with her heart. It was a vivid spot, as if she had seen her mother consumed by fire.

Lorna Moon (1886-1930)

The Games

(Shortly before the outbreak of the First World War)

The day of the games dawned modestly but cleared up to a brilliant noon, with the heat of the unclouded sun tempered by a gentle wind from the sea. The old people and I drove over to the games field in the gig and as we came through the wood we could see the tents on the level haugh beside the river, the bright colours of the dresses and the fantastic tower of a merry-go-round high over the heads of the crowd that were already gathering about an oval in the centre of the field. We unyoked the pony under a vast beech tree, hitched her to a post and went over to join our friends. I wish I could set down on paper, as I can see so clearly in my mind, the rural company who met that day, so secure in the enjoyment of their pleasant world and who were never to meet again in that or any other place this side of death. . . .

This is the old world as I remember it – farmers like Dungair and Thomas, slow footed and bent under a weight of years; my grandmother and Aunt Scott in black bonnets and black-trimmed capes, like pyramids in mourning, with wisps of white hair breaking from behind their velvet bows; young men like Uncle Sandy, in high waistcoats and higher collars, rather dashing in a clumsy way and smelling of hard yellow soap; handsome girls like Sally in yellow blouses and long skirts that swept the grass with incomparable and unconscious grace as they ran about in threes and fours; farm boys in their very tight Sunday trousers which made their legs seem quite inadequate for their slouching shoulders and their clumping feet; servant girls snatching a nervous pleasure by flirting with the men before the faces of their employers; and children everywhere, from babies to hulking brutes in knickerbockers. Some leaned against the ropes, some sat on forms, some lay in the grass, some walked slowly up and down, constantly stopping to greet a friend or pass a joke. A murmur of gossip and laughter, mingled with the shouts of the children, rose on every hand, while the sellers of candy and apples sang a song of 'three a penny' and the merry-go-round turned a sweet sentimental tune into acid drops of melody.

Three large tents stood in a shady corner of the field. One was for the Committee, one for the competitors, and the third for refreshments. As the Old Man was on the Committee we went to the first at once and the Old Man began to revive the glories of the days when he could toss the caber further than any other man in three parishes. Such memories were dry work. They demanded the refreshment of many drams, which led to a contest in another rural art, the drawing of the longbow. The old men would have argued all afternoon, but time was passing and, after the secretary had run himself almost off his feet, he managed to get the Committee out of the tent and the first competitors on to the field.

The next three hours saw a desperate but intimate struggle among the young men of the parish. They ran, leaped, threw hammers, tossed cabers, wrestled and cycled against each other, while their friends cheered them or shouted dry but not unkindly criticisms when they failed. To our great delight Tom threw the hammer a prodigious distance; "Donal' Dinnie couldna a deen better in his sleep, man"; and won the first prize with yards to spare. He and the other prizewinners became the heroes of the afternoon and, as soon as they drew their prize money from the Secretary, they made straight for the refreshment tent and the stalls, where they spent it on drinks all round and fairings for the girls. They owned the world that afternoon, and as evening came on the swagger of their shoulders told old men like Dungair that a new generation had taken their place and that there was nothing left for the old but a seat at the fire and then goodbye.

The games finished between five and six and those who had bicycles went home to supper. Those who had not, or who could not bear to leave the field, ate sandwiches in little groups under the trees or bread and cheese at the refreshment bar, and all washed down their meal with bottled beer. Many of the young fellows were already a little drunk and their careless spirits kindled a recklessness in the girls. Little squeals rose from the parties under the trees and some of the wenches even made so bold as to drink a few mouthfuls of beer out of the bottles, to the accompaniment of choking and laughter. Meantime the Old Man and his friends had some settling-up to do in the Committee's tent while my grandmother and the other ladies were accommodated with port wine and shortbread in the now empty competitors' marquee. When the Secretary had made sure that every cork had been well and truly drawn and when some of the Committee were beginning to stagger under the load of their responsibilities, the Old Man collected my grandmother and myself and we went off to tea with a friend nearby. As we left the field in the gig, the young people were returning from supper, ready for the evening's fun. A dancing board had been laid under the beeches and a small band consisting of a fiddle, two cornets, a clarionet and drums was tuning up for an eightsome reel. Meanwhile the sun was casting long shadows over the field and its light was tinged with a faint gold in transit to the rose, as afternoon passed into evening and the fiddle's thin music grew upon the air.

We visited the field again on our way home, for the Old Man could not pass the place where he had drunk so often and so deeply. The evening was very still and the music, augmented by the incongruous sounds of the merry-go-round and the drummling of the river, came loudly across the field while the feet of the dancers beat a heavy insistent rhythm on the board. That was a night to remember the old world by. The sun had gone down. Shadows were drawing in from the wood. Flares hung before the booths and lit a constellation of stars among the bottles in the refreshment tent. The young people and some who were not so young had gathered in well-defined blacks of shadow about the rings of light of the merry-go-round, the dancing board and the stalls, while some maintained a traffic to and fro between the entertainments, or stole away arm in arm into the privy wood. Others who had drunk wisely swaggered about with wide sweeping motions, now trying a snatch of song, now roaring out a challenge to the world, master of their fate for this one night; while a few who had drunk too well lay fast asleep where they had fallen. It was a pagan festival, dedicated to the old traditions of the countryside, and it centred around the dancing board, for the oldest game of all was being played out there. The technique may have varied, but the spirit was the same. Whether it was a tall young farmer with his black hair falling over his forehead as he whirled his partner masterfully round while his eyes burned above her upturned face, or a ploughman butting his wench in the clumsy motions of the waltz, like the movements of a rude stone idol, they had only one thought, – that they were young and the night was short, while the girls could only remember as desperately as they could that life is long and honour fleeting. So it had always been: so it would always be.

We did not leave the gig but drove to the whisky tent where the Old Man took a dram, then we made a round of the side-shows and finally drew up beside the board. I was all exclamations of wonder as I noticed dancers I knew and my grandmother talked to someone who was standing by. The Old Man did not speak at all. He sat very square in the gig, listened to the music of the country band and looked at the board where the couples circled round and round. I wonder what he saw there. Perhaps the shapes of the dancers dissolved and reformed as they might have been when he was twenty. Perhaps he felt the bitterness of age when youth is at its lusty pleasures. Or he may have thought that they would sometime be as old as he and that they were wise to enjoy themselves while they were able.

John R. Allan (1906-)

Bennygoak
The Hill of the Cuckoo

It wis jist a skelp o the muckle furth,
A sklyter o roch grun,
Fin granfadder's fadder bruke it in
Fae the hedder an the funn.
Granfadder sklatit barn an byre,
Brocht water to the closs,
Pat fail-dykes ben the bare brae face
An a cairt road tull the moss.

Bit wir fadder sottert i the yard
An skeppit amo' bees
An keepit fancy dyeuks an doos
'At warna muckle eese.
He bocht aul' wizzent horse an kye
An scrimpit muck an seed;
Syne, clocherin wi a craichly hoast,
He dwine't awa, an deed.

Midder's growin aul' an deen,
Dyle't an sma-bookit tee.
Bit stull, she's maister o her wark.
My wark, it maisters me.
Och, I'm tire't o plyterin oot an in
Amo' hens an swine an kye,
Kirnin amo' brookie pots
An yirnin croods an fye.

I look far ower by Ythanside
To Fyvie's laich, lythe lan's,
To Auchterless an Bennachie
An the mist-blue Grampians.
Sair't o the hull o Bennygoak
An scunnert o the ferm,
Gin I bit daar't, gin I bit daar't,
I'd flit the comin' term.

It's ull to thole on the first Spring day
Fin the black earth lies in clods,
An the teuchat's wallochin to the ploo

An the snaw-bree rins on the roads.
O, it's ull to thole i the stull hairst gloam,
Fin the lift's a bleeze o fire;
I stan an glower, the pail i ma han',
On ma road oot tull the byre.

Bit it's warst ava aboot Wutsunday
Fin the nichts are quaet an clear,
An the floo'erin curran's by i the yard
An the green corn's i the breer;
An the bird 'at gid this hull its name,
Yon bird ye nivver see,
Sits doon i the wid by the water-side
An laachs, laich-in, at me.

"Flit, flit, ye feel," says the unco bird,
"There's finer, couthier folk
An kin'lier country hine awa
Fae the hull o Bennygoak."
Bit ma midder's growein aul' an deen
An likes her ain fireside.
'Twid brak her hert to leave the hull:
It's brakkin mine to bide.

Flora Garry (1900-)

skelp: sizeable area
sklyter: expanse
faildykes: low turf walls
wizzent: shrunken
clocherin: coughing frequently
craichly hoast: catarrhal cough
dyl't: toilworn
sma-bookit: shrunken
plyterin: puddling
brookie: sooty
yirnin: curdling
lythe: shelter
scunnert: fed up
teuchat: lapwing

Lament for a Lost Landscape

The passing of a whole way of life with its associated rich culture of storytelling, ballads and music, is often regretted with the coming of mechanisation, oil and new lifestyles. It has, perhaps, been most eloquently expressed by David Kerr Cameron in his trilogy; The Ballad and the Plough, Willie Gavin: Crofter Man *and* The Cornkister Days.

The man who drives today's leviathan of the harvest field is a technician overall-suited, an oily rag in his hand as he walks round his monster machine at the *yoking's* end. It is a far cry now from the days when the Clydesdale team took the binder round the corn. The combine-harvester ushered in a change in country ways as far-reaching as the early machine-reaper did in its day. It divorced all but a few countrymen from the concerns of the *hairst* field. Old farmtoun men suddenly found themselves disfranchised by a clanking heap of metal that cut and cleaned and threshed the grain for the drier. For some, those grizzled men of the smaller two-pair touns, it took the meaning out of their *hairsts,* sweeping away as it did all the things that were dear to them, the things that justified their lives: the yellow sheaves, the stooks, the autumn glory of the cornyard. They had been fond of their stackyards, walking round them quietly in the end-of-*hairst* gloam as they took a last puff on their pipes before bedtime. The new farming that freed them was something else: less self-sufficient, demanding again some communal involvement, their participation in some new co-operative venture perhaps, in order to get their grain dried. They would not like it, labour-saving though it was: it was not their kind of *hairst.*

Looking back, men will see the coming of the "combine" for what it was: the instrument that severed the landsman's links with those ancestral harvests that knitted the generations and locked rural society in its frame. The language of the *hairst* field would become obsolete; the golden sheaf would lose its heavy symbolism, the Sunday Thanksgiving would become a little more remote in the fabric of the year. Yet the "combine" was a thing of our time: it conveniently displaced men. It had the enviable ability to snatch harvests that the binder might well have lost. It could tackle "laid" crops better than the binder ever could. Men did not have to "*redd* roads" – clear a path – for it. It made its own way in the world, coming in at the field gate to start work at once. Though it was harder on the farmer's purse, it was fine for his blood pressure. . .

So there faded from our view the world of Charles Murray, the red land of Lewis Grassic Gibbon, the land from which Flora Garry and John C. Milne distilled their poetry; it went with its seasons and its immutable rhythms, its pace of plodding change suddenly overtaken by the march of machines. As enclosure itself had brought forth the farmtouns so their mechanisation created the world of agri-business. The old cadences of the year – seedtime, summer and harvest and the ploughs of winter – with all the patterns and rituals they brought to the fields would diminish. Traditions and old work practices that had been enshrined in them would be forgotten by a folk who had no further use for them, uncherished by those who had not known them.

So there passed from the land a legion of folk once bound to it, whose destinies were intertwined with it. The hard men have gone. The cottar's house, the tied home of the man who drove a Clydesdale pair, is no longer needed. The old stables stand silent of man and beast. Once they were the centres of bustle morning, noon and night, of pawky argument and occasionally hot disputation.

The bothies above or beyond are as silent, bereft of the men who once lodged there. They were always drifters. Now there is only the smell of the dust gathering in the corners and of rampant woodrot. You will not hear the scrape of a wild fiddle or the wheezy notes of an old melodeon let alone the raucous refrain of a bothy ballad all those miles from Moray to the Mearns.

David Kerr Cameron (1928-)

BENNACHIE

There's Tap o' Noth, the Buck, Ben Newe,
Lonach, Benrinnes, Lochnagar,
Mount Keen, an' mony a Carn I trow
That's smored in mist ayont Braemar.
Bauld Ben Muich Dhui towers, until
Ben Nevis looms the laird o' a';
But Bennachie! Faith, yon's the hill
Rugs at the hairt when ye're awa'!

Schiehallion, – ay, I've heard the name –
Ben More, the Ochils, Arthur's Seat,

Tak' them an' a' your hills o' fame
Wi' lochans leamin' at their feet;
But set me doon by Gadie side,
Or whaur the Glenton lies by Don –
The muir-cock an' the whaup for guide
Up Bennachie I'm rivin' on.

Syne on the Mither Tap sae far
Win'-cairdit clouds drift by abeen,
An' wast ower Keig stands Callievar
Wi' a' the warl' to me, atween.
There's braver mountains ower the sea,
An' fairer haughs I've kent, but still
The Vale o' Alford! Bennachie!
Yon is the Howe, an' this the Hill!

Charles Murray (1864-1941)

Mormond Braes

As I gaed doon by Strichen toon,
I heard a fair maid mournin',
And she was makin' sair complaint
For her true love ne'er returnin'.
It's Mormond Braes where heather grows,
Where aftimes I have been cheery,
It's Mormond Braes where heather grows.
And it's there I've lost my dearie.

Sae fare ye weel, ye Mormond Braes,
Where aftimes I've been cheery,
Fare ye weel, ye Mormond Braes,
For it's there I've lost my dearie.

Oh, I'll put on my goon o' green,
It's a forsaken token,
And that will let the young men know
That the bands o' love are broken.
There's mony a horse has snappert and fa'en,

And risen and gane fu' rarely,
There's mony a lass has lost her lad,
And gotten anither richt early.

There's as guid fish into the sea
As ever yet was taken,
I'll cast my line and try again,
I'm only ance forsaken.
Sae I'll gae doon to Strichen toon
Where I was bred and born,
And there I'll get anither sweetheart,
Will mairry me the morn.

Anonymous

aftimes: *often* gaed: *went* snappert: *stumbled*
Mormond: *the Hill of Mormond lies about thirty miles north of Aberdeen*
Strichen: *a village about three miles from the Hill of Mormond*

THE LAST TRYST

William Thom, often known as the weaver poet, was born in Aberdeen in 1798 of humble stock. He became an apprentice weaver at the age of ten and his facility with verse became apparent at an early age. The most fruitful years in creative terms were 1840-44 when he lived in Inverurie, weaving by day and writing by night. In 1841 he found himself a patron and was feted in London and introduced to many of the great literary figures of the day.

This nicht ye'll cross the bosky glen,
Ance mair, oh, would you meet me then?
I'll seem as bygane bliss an' pain
    Were a' forgot.

I winna weep to weary thee,
Nor seek the love ye canna gie; –
Whaur first we met, oh, let that be
    The parting spot!

The hour jist when the faithless licht
O' yon pale star forsakes the nicht;

I wouldna pain ye wi' the blicht
    Ye've brought to me.

Nor would I that yon proud cauld ray
Should mock me wi' its scornfu' play; –
The sunken een and tresses gray
    Ye manna see.

Wi' sindered hearts few words will sair,
An' brain-dried grief nae tears can spare;
These bluidless lips shall never mair
    Name thine or thee.

At murky nicht, oh, meet me then!
Restore my plighted troth again;
Your bonnie bride shall never ken
    Your wrangs to me.

William Thom (1798-1848)

To Ugie Water

Peter Still was a friend and contemporary of Thom who lived in even humbler and more tragic circumstances. A deaf poet who lived in a silent world, he was taken by his father to the feeing market at the age of ten and hired out as a farm labourer in rural Aberdeenshire. In a short, desperately hard life the Bard of Ugieside wrote much fine verse and published two collections by public subscription (1842 and 1844).

Roll on – roll on, thou mem'ry-stirring stream!
  Thy daisied banks are deeply dear to me:
I gaze upon them, and again I seem
  A schoolboy, bathing gloriously in thee!
Swift as the wind, again my unshod feet
  Pursue by thee the gaudy butterfly;
Or on thy banks, with wild flowers scented sweet,
  At sunny noon, imparadis'd I lie.
But, turning round, the dear delusion's o'er –

My offspring, frolicsome, around me play;
In childhood's glee, they throng thy pebbl'd shore,
Such as I was, when in my early May.
Roll on, my Ugie! though I'm young no more,
Yet will I love thee till my dying day.

Peter Still (1814-1848)

The Harvest of the Sea

I make no apology for including this extended extract from The Christian Watt Papers. *Christian Watt was a remarkable woman by any standards; a Fraserburgh fishwife born in 1833, she died ninety years later having spent almost half her life in Aberdeen's Cornhill Asylum for the Insane, in which institution she set down her memoirs of a life full of incident and tragedy. What she wrote there constitutes a unique document now published and dramatised for both radio and the stage. The background is always one of the sea. The sea that took four of her seven brothers her husband and her favourite son at the age of only 13, and which, ultimately, was responsible for her own mental collapse.*

I had learned to gut when I was 10: curing had started in a big way. In 1844 during the summer, most Broadsea fishers went to the west coast and the Hebrides. We as lassies went to cook for the men. We lived in sodbuilt bothies on the shore, I shared one with Annie Rogie and Suffie Noble, at Loch Eishort in Skye.

The work was hard for children, but we had a lot of fun. I enjoyed the long sail round the north of Scotland hugging the coast, I was with my father, and had faith in his skeelie seamanship. The scenery was really bonnie. For some reason the Highland folk didn't trust us. You could not make friends with them easily, but a few I did, those who could speak a little English. Kate McLeod, a quinie who brought the milk from Susnish, gave us all the clake. We gutted the herring, and packed them in barrels and ships from Glasgow took them away.

Lord Macdonald of Slate was a greedy character. He charged a fortune for the bothy; the factor collected it every week – he lived in a place with trees called Ostaig. One day I noticed the factor and his groom lift a barrel of herring onto their gig. I asked what they were doing. They said, 'Just taking a barrel of herring'. I told them to put it down; if I stole vegetables from his garden he would have had me up before the court. He said, 'Didn't I know he was the factor?' I told him I did not care though he was Prince Albert: if he did not put it down I would go up to Broadford and get the police. Lord Macdonald was a handsome batchelor who lived in style at Armadale Castle. Folk told us his mother was an illegitimate daughter of His Royal Highness the Duke of Gloucester, he was a first cousin to the Queen. Later he married: local folk said he was a "droll hare" who took up with men, and was marrying only to get an heir.

Some of the tenants were very poor, an old wifie of over 80 we visited regularly in a hovel – she kept goats and hens, Annie Rogie gave her her mother's old kwite and I gave her a sark, Suffie gave her 2 pairs of worsted hose – this old creature was banished to Canada along with the whole of Sleat Peninsular when Lord Macdonald started the clearances with unbelievable cruelty. He drove the people out; when we returned in later years not a soul was to be seen for miles and miles. I met his Lordship on the pier at Kyleakin, he had a party of toffs with him. I was not going to lose the chance, I said to him before this audience, 'You are lower than the outscourings of any pigsty, causing all that human suffering to innocent people', – had he been on the east coast his fine castle would have been burned down; though I was a herring gutter I was as much a descendant of the Lord of the Isles as he was. We went to Lewis and Barra and Strathy in Sutherland. I liked travelling the fishing, for it gave a true picture of the highland way of life, and the clearances which the Government turned a blind eye to.

We went again and again to Skye. The coastline was dotted with the bothies of girls; it was hard work to bake wash and cook to 27 men. The catches were not big; at this time the fishermen did most of the gutting, it had not yet become wholly a female job. We were several times to Steen. The laird of Macleod was a better landowner all round, his wife was one of the most beautiful women I have ever seen. She was sweirt, bone idle and took him out of the door, for she fired away money as you would do foul water. She had a grand barge anchored in the loch, and huge tea parties took place every day. It was a show, with all the ladies satin tea gowns.

One of the young Dougals from Pitullie had a big row on the

boat with his father, and went ashore to get a job as kitchen steward in Dunvegan Castle. The Skye folk called the Macleod's wife Lady John, she had gone off in a huff to London, and he had gone after her. It was Sunday, our only free day. The whole staff of Dunvegan had gone to the Kirk for 2 hrs. Young Dougal had the skowth to show Annie, Suffie and me over the Castle. It was beautiful inside, a fortune was spent on rebuilding. Lady John had a room full of dresses and coats, I insisted on trying on a sable one and admiring myself in the looking glass.

Two years following each other the summer was scorching hot followed by constant wet. All over the north of Scotland the tatties had been devoured by weevils, the harvest was also nothing. All over folk were starving. Macleod was good to them, and to his credit he carried out no cruel evictions. I tried to fathom what was wrong with the whole set up. I questioned why one man should be in a position to subsidize thousands of folk; we were equally hard hit at home, yet I could never imagine Lord Saltoun dishing out meal, any more than I could imagine the least one of his tenants accepting it. Highland women worked hard, and often their men were prepared to stand by and watch them do it. Many were extremely good looking and intelligent, and what I saw wrong was they should have printed school books in the Gaelic, for I could always think much quicker in Buchan doric rather than English, a language I had to always learn. If they had teached them in their own tongue they would be more self reliant and have a greater pride in their heritage. In forcing them to learn English, Education was suppressing their self respect. It was said the Sleat folk were Picts, the same as us. I had visited Dunscath Castle which was linked with the cove "Kataritchie" at home, where Scathack the Queen who dwelt in the east of Alba was said to reside with her two sea monsters, Gropus and Pilgaupige. But the awful Macdonald had banished everybody: the folks were fools to go, for if somebody attempted to burn my house, I would have lifted their skull with the sharpest stone I could lay hands on, and organised the others to do the same. Kate Macleod, the quinie from Susnish, wrote to me for a lifetime; she had married later an evicted crofter from Mull and they settled in Wallaceburgh in Canada. Macdonald brought in English shepherds with their children which could have but a tragic effect on the Gaelic language and on the whole Scottish nation.

I liked August best. Then the whole coast of fishwives went into the Grampian Mountains to dispose of their summer cure of dried fish, barns were cleared out and wifies and their bairns moved in. My mother, my two youngest brothers and I always went to the barn at Corrybeg: young Charlie Forbes's wife was connected with us in some way. We paid a small rent for the barn where we slept, and our food was cooked on a fire outside. We had a lot of orders to deliver on our way out. Mistress Gordon at Crathes always gave us an order to deliver at Craigevar Castle. The change was so health giving, for the Highland air and the sun built you up to face the winter. We stayed two weeks till all our cure was sold. McGrigor, the horse hirer at Strichen, took about 10 tons of fish inland for us: I shall aye regard this as the happiest days of my life.

The folks on the upper reaches of the Dee spoke the Gaelic. They lived to awful long ages. Old Granny Betty who lived with the Stewarts in Linmuie was well over 100, she could remember the Hanoverian troops occupy Mar Castle and all the cruel things they did. Nellie Hunter in Lynohaun was an awful age, she spoke the Doric and Gaelic. Lamont, the gamekeeper's father in Corndavan Lodge, had a great memory. His father was a weaver in Auchendryne; and Meg Macgregor in the old Castletown of Mar, Mrs. Clark in Aberarder, must have been a century old also. An interesting wifie was Jean Macdougal in Crathy. She lived to be 105, and Betty Macdonald lived near her was almost as old; and very nice they all were.

The smell of the hills and the air was so wonderful, at night the whole valley was filled with sound of the bagpipes. This was long before the Queen came, I have joined in the dancing at Mar Castle on the green at night, I think I may have danced with John Brown, the gillie who the papers made so much speak of in later years. My mother and I had a creel on our backs, my brothers a clean pillowslip of dried fish. Along with folk from Cairnbulg, Rosehearty and everywhere we scoured the mountains to all our regular customers. Lady Janet Farquharson at Invercauld always took an order. We went to the McGilvies and Macallaspicks, and an old wifie Cattanach in Glen Quioch. The Duchess of Leeds in Dalmohr House always bought a big order. We had customers on both sides of the burn at Inverey. There were a family McArdie, and Ranaltoch, in Glen Eye, but the land was very poor. The folk in Altander ha' house always took fish, a few crofts in Glen

Derrie; here we reached Ben Macdui. In Glen Gedie and Glen Binyack there was Lord Fife's ha' House and very old black houses where the folk spoke mostly the Gaelic. They did not look like west of Scotland folk, with high cheekbones, but were dark and tall with inbred good looks and Aberdeenshire characteristics, for the young ones could all speak Doric apart from Gaelic, but a few understood English. They had the dry humour of that folk, and were hospitable and would detain you for hours. They were always eager for news of the outside world, but we couldn't spare the time. We were very, very far from the sea.

Inside houses were more comfortable than west of Scotland houses, with panelled breasting on the box beds, a deece, stools and usually an open dresser often with a lot of bonny dishes on it. Most were catholics but very poor, children were very mannerable and would come down with us to outlying places, for if the mist came down they knew the rocks and boulders like the back of their hand. My mother aye took a bag of our outgrown clothes to give to the bairns. Hanging lums in houses were often made of reindeer skins, stretched over a wooden frame, the fur still on the outer side. Deer and golden eagles abounded around Lochnagar and Cairngorm. Here we met the Buckie folk who came up the Spey to work from Calumbrig. In Glen Binyack we met Maggie Dovan, Isie Deedle and Jessie Dottie, wifies from Portgordon and the Sloch. The old Castletown of Mar was shifted a lot nearer to Auchendryne. Near the Clunie Briggie was an ancient ruin. All the entrances were blocked by fallen masonry. Local folk said it had been Malcolm Canmore's hunting castle; there was much more of it when we went first, but they cleared it away to build dykes when they made big parks. We got an order from the factor at Aldourie, we went right up Glen Cairn to Strathdon.

After Royalty came Deeside was ruined. The rich came and built huge palaces to try to outshine Easter Balmoral. Some of the ha' houses were very grand. In our fisher dress a group of us stood by the roadside near Crathie. The Queen came by, she looked so sour you could have hung a jug on her mouth. The carriage stopped and Prince Albert came down and spoke to us. He was very pleasant. The Prince of Wales was a bonny loon then, nobody would have thought he would turn out the foul bawdy man he did. The whole area was now invaded by the curious. Our hill trade was ruined, for we were no longer permitted to traverse the mountains after they made the deer forests. During stalking you might disturb the quarrie or get a bullet in your head. After the sport was properly organised we were officially banned. For all that hard work, after your expenses were paid, you had a few pounds to help educate your sons and see you through the winter. (I was always furious that girls were not allowed to be educated. It was assumed a man must work for a wife and needed learning, a lot of men I would not have seen in my way – I would have worked any of them blind.)

Years later a chap tapped me on the shoulder in Aberdeen, he said 'You are a Kirsty, the lassie who came with the fish wifies'. It was Andrew Coutts and his friend Alex Ruanach, now both granite masons, I had known them when we were all bairns. They told me Lord Fife had cleared the whole Glen to make a deer forest. All had to go on three months notice. Lord Fife's uncle was an honourable man who would never have evicted anybody, but now they were building vast palaces in relentless pursuit of pleasure, at the expense of a race who had probably been there since the end of the ice age. Both boys vowed vengeance, and said the day would come when the Skene Duffs would call on the mountains to fall upon them.

Christian Watt (1833-1923)

The Aberdeen Joke Factory

This is, of course, pure fantasy. . . Or is it? Over the years, H. V. Morton's account of his visit to the legendary Aberdeen joke factory has given me much pleasure and it is certainly regarded as an institution in Aberdeen itself. Aberdonians will gleefully direct you to it but somehow it remains elusive.

In Aberdeen is the most mysterious building in Scotland. It is a solid and impressive affair constructed, like the rest of Aberdeen, in grey granite, which after a rainstorm "sparkles as if powdered with diamonds". (I raise my hat to every writer on Scotland and return thanks for that phrase.)

The visitor, who can enter only with an introduction signed by the Lord Provost and countersigned by the Principal of the University and the Chief Constable, finds himself ascending a massive flight of stairs at the top of which is a swing door guarded by a tremendous commissionaire. He examines the credentials and then asks in the sharp voice of an ex-sergeant-major:

'Home or export?'

'Home,' you say.

'Tak' the lift tae the fir-r-st floor-r and tur-r-r-n tae the richt!'

On this floor granite gives way to the marble of long corridors. You turn to the right, and, passing doors, some marked 'Private', others named 'Professor MacDougal', 'Professor Epstein', 'Professor Frank P. Hicking', 'Professor Cheng', approach a room which resembles an American newspaper office or the sorting-room of a G.P.O. A hundred men sit at little desks all round the room. The centre is occupied by a horseshoe table at which sit men writing busily. Now and then one of the men at the small desks rises and approaching the book-cases, with which the room is lined, consults a volume, and returns thoughtfully to his work.

All the time there is much coming and going of officeboys in neat uniforms. They enter with empty wicker-work baskets, and approaching the man who sits at the head of the horseshoe table depart with their baskets filled with neatly folded slips of typescript. These they take to a carpeted ante-room. Here an official superior even to the man at the horseshoe table eagerly scans the typescript, some of which he destroys; the rest he stamps with a rubber imprint and, flinging it back into the baskets, says briefly:

'Sorting-room!'

The boys dart out with their baskets through another door. It is all very efficient, as silent as the British Museum reading-room, as deliberate as the Bank of England, until – and this to the visitor is always disconcerting – the great room suddenly rings with a yell of uncontrollable laughter! But no one shows any surprise! The men at the horseshoe table continue to write; the men at the little desks writhe slightly and proceed with their tasks. But in a corner of the room one occupant of a small desk rocks with wild mirth! He flings down his pen, jumps up, and cries:

'I've got it! What do you think of this?'

'Oh, go away!' shouts a companion to whom he has gone for encouragement.

'But listen . . .'

'*Will* you go away? I don't want to hear your filthy old chestnut!'

An awful pallor passes over the face of the man who laughed.

'It's not a chestnut,' he says gravely, but with a heart-catching uncertainty in his voice. 'It'a new one.'

'Well, don't bother me! Go and ask the professor.'

He crosses the room with dignity and goes up to the man at the horseshoe table.

'Sir,' he says deferentially, 'an Englishman, an Irishman, and an Aberdonian were having a drink of whisky. . .'

'Indeed,' remarks the professor blandly, looking over his spectacles. 'How remarkable.'

This seems to chill the young man, who gulps slightly and continues:

'Of whisky, you see, sir. . .'

'Continue.'

The young man falters.

'You haven't heard. . .'

'Proceed, my dear sir. It is never possible to deliver judgment on so familiar a beginning.'

'Well, sir, you see, as they were having a drink of whisky three flies fell, one into each glass.'

The professor's eyes become steely hard behind his glasses, but the young man, now committed, blunders on.

'The Englishman took a spoon and lifted his fly out, the Irishman dipped his finger in the whisky and took his fly out, and the Aberdonian. . .'

'*Wrung it out!*' shouts the professor in a voice of thunder.

Heads look up all over the room and work ceases.

'Mr. Johnson!' cried the professor, livid with passion, 'I am ashamed of you! That story was cabled back from Toronto last Thursday week. Come to me in my office to-morrow at twelve!'

The young man slinks back to his desk and buries his head in his arms. No one pays any attention to him. His companions now and then give way to laughter; there is a sudden clicking of a typewriter and a slip thrown into a basket. Sometimes a man approaches the professor and whispers. Sometimes the professor smiles broadly and pats his colleague on the back; sometimes he shakes his head doubtfully; sometimes he whispers: 'Go outside and try it!' and the man so instructed runs for his hat and leaves the building.

There is a lift. On the fourth floor a room runs the length of the building. Over the door is the notice:

EXPORT

NO ADMISSION EXCEPT ON BUSINESS

A travelling band runs round this room, laden with full wicker-work baskets. To each one has been fixed a label: 'Siam', 'Malay States', 'Kenya Colony', 'Mexico', 'Japan', 'India', 'Canada', 'United States of America' – the whole world is represented in this room. As the baskets move over the band they are snatched by men standing under labels which correspond with those on the baskets. They empty the contents out, pack them neatly in strong boxes, on them slap a label already addressed to distant parts of the earth, and shoot them into a lift which carries them to the postal department.

'So you are interested in Aberdeen Publicity,' says an alert man of middle age. This is Professor X (his name is never mentioned), the head of the department. 'Our production goes up by leaps and bounds. We are this year 500,000 new anecdotes ahead of last year. Now that Turkey has reorganized the alphabet we are finding an enormous field over there. Stories about Aberdeen are, in fact, used in the schools. Excuse me. . .'

An official holds out a slip of paper.

'Look at that, sir.'

'Good heavens! The old one about the weighing machine penny! Where did you find it?'

'Australian box, sir.'

'Terrible! Send it back to the Sorting Department and instruct them to have it translated into Chinese. It was sent round Australia six months ago.'

The official departs.

'That man is authorized to dip into the foreign jokes to test their freshness. There is always a chance that an old one may slip in by mistake.'

'What do you do with the old ones?'

'Come this way!'

He opens a door and you enter a room full of men working at top speed.

'This is the translation department. An Aberdeen joke is officially old in four weeks; in five weeks it is stale, in six weeks it is bad, in seven weeks it is dead – officially speaking, that is – actually an Aberdeen joke never dies: it is immortal. But when a joke has been launched it is immediately translated into every foreign language; and even then we are frequently beaten unless we employ the cable, which is a most expensive way of propagating a reputation for meanness. However. . .'

As you go towards the lift the professor pauses and asks:

'You have noticed, no doubt, that one of the characteristics of the city is that as soon as you arrive a fellow guest in the hotel seeks an opportunity of asking: 'Have you heard this one?'

'I have indeed!'

'Do you know how that is done? Well, I will show you one of our secrets. Many an Aberdonian is in ignorance of the thing you are now to see.'

We enter on the official side of a long counter. On the door is painted 'Out-Patients' Department'. The public side of the counter is divided into a series of small cabinets, so that the man in one cannot see the man on his left or right.

'This is carried out in the greatest secrecy,' says the professor. 'The source of a good story must always be mysterious. A good story should drop like manna from above. Now watch. . .'

The doors from the street open. Men enter the cabinets and rap on the counter as if demanding a railway ticket.

'*Got a good new one?*' they whisper anxiously.

A clerk picks up an envelope and swiftly passes it across.

'*Anything new about Jews and Aberdonians?*'

'Certainly, sir.'

So it goes on.

'The Out-Patients' Department is open all night,' explains the professor. 'We should lose a lot of publicity if we were not – people going on the night trains, you know.'

'What an amazing sight.'

'Yes, it is! Now if you dash round to your hotel at once you will just be in time to hear the stories which you saw handed over the counter. Well, I must say good-bye. By the way, this hasn't been put out yet: A Jew in Aberdeen for the first time noticed that there were few taxicabs, so. . .'

I said at the beginning that in Aberdeen is the most mysterious building in Scotland. I am sure it exists!

H.V. Morton (1892-1979)

CHAPTER 7

THE SABBATH

We arrived at Edinburgh on a Sunday, that is to say, on one of those days of strict observance, when every house is closed, every shop is impenetrable, and everybody is at prayers. The solitude was immense, absolute, and the first feeling we had of Edinburgh was, that this prodigious city had been anciently built by a race of giants who had long since vanished from the earth.

Charles Nodier (1780-1844)

M. C. Nodier and his friends, said the consul, arrived here one Sunday morning. They had the misfortune to lose almost all their hats on the way; they had only one remaining among four. The observation of the Sabbath is so strict in Edinburgh that they could not get any hatter to open shop till late in the day; and in order to lose no time, each of the party in his turn wore the preserved hat, and took a solitary walk through the town!

Amedée Pichot (1822)

Being Sunday, we saw many women in and near town, walking to church in their best apparel, and really very neatly dressed. White gowns, shawl, black velvet bonnet, gloves, and an umbrella, absolutely walking barefooted in the mud, very composedly, with their shoes and stockings in their hands. This custom is defended as clean, for they must wash their feet, – as wholesome, for they are sure of having dry shoes and stockings, – and it is certainly saving.

Louis Simond (1810)

'Presbyterianism is no fit religion for a gentleman.'

King Charles II (1630-85)

The Kirk

On Sundays we saw slightly more of our parents, because we went with them to church. Our family had a different religion from that of the people who lived on the estate, for we belonged to the Episcopalian church, whereas they were Presbyterians. Once a month a fat itinerant minister with dyed red hair visited us and held a service in our damp private chapel, but on three Sundays out of four we went to the Presbyterian kirk in the village.

By the time I was born, the kirk had been in continuous use as a place of worship for over seven hundred and fifty years; its bible, the tattered-edged leaves yellowed with age, belonged to the days of Charles II, and its communion register went back to 1630. When I was still quite small, restoration work on it revealed a perfect Norman arch, but – oblivious to its history – we children preferred the kirk simply because the form of service held there incorporated ad-lib prayers from the minister; mostly these were intercessions on behalf of sick or bereaved members of the congregation, but there was always a hope that the minister would pray for the salvation of a sinner, especially if the sinner's identity was not too difficult to guess.

If bored by the length of the sermon, my father would pull out his fob watch. This – hung on a gold chain which threaded through a button-hole, spanned his waistcoat from pocket to pocket – was of the type known as a "repeater", and when a button on top of its winder was pressed would chime not only the hour but also announce – by one, two or three notes of a higher pitch – the quarter hours. If the minister ignored this discreet but clearly audible reminder my father would leave our front-row family pew and ostentatiously poke the coals of the iron stove that was the kirk's only heating or, if the weather was warm, fetch a hook-ended pole from the vestry and noisily adjust the sashes of the tall arch-topped windows. Perhaps he felt an unconscious sense of unity with the congregation that had listened in this same kirk to the sermons of John Wesley, who wrote in 1766, after his third visit, 'I spoke exceedingly plain; yet the hearers did not appear to be any more affected than the stone walls.'

Christian Miller (1920-)

Censure from the Pulpit

Dean Ramsay's successful combination of pithy humour and keen observation of life in a Scottish village ensured that his classic Reminiscences of Scottish Life and Character *became a bestseller: in his own lifetime it went into more than 30 editions.*

A circumstance connected with Scottish church discipline has undergone a great change in my time – I mean the public censure from the pulpit, in the time of divine service, of offenders previously convicted before the minister and his kirk-session. This was performed by the guilty person standing up before the congregation on a raised platform, called the *cutty stool,* and receiving a rebuke. I never saw it done, but have heard in my part of the country of the discipline being enforced occasionally. Indeed, I recollect an instance where the rebuke was thus administered and received under circumstances of a touching character, and which made it partake of the moral sublime. The daughter of the minister had herself committed an offence against moral purity, such as usually called forth this church censure. The minister peremptorily refused to make her an exception to his ordinary practice. His child stood up in the congregation, and received from her agonised father a rebuke similar to that administered to other members of his congregation for a like offence.

The spirit of the age became unfavourable to the practice. The rebuke on the cutty stool, like the penance in a white sheet in England, went out of use, and the circumstance is now a matter of 'reminiscence.' I have received some communications on the subject which bear upon this point, and I subjoin the following remarks from a kind correspondent, a clergyman, to whom I am largely indebted, as indicating the great change which has taken place in this matter:

"Church discipline," he writes, "was much more vigorously enforced in olden time than it is now. A certain couple having been guilty of illicit intercourse, and also within the forbidden degrees of consanguinity, appeared before the Presbytery of Lanark, and made confession in sackcloth. They were ordered to return to their own session, and to stand at the kirk door, barefoot and barelegged, from the second bell to the last, and thereafter in the public place of repentance; and, at direction of the session, thereafter to go through the whole kirks of the Presbytery, and to satisfy them in like manner. If such penance were now enforced for like offences, we believe the registration books of many parishes in Scotland would become more creditable in certain particulars than they unfortunately are at the present time."

But there was a less formidable ecclesiastical censure occasionally given by the minister from the pulpit against lesser misdemeanours, which took place under his own eye, such as levity of conduct or *sleeping* in church.

A most amusing specimen of such censure was once inflicted by the minister upon his own wife for an offence not in our day visited with so heavy a penalty. The clergyman had observed one of his flock asleep during his sermon. He paused, and called him to order. "Jeems Robson, ye are sleepin'; I insist on your waukin' when God's word is preached to ye." "Weel, sir, you may look at your ain seat, and ye'll see a sleeper forbye me," answered Jeems, pointing to the clergyman's lady in the minister's pew. "Then, Jeems," said the minister, "when ye see my wife asleep again haud up your hand." By and by the arm was stretched out, and sure enough the fair lady was caught in the act. Her husband solemnly called upon her to stand up and receive the censure due to her offence. He thus addressed her: "Mrs. B——, a'body kens that when I got ye for my wife, I got nae beauty; yer frien's ken that I got nae siller; and if I dinna get God's grace, I shall hae a puir bargain indeed."

Dean Ramsey (1793-1876)

Dressed for the Sabbath

It is the Sabbath.

I lie in bed for a time listening to it. You can feel the Sabbath in the Highlands of Scotland just as in cities you can feel a fall of snow: the world is wrapped in a kind of soft hush; normal early morning noises are muffled or absent.

I sing in my bath; then, remembering with a shock that I am breaking the Sabbath, stop and feel criminal. I slink down to breakfast and eat, gazing across the narrow street at the closed shop fronts opposite and the big bow-fronted parlour windows with the sun on them. I can see inside. Shafts of sunlight lie over horsehair sofas, or, wandering, splash the walls with light, illuminating the hideous coloured photographic enlargements of grandfather and grandmother which gaze grimly down from so many Scottish parlour walls. Grandfather looks out from a hedge of whisker with an expression like a granite quarry; grandmother, wearing a lace cap on her thin, parted hair, looks down on the younger generations with an expression which is something between a rebuke and an accusation. The older Scottish generation must have been singularly alike. I would guarantee to take away these pictures of grandparents and replace them with other grandparents lower down the street and no one would notice!

The rooms are all empty. The little town is lying reverently in bed.

There are footsteps in the street. I look down with interest. A young man comes along dressed in abnormal clothes. There is a small boy with him wearing a kilt. They have the appearance of being strangers, but they are merely dressed for the Sabbath.

H.V. Morton (1892-1979)

A Capital Sabbath

The one outstanding difference I perceived between religious life in Auld Reekie and that of the Highlands was that I now heard less of eternal damnation, less of an infuriated and avenging God, and more of the sort of God one might like to meet in Heaven. The prospect of my being there with Him one day certainly brightened on reaching the Lowlands. The Day of Doom, the inevitability of which I had accepted without question since cradle days, now appeared less imminent. For the mental relief this brought, I felt truly thankful. It was comforting to be able to join in public worship in an atmosphere not so charged as heretobefore with the fumes of brimstone. For the first time in my life, it would seem, I was in the way of hearing a little more about the God of Love, and correspondingly less about the God of Vengeance. Auld Reekie then, as ever, was much given to sermons, but these had a touch of charity about them. Furthermore, they had a contributory virtue in their being less protracted than those to which, in childhood, I had been subjected.

For all that, churches and the precincts and premises appurtenant thereto were held in much greater veneration in Auld Reekie than to-day. When we arrived but a few years before the Great War, there was raging a controversy as to whether it was seemly to use church-halls for badminton and amateur dramatics and suchlike. The Roman Catholics, taking a more metallic view of the church's function in this connection, had long been letting its properties for cold cash. That, in itself, was sufficient to intensify any logomachy in our ultra-Calvinist city. The sterner brethren especially those of the Free Church, refused to countenance such "a carry-on". They questioned the legality even of soirees and cantatas on church premises. About this time, Coleridge-Taylor's *Hiawatha* was enjoying a considerable measure of popularity among guilds and choirs; and it was no unusual occurrence to find half a dozen dramatic societies connected with the city surfeit of kirks all rehearsing feverishly, vieing with the other in its performance, spite the disapproval of the purists who, interested primarily in the propagation of the Gospel through such channels as the Sunday-school and the Bible-class, held out against this monstrous desecration of sanctified stone and lime. The purists, in the end, were routed completely, since the churches, never able to withstand for long the temptation of the bawbees, found it commercially advantageous to let their halls, especially at this time, when musical and dramatic societies, springing up all over the city, were experiencing difficulty in finding premises in which they could display their talent not too expensively.

Notwithstanding, the religious life of the city proceeded apace; and the clamour of competing bells remained a resounding feature of its Sabbath. Right from the pious purlieu of Morningside to the sea's edge at Leith or Granton, they could be heard, announcing, in challenging tones, a score of incongruous orthodoxies. Inwardly fortified by the matutinal bacon-&-eggs, male representatives of all denominations trooped out in frock-coat and top-hat or Sunday bowler, followed a pace or two behind by their womenfolk and bairns. Umbrellas were always an indispensable adjunct, even in midsummer sunshine; and a pair of gloves, worn but infrequently, dangled from the hand with conventional precision. One would as readily have gone to church without umbrella or bowler as without trousers in those days. God had to be worshipped in correct habit. Upon this He insisted. Nowadays, so few disport any of these formal appurtenances that the clergy is glad to welcome us without them. So serious, indeed, has been the decline in church attendance that one minister actually announced in staid Auld Reekie (though not without incurring the displeasure of a section of his congregation) that he did not mind if young men came to church in plus-fours, so long as they had the decency to leave their golf-clubs outside.

Alasdair Alpin MacGregor (1889-1970)

A Jewish Sabbath in Edinburgh

David Daiches grew up in an orthodox Jewish household, the son of a Rabbi, in the Edinburgh of the 1920s. At home, the existence of the family was governed by the solemn rituals of Judaism while all around were the often conflicting influences of a Scottish, deeply Protestant city. The writer looks back on this time with warmth and humour.

There were some things of course, that one did not talk about to one's school fellows, because they would never have understood. And, while at home we never called Saturday 'Saturday' but always *Shabbos* (the Hebrew for Sabbath in the 'Ashkenazi, pronunciation used by most European Jews before the 'Sephardi' pronunciation of the Palestinian Jews came to be associated with the Zionist movement and with modern Hebrew culture), I was always careful to say 'Saturday' at school. Only once do I remember making a mistake in vocabulary, and that was because I did not know that the Hebrew word *yomtov* (festival) was not current English usage. I was taking off my coat in the school cloakroom and chatting to a red-headed boy named Cunningham. It was one of the intermediate days of Passover, when we could go to school though of course we still ate only 'Pesachdick' food. Cunningham offered me a sweet – it was a red jujube, as I clearly recall, though the incident happened in 1920 – and, momentarily forgetting that it was Passover and that I could not eat any food that had not been specially prepared under rabbinical auspices, I popped it into my mouth. A second after I had done so, I realised what I had done, and hastily spat it out on the floor. Cunningham watched in amazement, and I tried to explain: 'It's a Jewish *yomtov*, when we can only eat unleavened bread and specially prepared food that hasn't been near anything leaven.' It was the utterly bewildered look on Cunningham's face that first taught me that *yomtov* was not a regular English word.

This was an exceptional incident, which accounts for its having stuck so clearly in my memory. Normally I had no difficulty at all in living in two worlds at once; both seemed to be satisfactorily related to the physical environment of Edinburgh. The synagogue in Graham Street – it had once been some sort of a chapel and had been made over – was in a decayed but fascinating part of the city; behind it the old streets tumbled down into the Grassmarket and Johnstone Avenue and the southern, precipitous side of Edinburgh Castle, and the approach from the east was by a picturesque narrow lane known as the Vennel, flanked by part of the old city wall. Many years later, when I was a student at Edinburgh University, my father's efforts resulted in the building of a fine new synagogue in a less run-down part of the city, and though like everyone else I hailed the new building with satisfaction, the move was for me a disturbing break with my childhood and coincided (whether by chance or not I am sure) with a far-reaching revaluation on my part of the relation between the two elements in my background.

But in 1919 I was untroubled by any conflict of beliefs or loyalties. The streets and meadows and hills of Edinburgh represented the timeless world, while my religion, with its fixed times and seasons, its recurring sabbaths and feasts and fasts, each with its own synagogue and domestic ritual, was a world strictly divided into temporal units. On Saturday nights we would watch until three stars appeared in the sky, and then we knew that the sabbath was over – *shabbos* was 'out', as we put it – and one could strike a match or play the piano or revert to any of the usual weekday activities, even if my father, holding a lighted torch of twisted tapers, had not yet formally announced the change with a blessing over a glass of warm milk and a sniff at the silver spice-box whose comforting odour was supposed to console one for the departure of the Princess Sabbath. In summer, no matter how late we stayed up, we were in bed before the dividing line (one could bring *shabbos* in earlier than the legal time on

Friday evening, but one could not send it out on Saturday night before the sun had completely set): in winter it came early, and in the short days of December and January there was a whole secular evening to follow, just as the previous evening, candles were lit and the curtains drawn and the world of Jewish time established the moment we got home from school.

In the long summer evenings, when the sabbath seemed to be stretching on for ever, we would go for sedate walks through the more genteel streets to the south, carrying a sort of invisible wall with us as we moved through a working and playing world. It never occurred to me to resent this restriction on my freedom, to feel ill-used because I could not join the wild street play of the children who were often my casual playmates on other days of the week. But I preferred to avoid passing them, and to walk in the quieter ways where they were not likely to be. This was because I would be wearing my best clothes, and I disliked to be seen dressed up by boys who were in their ordinary weekday attire. This matter of clothing was the only thing that I remember disturbing my relations with the non-Jewish world in my childhood, and this was especially so after my mother had come home from the nursing home (I think in the middle or late summer of 1919) and briskly undertook the improvement of our dress. I had no objection to wearing neater and cleaner school clothes, because they were the same kind of clothes that the other boys at school wore, but I did occasionally feel uncomfortable when, dressed in a dark suit on a Saturday or a festival, I passed some of my friends wearing open cricket shirts or jerseys and blazers. . .

The most serious problem that arose when we had no maid was the lighting of fires and the turning on of the gas on the Sabbath, when such activity was forbidden. There was a little grocery shop, Cameron's, round the corner, where we used to get some of our groceries, and they had a messenger boy ('message boy' was the term we used) whom we were sometimes able to get to come in and put a match to the fire or the gas stove. The boy regarded us as quite mad. 'See,' he said to my mother the first time he was asked to come in and light the gas, 'it's quite easy. Ye just turn this wee handle and then pit the light tae the wee holes.' 'I know how to do it,' replied my mother calmly, 'but this is the Jewish sabbath and I may not strike a light.' The boy's jaw dropped, and he looked at her sideways, half scared. But later he came to take it all for granted. Sometimes, when Cameron's boy was not available, my mother would go into the street and ask anyone she could find to come in and light the gas. I remember an occasional bewildered stranger being led into the kitchen to put a match under the soup. When I was a little older I would ask my father what one was supposed to do in a community where everybody was Jewish and there were no '*goyim*' to light the gas, but I cannot remember ever receiving a satisfactory answer. The logical answer, I suppose, would have been that everybody would have to stay cold, and we had some experience of that state on winter Saturday afternoons when there was no maid and no temporary substitute.

David Daiches (1912-)

SUNDAYSONG

its about time
it came back again
if it was going to.
yes   something's nesting
in the tentative creeper scribbling
Kellygreen felt tip
across our bedroom window.
hello.
its a lovely morning.   we've got
full french roast for the enamelled yellow coffee pot.
there'll be transistors in the botanics
and blaring notes of blossom.
let's walk.   let's talk.
let the weekend watch wind down.
let there be sun
let first you and me
and then breakfast and lunch be
rolled into one.

Liz Lochead (1947-)

The Collection

An encounter of wits between a laird and an elder: A certain laird in Fife, well known for his parsimonious habits, whilst his substance largely increased, did not increase his liberality, and his weekly contribution to the church collection never exceeded the sum of one penny. One day, however, by mistake he dropped into the plate at the door a five-shilling-piece, but discovering his error before he was seated in his pew, hurried back, and was about to replace the dollar by his customary penny, when the elder in attendance cried out, 'Stop, laird; ye may put *in* what ye like, but ye maun tak' naething *out*!' The laird, finding his explanations went for nothing, at last said, 'Aweel, I suppose I'll get credit for it in heaven.' 'Na, na, laird,' said the elder, 'ye'll only get credit for the *penny*.'

Dean Ramsay (1793-1876)

An Edinburgh Sunday in the '80's

One awoke on Sunday morning to a city of silence. No sound in the streets of trams or carts, and no cries of coalmen. The rare rattle of a cab and the clip-clop of the horse's feet on the stones have an ungodly ring. For to drive in a cab on Sunday, except in a case of "needcessity", as Ann would say, was to break the Sabbath, and to break the Sabbath was to imperil the soul, *and* to pay double fare into the bargain, and I really don't know which we in Scotland considered the worse penalty of the two.

No sweet chimes usher in the morn as in lighter-minded lands. Early church-goers, Catholic or 'English Church', must walk in quietness. Not till the forenoon is well advanced, when every steeple and tower will set harsh bells a-clanging, must there be any disturbance of the Presbyterian Peace.

The signs of Sunday are all about me as I run downstairs, dressed in my Sunday frock. The shine and polish of yesterday, but no bustle of today. I hear Forbes in the kitchen grinding the coffee-beans in the little coffee-mill. The beans make a scrunchy sound and the smell is delicious.

The round table in the dining-room is laid for breakfast and the big brass kettle is beginning to sing on its gas ring attached by rubber piping to one of the jets of the chandelier. My father has cleared a space for the enormous fat family Bible and found his place. The first bell is rung, for prayers. The second bell will mean breakfast. On week-days there is a third bell, for porridge, between prayers and breakfast proper. Very confusing for the stranger within our gates.

Forbes and Christina come in and sit near the door in their clean prints and aprons, their hands folded primly in their laps, their fine thin Scottish faces models of Sabbath solemnity. Ann slips unobtrusively into a corner and shakes her head at Louis and me as a warning to behave properly. If Aunt Louisa is there, she sits in the velvet armchair, her mouth drawn down, her face grim with disapproval of my father's method of reading the psalms and prayers, which is scholarly but breezy. When we say the Lord's Prayer she does her protesting best to slow down the pace, and caps my father's cheerful "A-men" with an evangelically emphatic "*Ay*-men", and I feel quite sure that "*Ay*-men" is more religious than "A-men".

No emotional memory of family prayers stirs in me. But one picture remains of a happening brought about by our custom of the three bells.

A morning in summer when Madame Davy was our guest. She was a Catholic, so did not come in to prayers, and being French she was not expected to like Scotch porridge. So she had been bidden to wait until the third bell had sounded before joining us in the dining-room. But this morning she must have forgotten which bell meant which. My father had finished the psalm and shut the Bible with his characteristic gesture of decision, not to say with a bang, at which signal we all with one accord turned our backs on him and knelt down. I counted the buttons on the leather padding of the chairs the while I let the words of the General Confession creep in my ears. Suddenly I heard the door open, and turned my head to see Madame Davy standing there irresolute, startled by this unusual and peculiar back-view of the household.

Now I knew all about Roman Catholics from Aunt Louisa, and conceived of them as people plunged in the darkness of superstition. What would Madame Davy do? Would she turn and flee as from mortal sin, or would she stay and risk damnation? I watched, fascinated. And then I saw her close the door softly and kneel down, in her black gown and her wondrous snow-white coiffure, and with bent head and meek devotion join in our Protestant prayers. My childish mind, imbued with prejudice, took a leap forward, and I saw a new vision of understanding and tolerance.

Eleanor Sillar (1870-?)

The Lords Prayer

"Uor fader quhilk beest i' Hevin, Hallowit weird thyne nam. Cum thyne kinrik. Be dune thyne wull as is i' Hevin, sva po yerd. Uor dailie breid gif us thilk day. And forleit us our skaths, as we forleit then quha skath us. And leed us na intil temtation. Butan fre us fra evil. *Amen.*"

Old Scots version

An Invocation

Frae Witches, Warlocks, an' Wurricoes,
An' Evil Spirits, an' a' Things
That gan Bump i' the nicht,
Guid Lord, deliver us!

Traditional

CHAPTER 8

Of Rebellions Past & Present

As long as there shall but one hundred of us remain alive, we will never subject us to the dominion of the English. It is not glory, it is not riches, neither is it honour, but it is liberty alone that we fight and contend for, which no honest man will lose but with his life.

The Parliament of Arbroath's message to the Pope (1320)

Few in numbers, uneasy in their novel quarters, all that they see around them, the very sea and sky, strange to their eyes – the gods have delivered the Romans into our hands as though they were caged prisoners.

Speech of Calgacus the Caledonian before the Battle of Mons Graupius as reported by Tacitus (55-120)

On the Union of the Parliaments

'All the advantages we shall have will be no more than what a man gets by marrying a beggar.'

Sir Edward Seymour, Member of the English Parliament (1633-1708)

The Massacre of Glencoe

To Captain Robert Campbell of Glenlyon 'For Their Majesties' Service.'

Sir, – You are hereby ordered to fall upon the rebels, the M'Donalds, of Glencoe, and putt all to the sword under seventy. You are to have special care that the old fox and his sons doe upon no account escape your hands. You are to secure all the avenues, that no man escape. This you are to put in execution att five o'clock in the morning precisely, and by that time, or very shortly after it, I'll strive to be att you with a stronger party. If I doe not come to you att five, you are not to tarry for me, but to fall on. This is by the king's special command, for the good and safety of the country, that these miscreants be cutt off root and branch. See that this be putt in execution without feud or favour, else you may expect to be treated as not true to the king's government, nor a man fitt to carry a commission in the king's service. Expecting you will not faill in the fulfilling hereof as you love yourself, I subscribe these with my hand.

ROBERT DUNCANSON.

Ballacholis, 12th February, 1692.

GLORIOUS FAILURE

Suppose that the Easter Rising of 1916 in Dublin had failed in its ultimate effect, suppose that Ireland had after this brief glorious flash subsided into a torpid acceptance of British rule, and suppose that years, decades afterwards the drawing-rooms of Dublin were tinkling to the sounds of songs about the bravery of 'the boys of '16'. Suppose, finally, that in an Ireland in which the British still ruled, advertisement hoardings proclaimed the virtues of various drinks and other goods linked with the heroes of Easter in 1916. Would not every decent Irish stomach be turned?

That is all that the popular form of Bonnie-Prince-Charleyism is in Scotland today. The rising which Charles Edward Stuart led had as its proclaimed aim the restoration of the House of Stuart, and the character of the young Stuart Prince had much to do with the devotion to his own personal cause. The real fact behind the rising was that it was Celtic Scotland's last stand by the force of arms in its own independence. It failed, and its failure undoubtedly produced some poignant song, balladry and legend. The tradition of that inheritance is now debauched, deboshed and worthless.

This is not to say that anyone really interested in Scotland's past and in her last bid by force of arms for independence cannot follow the footsteps of the Prince in the Western Highlands and inspect his memorials with genuine emotion. But that is a very different thing from a 'Jacobite concert' in the 'tartan-lounge' of a modern Scottish hotel.

Moray McLaren (1901-71)

Perth

A Tour through the Whole Island of Great Britain (1724-7)
This Town was unhappily for some time, the Seat of the late Rebellion; but I cannot say it was unhappy for the Town; For the Townsmen got so much Money by both Parties, that they are evidently enriched by it; and it appears not only by the particular Families and Persons in the Town, but by their publick and private Buildings which they have rais'd since that; as particularly a new *Tolbooth* or *Town-Hall*. . . . It seems a little Enigmatick to us in the South, how a Rebellion should enrich any Place.

Daniel Defoe (1661-1731)

Prince Charles Edward

Do not the pulpits and congregations of the clergy, as well as your weekly papers, ring with the dreadful threats of popery, slavery, tyranny, and arbitrary power, which are now ready to be imposed upon you by the formidable powers of France and Spain? Is not my royal father represented as a bloodthirsty tyrant, breathing out nothing but destruction to all who will not immediately embrace an odious religion? Or have I myself been better used? But listen only to the naked truth.

I, with my own money, hired a small vessel. Ill-supplied with money, arms, or friends, I arrived in Scotland attended by seven persons. I publish the King my father's declaration, and proclaim his title, with pardon in one hand, and in the other liberty of conscience, and the most solemn promises to grant whatever a free parliament shall propose for the happiness of a people. I have, I confess, the greatest reason to adore the goodness of Almighty God, who has in so remarkable a manner protected me and my small army through the many dangers to which we were at first exposed, and who has led me in the way to victory, and to the capital of this ancient kingdom, amidst the acclamations of the King my father's subjects. Why, then, is so much pains taken to spirit up the minds of the people against this my undertaking?

The reason is obvious; it is, lest the real sense of the nation's present suffering should blot out the remembrance of past misfortunes, and of outcries formerly raised against the royal family. Whatever miscarriages might have given occasion to them, they have been more than atoned for since; and the nation has now an opportunity of being secured against the like in the future.

That our family has suffered exile during these fifty-seven years, everybody knows. Has the nation, during that period of time, been the more happy and flourishing for it? Have you found reason to love and cherish your governors as the fathers of the people. . . . Has a family, upon whom a faction unlawfully bestowed the diadem of a rightful prize, retained a due sense of so great a trust and favour? . . . Have their ears been open to the cries of the people? . . . Have you reaped any other benefit from them than an immense load of debt? If I am answered in the affirmative, why has their government been so often railed at in all your public assemblies? Why has the nation been so long crying out in vain for redress against the abuse of parliaments, upon account of their long duration, the multitude of placemen, which occasions their venality, the introduction of penal laws, and, in general, against the miserable situation of the kingdom at home and abroad?

It is now time to conclude; and I shall do it with this reflection: Civil wars are ever attended with rancour and ill-will. . . . I, therefore, earnestly require it of my friends to give as little loose as possible to such passions: this will prove the most effectual means to prevent the same in the enemies of my royal cause. And this my declaration will vindicate to all posterity the nobleness of my undertaking, and the generosity of my intentions. . . .

From the Edinburgh Declaration of Prince Charles Edward, issued on the 10th of October, 1745.

Scottish Nationalism

Scottish Nationalism is apt to assert itself in queer and unexpected ways. Some years ago, an English friend of mine, when an undergraduate at Oxford, accepted the invitation of a Scots fellow-undergraduate to spend a few weeks with him in the Highlands, where his people owned a small estate. Reared in rural surroundings, and coming of farming stock, the Englishman had been taught that good husbandry required the beheading of thistles before they seeded. He therefore had formed the habit of decapitating every specimen of the Scottish national emblem that lay in his way.

One day, while out walking, he found his Scots contemporary very dour. Uncomfortable about his position, and anxious to know whether anything he had said or done had given offence, he ventured to enquire, and was met with the indignant rejoinder: 'You seem to have forgotten that the thistle is our national emblem; and you've done nothing since you arrived but swipe the head off every one you've seen. How would you like if I came to *your* place, and sloshed all the roses I saw?'

Alasdair Alpin MacGregor (1889-1970)

A General Discontent

There seems now, whatever be the cause, to be through a great part of the Highlands a general discontent. That adherence, which was lately professed by every man to the chief of his name, has now little prevalence; and he that cannot live as he desires at home, listens to the tale of fortunate islands, and happy regions, where every man may have land of his own, and eat the product of his labour without a superior.

Those who have obtained grants of American lands, have, as is well known, invited settlers from all quarters of the globe; and among other places, where oppression might produce a wish for new habitations, their emissaries would not fail to try their persuasions in the Isles of Scotland, where at the time when the clans were newly disunited from their Chiefs, and exasperated by unprecedented exactions, it is no wonder that they prevailed.

Whether the mischiefs of emigration were immediately perceived, may be justly questioned. They who went first were probably such as could best be spared; but the account sent by the earliest adventurers, whether true or false, inclined many to follow them; and whole neighbourhoods formed parties for removal; so that departure from their native country is no longer exile. He that goes thus accompanied, carries with him all that makes life pleasant. He sits down in a better climate, surrounded by his kindred and his friends: they carry with them their language, their opinions, their popular songs, and hereditary merriment: they change nothing but the place of their abode; and of that change they perceive the benefit.

This is the real effect of emigration, if those that go away together settle on the same spot, and preserve their ancient union. But some relate that these adventurous visitants of unknown regions, after a voyage passed in dreams of plenty and felicity, are dispersed at last upon a Sylvan wilderness, where their first years must be spent in toil, to clear the ground which is afterwards to be tilled, and that the whole effect of their undertaking is only more fatigue and equal scarcity.

Both accounts may be suspected. Those who are gone will endeavour by every art to draw others after them; for as their numbers are greater, they will provide better for themselves. When *Nova Scotia* was first peopled, I remember a letter, published under the character of a New Planter, who related how much the climate put him in mind of Italy. Such intelligence the *Hebridians* probably receive from their trans-marine correspondents. But with equal temptations of interest, and perhaps with no greater niceness of veracity, the owners of the Islands spread stories of American hardships to keep their people content at home.

Some method to stop this epidemick desire of wandering, which spreads its contagion from valley to valley, deserves to be sought with great diligence. In more fruitful countries, the removal of one only makes room for the succession of another: but in the *Hebrides*, the loss of an inhabitant leaves a lasting vacuity; for nobody born in any other parts of the world will choose this country for his residence, and an Island once depopulated will remain a desert, as long as the present facility of travel gives every one, who is discontented and unsettled, the choice of his abode.

James Boswell (1740-95)

A Public Statement

During the Crimean War army recruiters scoured the Highlands unsuccessfully for men willing and able to fight; but they went away largely empty handed. The reason is made plain in this address by the men of Sutherland who met and issued it lest they be thought of as cowards.

"We have no country to fight for, as our glens and straths are laid desolate, and we have no wives nor children to defend as we are forbidden to have them. We are not allowed to marry without the consent of the factor, the ground officer being always ready to report every case of marriage, and the result would be banishment from the county. Our lands have been taken from us and given to sheep farmers, and we are denied any portion of them, and when we apply for such, or even a site for a house, we are told that we should leave the country. For these wrongs and oppressions, as well as for others which we have long and patiently endured, we are resolved that there shall be no volunteers or recruits from Sutherlandshire. Yet we assert that we are as willing as our forefathers were to peril life and limb in defence of our Queen and country were our wrongs and long-endured oppression redressed, wrongs which will be remembered in Sutherlandshire by every true Highlander as long as grass grows and water runs."

An address to the newspapers by the men of Sutherland

University Installation Riot

For generations students at Aberdeen University have been allowed special licence to indulge in all manner of jokes, stunts, fun and merriment at the election and installation of their Rector – a lay person elected democratically by the students to represent their interests on the University Court, the governing body of the University. There is much competition among the various factions who are, to this day, virtually at war for the duration of the election campaign. The riot reported below occurred on March 16, 1861, but I can attest to the fact that things had changed only slightly for the better 100 years later!

The agitation which has been kept up with more or less intensity among the students ever since the election, seemed to be brought to a climax, in the case of those who opposed Mr. Maitland, by the ceremony of his induction; for, on entering the hall, greatly more than the wonted noise and excitement prevailed. . . . Not only did the usual variety of sounds – some of them comical enough – greet the ear, but sticks were pitched about freely, without any regard to where they fell. No kind of missile, so far as could be seen, was allowed to be taken into the hall; but some of the malcontents had brought hammers or some kind of tool in their pockets, and they speedily smashed up the seats, and converted them into fragments quite handy for throwing about. The forms had been, as usual, nailed to the floor, but this did not prevent the operation referred to.

When the procession, consisting of the Magistrates and Council, and the Professors, along with members of the University Council, entered with the Lord Rector, the cheering, hissing, hooting, and yelling were loud and prolonged, and a shower of sticks, which seemed to have been reserved for this moment, fell, without respect of persons or places. Principal Campbell having taken his place at the rostrum, called on the meeting to engage with him in prayer. A number of the medical students, however, seemed to evince a determination that the proceedings should not be allowed to commence, for they hooted, whistled, etc., for several minutes. At length, at a moment when some measure of calm was restored, the Principal commenced a Latin prayer, which was interrupted more than once by ejaculatory sounds . . . which caused laughter. . . . The prayer over, the hooting and uproar recommenced, during which the oath was administered to Mr. Maitland.

A protest against the election of Mr. Maitland having been read by a Divinity student, instruments were taken in the hands of a Notary Public.

Principal Campbell then shook hands with Mr. Maitland, congratulating him on his appointment, and the Rector thereafter ascended to the desk, upon which he placed the manuscript of his address, during which time the uproar continued unabated. The Rector in vain beckoned for silence, and stood for a time smiling at the hurricane of noise, which prevented him getting further in his address than the first word – 'Gentlemen.'

At this stage a student mounted on a form and, addressing the

Rector said – 'I am requested to inform you by the students of the University of Aberdeen that they hope you will not think of addressing them, as they——.' But the noisy portion of the audience did not feel more disposed to hear the student than the Rector, and the Professors began to move off the platform and to remonstrate personally with those taking a leading part in the row. At this time the hooting and whistling had an instrumental accompaniment, sounds like those of drums beating starting out from the other noises; and pease in handfuls and lesser quantities, and occasionally sticks and pieces of wood, were thrown. The Rector kept smiling, and went on – 'Gentlemen, I accept – (cheers, hisses, and interruptions) – as frankly as – (hooting) – the protest – (great uproar) – which you (looking to the demonstrators) have just offered.' (Uproar.) The protest was here handed to Principal Campbell, who received it. The Rector, still looking blandly, endeavoured to proceed thus – 'Gentlemen, I should be entirely——' (hooting and interruption). Here it was observed by those near the Rector that blood trickled down the learned gentleman's face, suggesting that he must have been struck by some of the missiles flying about. The younger, and quieter students attempted, by hissing, to shame down the rioters; and a voice was heard from the platform to 'call in the police.'

Principal Campbell, advancing to the end of the platform, exclaimed – 'I will take other means to put an end to this disgraceful scene. The names of two or three gentlemen who have been taking an active part in these proceedings have been recorded, and——' (cries of 'Out with them!' 'Expel them!' concluded the sentence). But the row abated not, and someone exclaimed – 'Call in the police!' (Great shouting, and cries of 'Oh! oh!') The Principal continued – 'I am sorry to say some of you have to-day . . . your prospects in life are ruined by the proceedings of to-day; some of you not only make use of expressions of opinion, but use dangerous missiles.'

The tumult continued, a diversion arising through the protesting students making a rush to leave the hall, which a number of them accomplished. The Principal ordered the door to be locked, which was done. The police were sent for, and several were brought up to the hall door, but no force was used by them. Some of the students outside, in their determination to keep matters lively, commenced throwing stones at the hall windows.

Ultimately they forced open the door and re-entered. Pandemonium again reigned supreme, and the proceedings had perforce to be brought to an abrupt termination.

The Aberdeen Journal, March 20 1861

Skye Boat Song

Chorus

Speed bonnie boat like a bird on the wing,
'Onward' the sailors cry;
Carry the lad that's born to be king
Over the sea to Skye.

Loud the winds howl, loud the waves roar,
Thunderclaps rend the air;
Baffled our foes stand by the shore,
Follow they will not dare.

Chorus

Though the waves leap, soft shall ye sleep,
Ocean's a royal bed.
Rocked in the deep Flora will keep
Watch by your weary head.

Chorus

Many's the lad fought on that day
Well the claymore could wield
When the night came silently lay
Dead on Culloden's field.

Chorus

Burned are our homes, exile and death
Scatter the loyal men;
Yet, ere the sword cool in the sheath,
Charlie will come again.

Chorus

Sir Harold Boulton (1933)

The Wee Wee German Lairdie

Wha the deil hae we gotten for a king,
  But a wee wee German lairdie?
And when we gade to bring him hame,
  He was delving in his kail-yardie;
Sheughing kail, and laying leeks,
  Without the hose and but the breeks;
And up his beggar duds he cleeks,
  The wee wee German lairdie.

And he's clappit down in our gudeman's chair,
  The wee wee German lairdie,
And he's brought fouth o' foreign trash,
  And dibbled them in his yardie;
He's pu'd the rose o' English loons,
  And broken the harp o' Irish clowns,
But our Scots thristle will jag his thumbs,
  The wee wee German lairdie.

Come up amang our Highland hills,
  Thou wee wee German lairdie,
And see how the Stuarts' lang-kail thrive,
  They dibbled in our yardie;
And if a stock ye dare to pu',
  Or haud the yoking o' a plough,
We'll break your sceptre o'er your mou',
  Thou wee bit German lairdie!

Our hills are steep, our glens are deep,
  Nae fitting for a yardie;
And our norland thristles winna pu',
  For a wee bit German lairdie;
And we've the trenching blades o' weir,
  Wad glib ye o' your German gear,
And pass ye 'neath the claymore's shear,
  Thou feckless German lairdie!

Auld Scotland, thou're o'er cauld a hole
  For nursing siccan vermin;
But the very dogs o' England's court,

They bark and howl in German.
Then keep the dibble i' thy ain hand,
Thy spade but and thy yardie;
For wha the deil now claims your land,
But a wee wee German lairdie?

Allan Cunningham (c. 1840)

blades o' weir: *(blades of war) swords*
cleeks: *clutches*
dibble: *short, thick stick with a handle used for planting kail, cabbages, etc.*
fouth: *abundance*
gade: *went*
glib: *strip*
norland: *north country*
sheughing: *planting*
siccan: *such*

The Canadian Boat Song

Listen to me, as when ye heard our father
Sing long ago the song of other shores!
Listen to me, and then in chorus gather
All your deep voices as ye pull your oars!

Fair these broad meads, these hoary woods are grand;
But we are exiles from our fathers' land.

From the lone shieling and the misty island
Mountains divide us, and a waste of seas;
Yet still the blood is strong, the heart is Highland,
And we, in dreams, behold the Hebrides.

Fair these broad meads, these hoary woods are grand;
But we are exiles from our fathers' land.

We ne'er shall tread the fancy-haunted valley,
Where, 'tween the dark hills, creeps the small, clear stream,
In arms around the patriarch banner rally,
Nor see the moon on royal tombstones gleam.

Fair these broad meads, these hoary woods are grand;
But we are exiles from our fathers' land.

When the bold kindred, in the time long-vanished,
  Conquered the soil and fortified the keep,
No seer foretold the children would be banished,
  That a degenerate Lord might boast his sheep.

Fair these broad meads, these hoary woods are grand;
But we are exiles from our fathers' land.

Come foreign rage! Let discord burst in slaughter!
  O then for clansmen true, and stern claymore:
The hearts that would have given their blood like water
  Beat heavily beyond the Atlantic roar.

Fair these broad meads, these hoary woods are grand;
But we are exiles from our fathers' land.

Anonymous

A Military Riot in Aberdeen

June 4, 1802.

On Friday last the anniversary of his Majesty's Birthday was observed in this city with the usual marks of joy. At twelve, three volleys were fired by the Ross and Cromarty Rangers in the Barrack-yard; and the young men of the different Incorporations made a procession through the town with their colours and the insignia of their different trades, and made a very showy appearance. At six o'clock the magistrates and principal inhabitants assembled in the Town Hall, where the usual healths and other appropriate toasts were drank, followed by repeated volleys of musketry by a detachment of the military drawn up on the Plainstones. Thus far the day was spent with that festivity which has long distinguished the inhabitants of this loyal city. But it now becomes our painful duty to relate the melancholy events of the evening, which led to consequences that we can never sufficiently deplore. An unfortunate affray took place between the boys in the street and some of the officers and privates of the Ross and Cromarty Rangers, then on guard in

Castle Street, who, being joined by the rest of the corps from the barracks, ran upon the people in the street with their arms in their hand, and began firing upon them with ball, indiscriminately and in every direction, and some were even seen taking deliberate aim at individuals. Many of the bullets went through windows and doors in the west end of Castle Street and in the head of the Shiprow and Narrow Wynd, and others were found at a greater distance through the town. As far as we can learn, the following were the fatal consequences that ensued – One man, a native of this place, and a private in the Rifle corps recruiting here, who was standing at the corner of the Planestones, was shot through the head, and instantly died on the spot. Thomas Milne, a mason; John Moir, a young boy, and only son of a widow; and William Gibb, apprentice to a barber, were all mortally wounded, and died next day; and ten more persons, as near as we can learn, were variously wounded. Upon being informed of the unhappy affair, the Provost and Magistrates, with becoming spirit, instantly interfered, and the whole corps were ordered into the barracks. A sufficient guard of armed citizens was immediately mounted, to prevent all communication with the regiment, which, in the irritated state of the public mind, might have led to further fatal consequences. An investigation of this lamentable affair was instantly set on foot by the magistrates, and is now going on. . .

On Saturday at twelve o'clock an express was sent off to Edinburgh to the Commander in Chief. The person, who carried it with an alacrity which did him much credit, returned again by three o'clock on Monday morning with the necessary orders; and yesterday morning about one o'clock the regiment marched out of town in dead silence and without beat of drum by the way of the Broadhill and Old-town Links, on their route northwards. . . .

The Aberdeen Journal, June 1802

A Time to Dance

The hero of this tale, young Nelson, is in the midst of his own personal rebellion, but things do not quite turn out as he intended.

Nelson, with a patch over one eye, stood looking idly into Mothercare's window. The sun was bright behind him and made a mirror out of the glass. He looked at his patch with distaste and felt it with his finger. The Elastoplast was rough and dry and he disliked the feel of it. Bracing himself for the pain, he ripped it off and let a yell out of him. A woman looked down at him curiously to see why he had made the noise, but by that time he had the patch in his pocket. He knew without looking that some of his eyebrow would be on it.

He had spent most of the morning in the Gardens avoiding distant uniforms, but now that it was coming up to lunchtime he braved it on to the street. He had kept his patch on longer than usual because his mother had told him the night before that if he didn't wear it he would go 'stark, staring blind.'

Nelson was worried because he knew what it was like to be blind. The doctor at the eye clinic had given him a box of patches that would last for most of his lifetime. Opticludes. One day Nelson had worn two and tried to get to the end of the street and back. It was a terrible feeling. He had to hold his head back in case it bumped into anything and keep waving his hands in front of him backwards and forwards like windscreen wipers. He kept tramping on tin cans and heard them trundle emptily away. Broken glass crackled under his feet and he could not figure out how close to the wall he was. Several times he heard footsteps approaching, slowing down as if they were going to attack him in his helplessness, then walking away. One of the footsteps even laughed. Then he heard a voice he knew only too well.

'Jesus, Nelson, what are you up to this time?' It was his mother. She led him back to the house with her voice blaring in his ear.

She was always shouting. Last night, for instance, she had started into him for watching T.V. from the side. She had dragged him round to the chair in front of it.

'That's the way the manufacturers make the sets. They put the picture on the front. But oh no, that's not good enough for our Nelson. He has to watch it from the side. Squint, my arse, you'll just go blind – stark, staring blind.'

Nelson had then turned his head and watched it from the front. She had never mentioned the blindness before. Up until now all she had said was, 'If you don't wear them patches that eye of yours will turn in till it's looking at your brains. God knows, not that it'll have much to look at.'

His mother was Irish. That was why she had a name like Skelly. That was why she talked funny. But she was proud of the way she talked and nothing angered her more than to hear Nelson saying 'Ah ken' and 'What like is it?' She kept telling him that someday they were going back, when she had enough ha'pence scraped together. 'Until then I'll not let them make a Scotchman out of you.' But Nelson talked the way he talked.

His mother had called him Nelson because she said she thought that his father had been a seafaring man. The day the boy was born she had read an article in the *Reader's Digest* about Nelson Rockefeller, one of the richest men in the world. It seemed only right to give the boy a good start. She thought it also had the advantage that it couldn't be shortened, but she was wrong. Most of the boys in the scheme called him Nelly Skelly.

He wondered if he should sneak back to school for dinner then skive off again in the afternoon. They had good dinners at school – like a hotel, with choices. Chips and magic things like rhubarb crumble. There was one big dinner-woman who gave him extra every time she saw him. She told him he needed fattening. The only drawback to the whole system was that he was on free dinners. Other people in his class were given their dinner money and it was up to them whether they went without a dinner and bought Coke and sweets and stuff with the money. It was a choice Nelson didn't have, so he had to invent other things to get the money out of his mother. In Lent there were the Black Babies; library fines were worth the odd 10p, although, as yet, he had not taken a book from the school library – and anyway they didn't have to pay fines, even if they were late; the Home Economics Department asked them to bring in money to buy their ingredients and Nelson would always add 20p to it.

'What the hell are they teaching you to cook – sides of beef?' his mother would yell. Outdoor pursuits required extra money. But even though they had ended after the second term, Nelson went on asking for the 50p on a Friday – 'to go horse riding'. His mother would never part with money without a speech of some sort.

'Horse riding? Horse riding! Jesus, I don't know what sort of a school I've sent you to. Is Princess Anne in your class or something? Holy God, horse riding.'

Outdoor pursuits was mostly walking round museums on wet days and, when it was dry, the occasional trip to Portobello beach to write on a flapping piece of foolscap the signs of pollution you could see. Nelson felt that the best outdoor pursuit of the lot was what he was doing now. Skiving. At least that way you could do what you liked.

He groped in his pocket for the change out of his 50p and went into a shop. He bought a giant thing of bubble-gum and crammed it into his mouth. It was hard and dry at first and he couldn't answer the woman when she spoke to him.

'Whaaungh?'

'Pick the paper off the floor, son! Use the basket.'

He picked the paper up and screwed it into a ball. He aimed to miss the basket, just to spite her, but it went in. By the time he reached the bottom of the street the gum was chewy. He thrust his tongue into the middle of it and blew. A small disappointing bubble burst with a plip. It was not until the far end of Princes Street that he managed to blow big ones, pink and wobbling, that he could see at the end of his nose, which burst well and had to be gathered in shreds from his chin.

Then suddenly the crowds of shoppers parted and he saw his mother. In the same instant she saw him. She was on him before he could even think of running. She grabbed him by the fur of his parka and began screaming into his face.

'In the name of God, Nelson, what are you doing here? Why aren't you at school?' She began shaking him. 'Do you realise what this means? They'll put me in bloody jail. It'll be bloody Saughton for me, and no mistake.' She had her teeth gritted together and her mouth was slanting in her face. Then Nelson started to shout.

'Help! Help!' he yelled.

A woman with an enormous chest like a pigeon stopped. 'What's happening?' she said.

Nelson's mother turned on her. 'It's none of your bloody business.'

'I'm being kidnapped,' yelled Nelson.

'Young woman. Young woman . . .' said the lady with the large chest, trying to tap Nelson's mother on the shoulder with her umbrella, but Mrs. Skelly turned with such a snarl that the woman edged away hesitatingly and looked over her shoulder and tut-tutted just loudly enough for the passing crowd to hear her.

'Help! I'm being kidnapped,' screamed Nelson, but everybody walked past looking the other way. His mother squatted down in front of him, still holding on to his jacket. She lowered her voice and tried to make it sound reasonable.

'Look Nelson, love. Listen. If you're skiving school, do you realise what'll happen to me? In Primary the Children's Panel threatened to send me to court. You're only at that Secondary and already that Sub-Attendance Committee thing wanted to fine me. Jesus, if you're caught again . . .'

Nelson stopped struggling. The change in her tone had quietened him down. She straightened up and looked wildly about her, wondering what to do.

'You've got to go straight back to school, do you hear me?'

'Yes.'

'Promise me you'll go.' The boy looked down at the ground. 'Promise?' The boy made no answer.

'I'll kill you if you don't go back. I'd take you myself only I've my work to go to. I'm late as it is.'

Again she looked around as if she would see someone who would suddenly help her. Still she held on to his jacket. She was biting her lip.

'Oh God, Nelson.'

The boy blew a flesh-pink bubble and snapped it between his teeth. She shook him.

'That bloody bubble-gum.'

There was a loud explosion as the one o'clock gun went off. They both leapt.

'Oh Jesus, that gun puts the heart sideways in me every time it goes off. Come on, son, you'll have to come with me. I'm late. I don't know what they'll say when they see you but I'm bloody taking you to school by the ear. You hear me?'

She began rushing along the street, Nelson's sleeve in one hand, her carrier bag in the other. The boy had to run to keep from being dragged.

'Don't you dare try a trick like that again. Kidnapped, my arse. Nelson, if I knew somebody who would kidnap you - I'd pay *him* the money. Embarrassing me on the street like that.'

They turned off the main road and went into a hallway and up carpeted stairs which had full-length mirrors along one side. Nelson stopped to make faces at himself but his mother chugged at his arm. At the head of the stairs stood a fat man in his shirtsleeves.

'What the hell is this?' he said. 'You're late, and what the hell is that?' He looked down from over his stomach at Nelson.

'I'll explain later,' she said. 'I'll make sure he stays in the room.'

'You should be on *now*,' said the fat man and turned and walked away through the swing doors. They followed him and Nelson saw, before his mother pushed him into the room, that it was a bar, plush and carpeted with crowds of men standing drinking.

'You sit here, Nelson, until I'm finished and then I'm taking you back to that school. You'll get nowhere if you don't do your lessons. I have to get changed now.'

She set her carrier bag on the floor and kicked off her shoes. Nelson sat down, watching her. She stopped and looked over her shoulder at him, biting her lip.

'Where's that bloody eyepatch you should be wearing?' Nelson indicated his pocket.

'Well, wear it then.' Nelson took the crumpled patch from his pocket, tugging bits of it unstuck to get if flat before he stuck it over his bad eye. His mother took out her handbag and began rooting about at the bottom of it. Nelson heard the rattle of her bottles of scent and tubes of lipstick.

'Ah,' she said and produced another eyepatch, flicking it clean. 'Put another one on till I get changed. I don't want you noseying at me.' She came to him, pulling away the white backing to the patch, and stuck it over his remaining eye. He imagined her concentrating, the tip of her tongue stuck out. She pressed his eyebrows with her thumbs, making sure that the patches were stuck.

'Now don't move, or you'll bump into something.'

Nelson heard the slither of her clothes and her small grunts as she hurriedly got changed. Then he heard her rustle in her bag, the soft pop and rattle as she opened her capsules. Her 'tantalisers' she called them, small black and red torpedoes. Then he heard her voice.

'Just you stay like that till I come back. That way you'll come to no harm. You hear me, Nelson? If I come back in here and you have got those things off, I'll *kill* you. I'll not be long.'

Nelson nodded from his darkness.

'The door will be locked, so there's no running away.'

'Ah ken.'

Suddenly his darkness exploded with lights as he felt her bony hand strike his ear.

'You don't ken things, Nelson. You *know* them.'

He heard her go out and the key turn in the lock. His ear sang and he felt it was hot. He turned his face up to the ceiling. She had left the light on because he could see pinkish through the patches. He smelt the beer and stale smoke. Outside the room pop music had startd up, very loudly. He heard the deep notes pound through to where he sat.

Bernard MacLaverty (1942-)

CHAPTER 9

Of Daily Bread & the Water of Life

Good Ale

He that buys beef buys banes;
He that buys land buys stanes;
He that buys nuts buys shells;
He that buys guid ale buys naething else.

Traditional

The Covenanter's Grace

When Burns dined with the Earl of Selkirk, at St Mary's Isle, he repeated these lines, which have been considered as his own. In fact, he must have given them from memory, for a correspondent remembers their being popular in the south-western province of Scotland before the days of Burns and they were always called the Covenanter's Grace.

Some hae meat that canna eat,
  And some wad eat that want it;
But we hae meat, and we can eat,
  For which the Lord be thankit!

A Galloway Grace

Bless the sheep for Dauvid's sake, he herdit sheep himsel;
Bless the fish for Peter's sake, he gruppit fish himsel;
Bless the soo for Satan's sake, he was yince a soo himsel.

Traditional

Haggis

Fair fa' your honest, sonsie face,
Great chieftain o' the pudden race

Clean a sheep's pluck thoroughly. Make incisions in the heart and liver to allow the blood to flow out, and parboil them, letting the windpipe lie over the side of the pot to permit the phlegm and blood to disgorge from the lungs; change the water after a few minutes boiling for fresh water. Another half hour's boiling will be sufficient; but throw back the half of the liver to boil until it will grate easily. Take the heart, the half of the liver and the lungs, trimming away all skins and black-looking parts, and mince them together along with a pound of good beef suet. Grate the other half of the liver. Have eight onions peeled and scalded in two waters, which chop and mix with this mince. Toast some oatmeal before the fire till it is of a light brown colour and perfectly dry. Less than two teaspoonfuls of meal will do for this quantity of meat. Spread the mince on a board and strew the meal lightly over it, with a high seasoning of pepper, salt, a little cayenne and marjoram, well mixed. Have a sheep's stomach perfectly clean, and see that there is no thin part in it in case of its bursting. Put in the meat with a half-pint of good beef gravy, or as much strong broth and the juice of a lemon or a little good vinegar as will make a thick stew. Be careful not to fill the bag too full so as to allow the meat room to swell. Press out the air and sew up the bag; prick it with a large needle when it first swells in the pot, to prevent bursting; let it boil slowly for three hours if large.

Robert H. Christie (1911)

The Scottish Cuisine

Not long after the dram, may be expected the breakfast, a meal in which the Scots, whether of the lowlands or mountains, must be confessed to excel us. The tea and coffee are accompanied not only with butter, but with honey, conserves, and marmalades. If an epicure could remove by a wish, in quest of sensual gratifications, wherever he had supped he would breakfast in Scotland.

In the islands however, they do what I found it not very easy to endure. They pollute the tea-table by plates piled with large slices of cheshire cheese, which mingles its less grateful odours with the fragrance of the tea.

Where many questions are to be asked, some will be omitted. I forgot to inquire how they were supplied with so much exotic luxury. Perhaps the French may bring them wine for wool, and the Dutch give them tea and coffee at the fishing season, in exchange for fresh provision. Their trade is unconstrained; they pay no customs, for there is no officer to demand them; whatever therefore is made dear only by impost, is obtained here at an easy rate.

A dinner in the Western Islands differs very little from a dinner in *England*, except that in the place of tarts, there are always set different preparations of milk. This part of their diet will admit some improvement. Though they have milk, and eggs, and sugar, few of them know how to compound them in a custard. Their gardens afford them no great variety, but they have always some vegetables on the table. Potatoes at least are never wanting, which, though they have not known them long, are now one of the principal parts of their food. They are not of the mealy, but the viscous kind.

Their more elaborate cookery, or made dishes, an English man at the first taste is not likely to approve, but the culinary compositions of every country are often such as become grateful to other nations only by degrees; though I have read a French author, who, in the elation of his heart, says that French cookery pleases all foreigners, but foreign cookery never satisfies a Frenchman.

Their suppers are, like their dinners, various and plentiful. The table is always covered with elegant linen. Their plates for common use are often of that kind of manufacture which is called cream coloured, or queen's ware. They use silver on all occasions where it is common in *England*, nor did I ever find the spoon of horn, but in one house.

The knives are not often either very bright, or very sharp. They are indeed instruments of which the Highlanders have not been long acquainted with the general use. They were not regularly laid on the table, before the prohibition of arms, and the change of dress. Thirty years ago the Highlander wore his knife as a companion to his dirk or dagger, and when the company sat down to meat, the men who had knives, cut the flesh into small pieces for the women, who with their fingers conveyed it to their mouths.

James Boswell (1740-95)

A Shetland Dish

Sassermaet and Brönies

The Sassermaet mixture is a kind of preserved beef mince. About 6lb (3kg) of mince is spiced and salted and kept in a cool place. This is used with an equal quantity of fresh mince, breadcrumbs and onions and made into cakes and fried; it is then known as Brönies. The following recipe has been adapted to combine the two processes.

1lb minced beef (500g)
1oz breadcrumbs (25g)
1 egg
1 small onion, finely chopped
Seasoning mixture –
1 level dsp salt
a large pinch of the following –
Mixed spice, freshly ground black pepper, white pepper, ground cloves and cinnamon
Oil or butter for frying

Put the minced beef, breadcrumbs, egg and onions into a large bowl. Make up the seasoning mixture and mix with all the other ingredients.

Put some flour onto a board. Divide the mixture into 4 and shape into round patties 1in (2½cm) thick, coating with flour to prevent them sticking.

Melt oil or butter in a frying pan and fry them gently for 5-10 minutes on both sides. Serve with some warm bannocks.

Catherine Brown (1981)

An Aberdeen High Tea

High tea in Aberdeen is like no other meal on earth. It is the meal of the day, the meal par excellence, and the tired come home to it ravenous, driven by the granite streets, hounded in for energy to stoke against that menace. Tea is drunk with the meal, and the order of it is this: First, one eats a plateful of sausages and eggs and mashed potatoes; then a second plateful to keep down the first. Eating, one assists the second plateful to its final home by mouthfuls of oatcake spread with butter. Then you eat oatcake with cheese. Then there are scones. Then cookies. Then it is really time to begin on tea – tea and bread and butter and crumpets and toasted rolls and cakes. Then some Dundee cake.

Then – about half-past seven – someone shakes you out of the coma into which you have fallen and asks you persuasively if you wouldn't like another cup of tea and just *one* more egg and sausage . . .

And all night long, on top of this supper and one of those immense Aberdonian beds which appear to be made of knotted ship's cable, the investigator, through and transcending the howl of the November sleet-wind, will hear the lorries and the drays, in platoons, clattering up and down Market Street. They do it for no reason or purpose, except to keep you awake. And in the morning when you descend with a grey face and an aching head, they provide you with an immense Aberdeen breakfast; and if you halt and gasp somewhere through the third course they send for the manager who comes and questions you gravely as to why you don't like the food? – should he send for a doctor?

Lewis Grassic Gibbon (J. Leslie Mitchell, 1901-35)

Dinner at Inveraray Castle

Towards the end of the dessert the ladies withdrew, in conformity with the custom of the country. The toasts then commenced, and a great number was drank with spirit and vivacity. The English [*sic*] provide for everything; and if the diuretic influence of the liquors is felt, there are certain utensils at hand, which are used without ceremony; and as the ladies here are extremely delicate, this may be the reason for their withdrawing before the toasts begin.

Faujas de Saint-Fond (1784)

Highland Hospitality

One thing I should have told you was intolerable, viz., the number of Highlanders that attended a table, whose feet and foul linen, or woollen, I don't know which, were more than a match for the odour of the dishes.

Edward Burt (d.1755)

Food in These Parts

The author of these observations, made around 1937, was a well known civic figure in Edinburgh, a fashionable draper and a most distinguished figure in Princes Street where he would daily appear at his emporium immaculately dressed with fresh buttonhole.

The phrase, 'The wine of the country,' is familiarly on the lips – and it might be added, the palates – of all travellers, and Scotland does not lack in appropriate beverages. The Usquebaugh of Scotland is assuredly the world's most unique beverage, for no other beverage is produced within such a limited area to the exclusion of all others.

The wines of France have their kin in Belgium, Germany, Switzerland, Italy and Greece, not to speak of South Africa and Australia; but the native drink of Scotland is so unique that in recent months a daring Canadian producer of the beverage has established himself in Scotland in order that what was formerly, at best, a good imitation, may now become 'the real Mackay.'

The Scots economist feels very keenly that this unique product of Scottish industry should be made the basis of what is not unfairly described as 'Penal Taxation.' The Scotsman perhaps is so accustomed to giving generously to the world that he does not feel it as keenly as, for example, the people of Lancashire or Yorkshire would if their native product were made to such a large extent one of the principal elements of national taxation.

This essay is intended to deal principally with Scottish food, but one cannot divorce, fortunately, food from drink so easily and a word must be said about Scottish beer.

The increasing export business which is done in Scottish beer justifies the claim that it is unequalled in the world. Edinburgh, Glasgow, Falkirk, Alloa – these are four centres where this glorious beverage is brewed.

The narrow days of teetotal agitation are fortunately past, and now one can look upon both these beverages with almost a vegetarian eye. After all, they are vegetable products. They follow in analogy the making of tea – they are immersed in boiling water and the result is a beverage which makes glad the heart of man.

If whisky and beer are Scotland's two leading drinks, milk certainly is entitled to a third place; and Scotland produces, from the finest herds in the world, easily the best milk, despite machinations of the Milk Marketing Boards and similar large scale organisations.

Milk is the basis too of some of Scotland's most famous dishes. Whisky and milk – there has already been enough said about whisky, we will leave it on one side – curds and cream – porridge and milk – and cheese – and butter. The individual qualities of all these Scottish milk products are perhaps not appreciated as highly as they should be by Scotsmen. The present writer knows a Frenchman who journeys once a year to Scotland in order to please his palate with the cheese and butter of Scotland as a contrast to Camembert and Normandy. This distinctiveness we who live in Scotland perhaps do not rate sufficiently highly.

Scottish bread – ordinary baker's bread – has a definite flavour of its own in which the visitor finds a new delight. The traveller in England must have been struck by the occasional sight of a sign above a baker's door, 'Scottish Bakery,' and this is a tribute to Scottish achievement in this field.

Scottish cakes, scones, pastry, made from Scottish butter and Scottish milk take as high a place in the minds of international epicures as the *pâtisseries* of Brussels or Vienna. No country makes oatcakes and scones as Scotland does, and if a unanimous vote on Scottish food were sought, it would probably be to these that the Scottish epicure would point with the greatest pride.

From the point of view of the tourist, however – and from his point of view rather than that of the Scots themselves – haggis, shortbread, and currant bun make the readiest appeal. They have the merit of convenience, when enclosed in the appropriate tin, of being more portable than the scones, and it is this merit, perhaps, which has tended to make them universally eaten from one Pole to the other and right round the Equator and back again.

It is climate ultimately which determines the kind of food which folk eat.

The Scottish climate makes men hungry, and hungry folk like starchy foods, 'filling foods' as they are called – breads and scones and thick soups. Scottish broth is different from and better than any vegetable soup made anywhere. The quality of the vegetables as well as the stock which is its base has everything to do with it. The vegetables grown in the hard, trying and difficult climate of Scotland have a quality almost personal to themselves. You cannot make Scotch broth with English turnips and French onions. The vegetables must be, like the meat and bones which are the basis of the stock, Scottish grown.

The meats of Scotland have commanded the attention of Smithfield, and no higher commendation can come from the Englishman than the tribute of his belly. Scotch beef and Scotch mutton hold pride of place and none approach or challenge them, while Scotch venison and Scotch small game generally always find the first place in the market and the highest place in the opinion of the buyer.

Then there are the fish – the salmon, the trout and the herring, the lobsters and the crabs – all distinctively different and all pre-eminently Scottish.

It will be observed that there is no order in this catalogue of Scottish Food. The items do not follow the bill of fare; they come as nature brings them in season and out of season, always stimulating to the imagination and exciting to the appetite.

But one must begin to put these ideas in some sort of view.

Let us begin the day from the visitor's point of view.

Let him call for a glass of hot water wherewith to clean the palate and stimulate the digestion.

The waters of Scotland, whether they be from Strathpeffer, St Ronan's Well, or from the Highland stream, are not as the waters of other lands. Scotsmen may well say, 'Are not the rivers of Scotland more than the rivers of Babylon?' – and if they did say so they would say so in truth.

Begin the day, therefore, my dear visitor to Scotland, with the glass of hot water and proceed an hour later to a noble breakfast commencing with porridge from Scottish oats, milk or cream from Scottish cows, and – if you must sweeten the dish – there are sugars which are made in Scotland, but let me commend to you the golden syrup or treacle of Greenock – a Scottish production of over a hundred years.

From the porridge you will proceed to the finnan haddock or the grilled trout, and then to the Ayrshire bacon, Lanarkshire tomatoes and eggs from the farm over the hill. If you must drink a beverage, they do tea better in Scotland than they do coffee as a rule, and much talent and genius has been put to the task of blending teas – grown by Scotsmen in India and Ceylon – with the waters of the native land – for which in their exile they pine.

You will smoke after your breakfast and do not forget that Scotland has its own tobacco industry, having produced on the Clyde and in Edinburgh better tobaccos long before ever Bristol became the principal centre of that industry.

You may spend the morning as you like, but when you return for your luncheon some Scottish ale or a glass of whisky will make the only *apéritif* that is appropriate to the climate.

Luncheon may consist of Scottish broth, boiled salmon – pastry or tart, followed by a whang of Dunlop or Scottish Cheddar cheese.

You will not want any tea. This is an English meal and you can dispense with it. The ladies of the party will desire it and you should see that they have some scones and tarts and perhaps these 'Petticoat Tails' which the romantics tell us are a recipe handed down from Queen Mary's days when they were known as 'petit gatelles.'

You will scorn the tea, doubtless; and, striding again across the moors and mountains or charging the bunkers, at seven you will be ready for the evening meal. Let it be worthy of yourself and of the land in which you find yourself.

Having lunched as you have done, an alternative menu must be provided. Smoked salmon as a *hors-d'œuvre* followed by hare soup: you would then have grilled Moray Firth soles and proceed to the roast mutton. You may prefer the loin, but for the grand meal the saddle is indicated, especially if you will support it with that distinctive quality of claret which, imported through Leith, is a different beverage altogether from what one drinks in France.

You will have the red currant jelly and baked potatoes and the appropriate sprouts, cabbage or cauliflower. Your sweet should be a substantial one and your fancy might turn to Scottish triffle made of Scottish sponge cakes, heightened with port or sherry, or you might prefer a couple of good Scotch apples, well baked. In any case, the joys of the table are not over with that course, for a Scottish savoury awaits your further delectation. It might well be a croute of herring or a cheese and bacon savoury, or you might resume again the acquaintance which you made at luncheon with the Scottish Cheddar.

Claret I have commended; but for this meal too – only if you feel like it – there is the aforementioned whisky, beer, and certainly the liqueur. You might do a great deal worse than sample the well-known Scottish liqueur, Drambuie, made of honey and whisky, in which Prince Charlie himself toasted his fortune in the '45.

The great satisfactions of life are not in the achievements of the

League of Nations nor in the balanced budgets of National Governments, nor the revolutionary proposals of reformers. You know dear reader, that happiness is a smaller thing than these. It consists in a day well spent, and the essential of a day well spent is a day with good digestion, a day in which appetite has been satisfied but not sated. Such is the achievement of Scottish food; it invokes the appetite and it gives a satisfaction which is among the world's greater contentments.

Will Y. Darling (1937)

SCOTCH OATMEAL

When Dr. Johnson described oatmeal as 'Food for horses in England and men in Scotland,' a witty Scot quickly remarked – 'Ay! and whaur will ye get sic horses and sic men?'

The fouk wha say oatmeal's nae guid
Maun hae carbuncles in their heid;
I'll prove to a' wha care to read
    This plain appeal,
They can on naething better feed
    Than Scotch oatmeal.

What Scotchman is't that does na min'
On youthfu' days o' auld lang syne,
His humble joys, maist a' divine,
    In some sma' biel';
The frugal fare he thocht sae fine –
    Ev'n Scotch oatmeal?

Though aince denounced wi' Cockney shout
As only fit for horse or nowte,
Ere Johnson turned his classic snout,
    He saw, puir chiel!
How horses throve and men grew stout
    On Scotch oatmeal.

Whan Bruce, at glorious Bannockburn,
Made England's proud batalions mourn,
What made the cowardly rascals turn
    On hasty heel?
'Twas sturdy bane-and-muscle corn,
    Or Scotch oatmeal.

What won auld Scotland back her rights?
What bore the Scots through countless fights?
What led the kilts up Alma's heights?
    Made Russians reel? –
What else but timely sups and bites
    O' Scotch oatmeal?

Whan Burns and Scott triumphant sang
Their native hills and glens amang,
In deathless notes their numbers rang,
    Proud to reveal
What wondrous gifts o' genius sprang
    Frae Scotch oatmeal.

Victoria, Britain's honoured Queen,
To Scotland aye a trusty frien',
Had routh o' dainties mony a ane,
    Yet was sae leal;
Ae favourite dish she trocked for nane –
    'Twas Scotch oatmeal.

Whan fashed wi' nyattery colic pain,
Douce, canny Scotchmen ne'er complain,
John Barleycorn, sweet juice o' grain,
    Soon mak's them weel;
They need nae drugs wha life sustain
    On Scotch oatmeal.

But English fouk, whan they grow ill,
Maun lie in bed for cough or chill,
Wi' poultice, powder, paste, or pill
    To soothe and heal;
Gweid help them! but commend me still
    To Scotch oatmeal.

Your West-End Anglo-Scotch M.D.,
O' therapeutic pedigree,
A true-blue Scot he canna be,
    But some saft chiel,
Whase stamack, hoven wi' windy tea,
    Spews Scotch oatmeal.

William A. G. Farquhar (1904)

Ballade of Good Whisky

You whose ambition is to swim the Minch
Or write a drum concerto in B Flat
Or run like Bannister or box like Lynch
Or find the Ark wrecked on Mt. Ararat –
No special training's needed: thin or fat,
You'll do it if you never once supplant
As basis of your commissariat
Glenfiddich, Bruichladdich and Glengrant.

My own desires are small. In fact, I flinch
From heaving a heavenly Hindy from her ghat
Or hauling Loch Ness Monsters, inch by inch,
Out of their wild and watery habitat.
I've no desire to be Jehoshaphat
Or toy with houris fetched from the Levant.
But give to me – *bis dat qui cito dat* –
Glenfiddich, Bruichliddich and Glengrant.

I would drink down, and think the feat a cinch,
The Congo, Volga, Amazon, La Platte,
And Tweed as chaser – a bargain, this, to clinch
In spite of *nota bene* and *caveat*
(Though what a feast must follow after that
Of Amplex, the divine deodorant!)
If they ran – hear my heart go pit-a-pat! –
Glenfiddich, Bruichladdich and Glengrant.

Envoi

Chris! (whether perpendicular or flat
Or moving rather horrible aslant)
Here is a toast that you won't scunner at:
Glenfiddich, Bruichladdich and Glengrant!

Norman MacCaig (1910-)

Petticoat Tails

A baking speciality of the Edinburgh area, now made commercially, which takes its name from the shape of the petticoat hoops worn in the nineteenth century. The original recipe in Meg Dods' Cook and Housewife's Manual *included a little milk, which is not used today; otherwise it is simply a good shortbread with an interesting shape. It is a ladies' shortbread, as men usually prefer the thick fingers.*

7oz plain flour (200g)
3oz butter (75g)
1oz lard (25g)
2oz icing sugar (50g)
1 dsp caraway seeds *(optional)*

Preheat the oven to 350°F/180°C or gas mark 4.

Sift the flour and icing sugar into a bowl. Add the butter and lard and rub in fats till the mixture resembles fine breadcrumbs. Add caraway seeds and then turn the mixture out onto a board and knead together into a firm dough.

Roll out into a large round about ¼in (½cm) thick. Crimp the edges with your finger and thumb. Prick all over with a fork then cut a circle out of the centre. Divide the rest of the circle into either twelve, eighteen or twenty-four pieces, depending on the size you want. Bake on a greased baking sheet for 20-30 minutes or until they are a pale golden brown. Dredge with caster sugar while still hot.

Catherine Brown (1981)

CHAPTER 10

THE ARTS

A Gude Buke

Ah like a gude buke
a buke's aw ye need
jis settle doon
hiv a right gude read

Ay, a gude buke's rerr
it makes ye think
nuthin tae beat it
bar a gude drink

Ah like a gude buke
opens yir mine
a gude companion
tae pass the time

See mi wi a buke, bit
in a bus ur a train
canny whak it
wee wurld i yir ain

Ah, ah like a gude buke
widny deny it
dje know thon wan
noo – whit dje cry it?

Awright, pal, skip it
awright, keep the heid
howm ah tae know
yir tryin tae read?

Stephen Mulrine (1937-)

Oh Sir Walter, We Do Not Love You . . .

'A meeting of the Skene Reading Society was held on Monday last for the approving or disapproving of the Waverley Novels as forming part of their library . . . The arguments of the first party were that the books were full of oaths . . . that the works tended to debase Christianity; to uphold worldly motives of action, and that they were to the mind what cholera and pestilence were to the body . . . The argument on both sides being finished . . . a member, to procure unanimity, proposed to remit the forty-eight volumes to a committee to consider them . . . A committee of eleven was then appointed, and thus . . . are eleven of the good men of the parish of Skene to sit in judgement on the works of the master spirit of the age . . .'

The Inverness Courier, December 10, 1834

At The Orphanage

Young Janie has been removed from the squalors of life in The Lane and placed in the Orphanage of Skeyne, on Deeside. It is Trustees' Day and the day of decision for the future of the older children. Janie, however, has her own ideas about her future.

'And Janie? We're going to be losing Janie soon. How many years, Mrs Thane? How long have we had Janie?'

The Head Trustee rose to his feet. The gesture signalled the dismissal of the children, and cut off the flow of the small Trustee's words.

'Stay behind the others,' Mrs Thane whispered in Janie's ear. The children filed past her, their small, sidelong glances of awe lengthened her in spirit and in stature. The door closed behind them. Its click separated her from childhood.

'We've had a visit from your Schoolmaster, Janie.'

The Head Trustee was speaking long enough for Janie to know the sound of his voice for the first time.

'He tells us you have made excellent progress at school.'

'Did you know,' Mr McLaren, the Minister, leant forward, cutting Janie from the scene, 'that her English papers were the best in Aberdeenshire? Most unusual,' he explained, 'I read the particular essay. The lifetime of an old woman, complete in a single page. It was difficult to understand how anyone so young could have written it, without having possibly experienced it.'

'I didn't realise that Janie was in any way . . .' The small

Trustee faltered, his eyes searched Mrs Thane for aid. 'I always had the impression that she . . . well, that she . . .'

Mrs Thane came to his rescue.

'She's a puzzle. She can be as crude and knowing as they come. And, at the same time, she's less sophisticated and more sensitive than any of the other children, who haven't had such a deplorable background.'

'A disintegrated personality?' the Minister suggested.

'I'm afraid so,' the Head Trustee admitted. 'That's why this question of further Education presents a problem. The pity is that we sometimes get them too late to adjust the balance.'

'How old was Janie when she came to us, Mrs Thane?' The small Trustee put the question.

'Nine. Just on nine.'

'Give me a child till it is seven,' the small Trustee deplored. 'After that, any one can have it. What's bred in the bone, you know.'

'Well! What have you got to say for her, yourself, Mrs Thane?' The Head Trustee's breeziness drew Janie into their circle again.

'She's honest,' Mrs Thane agreed. 'She's very good with the younger ones. She's got a nice nature, she never sulks. She's an excellent milker. She can turn out a room well. Indeed, Janie can do anything well when she likes. But she doesn't always . . . like!'

'We're all inclined to be a bit like that, sometimes,' the Minister confessed. 'It's a very human failing.'

'What about an under-housemaid's job for her, Mrs Thane.' The small Trustee was struck with the idea and urged it lovingly.

'In some good household you know. Where they'll take an interest in her.'

'I'm no' so sure about that,' the Mannie intervened for the first time.

'Good, Mr Thane.' The small Trustee sounded as if he were aware of the Mannie for the first time, and was anxious to make up for it. 'It's excellent to have the practical opinion of a plain man. What would you suggest?'

'If Janie has to go into service at all,' the Mannie spoke unperturbed by Mrs Thane's alert attitude, 'I suggest that she works at a local farmhouse. She likes outside work. And she's good at it. She'll know where she is, and the folk that she's amongst. At least till she gets another year over her head.'

'What do you think, yourself, Janie?' The small Trustee put the question.

Don't fly up. Mrs Thane's eyes pleaded. Don't fly up just now. I tried to prepare you for this.

Janie found the small Trustee's face.

'I don't want to dust and polish,' she told it. 'And I don't want to work on a farm. I want to write poetry. Great poetry. As great as Shakespeare.'

Janie dismissed herself from the room. Surprise rooted Mrs Thane from preventing her. Her last Trustee's Day was over.

Jessie Kesson (1916-)

Shaw on Barrie

Barrie had that queer Scottish quality of likeability that seems to be quite independent of anything specially endearing in Scottish conduct . . . . Barrie had none of the Caledonian vices: he was not envious, nor greedy, nor jealous, nor sensitively egotistical, nor quarrelsome, nor drunken, nor a begetter of illegitimate children. It is possible to like a Scot who has all these failings; but in Barrie's case there was nothing to forgive: one liked him not only for his books and plays but because there was not the smallest reason for disliking him unless you disliked Scots as such . . . His plays and books must have made people happy; yet he was, as far as can be guessed, not much more of an optimist than Calvin. This may account partly for the sterility of his later years; for he was not lazy, and if he had found anything delightful to say he would certainly have said it.

George Bernard Shaw (1856-1950)

James Bridie

When Mrs Siddons played Isabella in *The Fatal Marriage* at the old Theatre Royal in Edinburgh, the gallery doors had to be guarded by soldiers against the crowd, porters and servants sat all night on the pavement to make sure of booking seats for the gentry, and ladies in the audience were so immoderately moved by the performance that many of them fainted. Miss Gordon of Gight, destined to become the mother of the poet Byron, was carried from her box one evening in hysterics; and such was the general perturbation, commotion, and rapture of the great audiences that a gang of London pickpockets arrived to take advantage of their distraction, and went off with a fine collection of wigs, watches, hats, and pocket-books as a reward for opportunism.

In spite of this vivacity, however, the theatre did not flourish in Scotland, and there was no native growth of drama. With a contrary and broader enthusiasm Scotland had adopted the religion of Calvin, which John Knox brought from Geneva in the sixteenth century, and Calvinism, as translated into Scottish Presbyterianism, was hostile to plays and regarded the stage as a pulpit for the Devil.

During the nineteenth century English touring companies could be seen in most of the larger towns, and some crudely dramatised versions of the novels of Sir Walter Scott were popular. But there was still no native theatre, and the Church, in general, maintained its disapproval. Scotland entered the twentieth century without a drama of its own. There was a lively and distinguished heritage of poetry; a great number of spirited tales and legends, and the Waverley novels; there were native songs in abundance, and native dances which, at their best, combined something of the grace of France with something of the vigour of Poland – but no native theatre, no Scottish plays except the few poor transcriptions from Sir Walter.

As the new century came in, the small but remarkable figure of J. M. Barrie appeared above its horizon, a pioneer though not recognisably heroic, and for a generation his very skilful comedies were immensely popular and fashionably successful. Their success did much to persuade Scotland that the theatre might become a respectable part of its life, but their immediate sequel was an undistinguished growth of domestic comedies, many of a humble sort that became known as 'kitchen comedy'; and as a serious influence Barrie did not survive the first Great War. After the surly discomfort of battles in the mud, and the disillusion of the years that followed, his whimsical fancy and his sentimentality were rejected – sternly by the stern and scornfully by the sophisticated – and of his pioneering little remained on which to build except a new awareness of the theatre, a familiar acceptance of it, which were his creation.

But the war which was about to rob Barrie of his fame was maturing the mind of a new dramatist . . .

The City Council of Glasgow once entertained at luncheon some distinguished guests, among whom were Mr. Bridie and Miss Edith Evans. Mr. Bridie was required to make a speech. He stood up, fumbled irresolutely with some notes, and put them in his pocket. 'I am not,' he said, 'going to deliver the very good speech which I had prepared. With Miss Evans in our company, all other subjects are irrelevant, and I have no interest in them. I shall speak about Miss Evans.'

And he spoke so aptly, with such judgement, eloquence, and so nice a warmth, that Dame Edith, when he had finished, rose impulsively and in the noble melody to which she alone can tune the human voice, declared: 'My Lord Provost! I apologise for what is, I cannot deny it, the gravest breach of decorum – for convention and common modesty both, in the ordinary way, require privacy for a proposal – yet I dare not lose this immediate opportunity, but must say now, before you all, that if Mr. Bridie's dear wife should ever decide to release him from his present engagement, I intend to marry him myself!'

'No Englishman unmoved that statement hears,' as W. S. Gilbert remarked on another occasion; but the record must not be too uniformly flattering. As a member of committee, I have heard, Mr. Bridie can be opinionative, wilful, and mulishly obstinate; and with his kindness goes his Calvinism which, like that of its author, is arbitrary.

Once, about ten years ago, I met him by accident in a train leaving Edinburgh. Now Mr. Bridie belongs to Glasgow, and every honest man in Glasgow believes that the people of Edinburgh are shallow, false, hard of heart, and paltry before God. I would ask you to remember this. – For as we quickly fell into conversation, our talk turned speedily to religion, and while we were still running through the suburbs of Edinburgh I said to Mr. Bridie, 'But do you really believe all that?'

'Of course I do,' he answered.

'And who,' I demanded, 'are the Elect? Who are those predestined for Heaven and Eternal Bliss?'

'You and I,' he calmly replied.

'Then who,' I enquired, 'are the damned? Who are those booked (so to speak) for everlasting torment?'

'All those damned fools walking up and down Princes Street,' he answered.

Eric Linklater (1899-1974)

Scotland's First Newspaper

The first newspaper supposed to have been printed in Scotland, was entitled, '*Mercurius Scoticus, or a true character of affairs in England, Ireland, Scotland, and other foreign parts, collected for publicque satisfaction,*' which was published weekly, and consisted of eight pages small quarto. The first number was issued on 5th August, 1651, but neither the place where it was printed, nor the name of the printer are mentioned in it, however, it is supposed to have been printed at Leith. It was but a short-lived publication, having, in November, 1652, given place to a paper published at London, and reprinted at Leith, entitled, '*A Diurnal of some passages and affairs.*' This paper was also of short duration, it having been superseded in less than a year by another, entitled, '*Mercurius Politicus,* comprising the sum of intelligence, with the affairs of England, Ireland, and Scotland, in defence of the commonwealth, and for information of the people, *Ita vertere seria, Hor. de art poet.* Printed at London, and reprinted at Leith.' This paper generally consisted of from eight to sixteen pages, and was, in 1655, reprinted in Edinburgh, which is said to have been the first time that a newspaper was put to press in the city.

Annals of Edinburgh

Embro To The Ploy

A brilliant satire of the annual Edinburgh International Festival when, for three brief weeks, the City goes mad with events, happenings and lunacies perpetrated by residents and visitors alike.

In simmer, whan aa sorts foregether
in Embro to the ploy,

fowk seek out friens to hae a blether,
or faes they'd fain annoy;
smorit wi British Railways' reek
frae Glesca or Glen Roy
or Wick, they come to hae a week
of cultivatit joy,
                    or three,
in Embro to the ploy.

Americans wi routh of dollars,
wha drink our whisky neat,
wi Sasunachs and Oxford Scholars
are eydent for the treat
of music sedulously high-tie
at thirty-bob a seat;
Wop opera performed in Eytie
to them's richt up their street,
                    they say,
in Embro to the ploy.

Furthgangan Embro folk come hame
for three weeks in the year,
and find Auld Reekie no the same,
fu sturrit in a steir.
The stane-faced biggins whaur they froze
and suppit puirshous leir
of cultural cauld-kale and brose
see cantraips unco queer
                    thae days
in Embro to the ploy.

The tartan tred wad gar ye lauch;
nae problem is owre teuch.
Your surname needna end in *-och;*
they'll cleik ye up the cleuch.
A puckle dollar bills will aye
preive Hiram Teufelsdrockh
a septary of Clan McKay,
it's maybe richt eneuch,
                    verfluch!
in Embro to the ploy.

The auld High Schule, whaur monie a skelp
of triple-tonguit tawse
has gien a hyst-up and a help
towards Doctorates of Laws,
nou hears, for Ramsay's cantie rhyme,
loud pawmies of applause
frae folk that pey a pund a time
to sit on wudden raws
                    gey hard
in Embro to the ploy.

The haly kirk's Assembly-haa
nou fairly coups the creel
wi Lindsay's Three Estaitis, braw
devices of the Deil.
About our heids the satire stots
like hailstanes till we reel;
the bawrs are in auld-farrant Scots,
it's maybe jist as weill,
                    imphm,
in Embro to the ploy.

The Epworth Haa wi wunner did
behold a piper's bicker;
wi *hadarid* and *hindarid*
the air gat thick and thicker.
Cumha na Cloinne pleyed on strings
torments a piper quicker
to get his dander up, by jings,
than thirty u.p. liquor,
                    hooch aye!
in Embro to the ploy.

The North – British Embro Whigs
that stayed in Charlotte Square,
they fairly wad hae tined their wigs
to see the Stuarts there,
the bleidan Earl of Moray and aa
weill-pentit and gey bare;
Our Queen and Princess, buskit braw,
enjoyed the hale affair

(see Press)
in Embro to the ploy.

Whan day's anomalies are cled
in decent shades of nicht,
the Castle is transmogrified
by braw electric licht.
The toure that bields the Bruce's croun
presents an unco sicht
mair sib to Wardour Street nor Scone,
wae's me for Scotland's micht,
says I
in Embro to the ploy.

A happening, incident, or splore
affrontit them that saw
a thing they'd never seen afore –
in the McEwan Haa:
a lassie in a wheelie-chair
wi naething on at aa.
jist like my luck! I wasna there.
it's no the thing ava,
tut-tut,
in Embro to the ploy.

The Café Royal and Abbotsford
are filled wi orra folk
whaes stock-in-trade's the scrievit word,
or twicet-scrievit joke.
Brains, weak or strang, in heavy beer,
or ordinary, soak.
Quo yin: This yill is aafie dear,
I hae nae clinks in poke,
nor fauldan-money,
in Embro to the ploy.

The auld Assembly-rooms, whaur Scott
foregethert wi his fiers,
nou see a gey kenspeckle lot
ablow the chandeliers.
Til Embro drouths the Festival Club

a richt godsend appears;
it's something new to find a pub
that gaes on sairvan beers
                    eftir hours
in Embro to the ploy.

Jist pitten-out the drucken mobs
frae howffs in Potterraw,
fleean, to hob-nob wi the Nobs,
ran to this Music Haa,
Register Rachel, Cougait Kate,
Nae-neb Nellie and aa
stauchert about amang the Great,
what fun! I never saw
                    the like,
in Embro to the ploy.

They toddle hame doun lit-up streets
filled wi synthetic joy;
aweill, the year brings few sic treats
and muckle to annoy.
There's monie hartsom braw high-jinks
mixed up in this alloy
in simmer, whan aa sorts foregether
in Embro to the ploy.

Robert Garioch (1909-81)

ploy: harmless frolic
routh: plenty
cleik: hook
coups: upsets
splore: frolic
fier: companion
tine: lose
smorit: smothered
steir: hurly-burly
cleuch: steep place
creel: basket
scrievit: written
kenspeckle: familiar
bield: shelter
eydent: eager
puirshous: precious
skelp: smack
stots: bounces
clinks: money
ablow: below
stauchert: staggered
furthgangan: exiled
leir: learning
tawse: strap
bawrs: jokes
poke: pouch

James McBey was born in 1883, the son of a village blacksmith in Newburgh, Aberdeenshire. He left school at the age of 15 and went to work in a bank in Aberdeen. His interest aroused by an article in BOY'S OWN PAPER, the young McBey taught himself to etch, producing the first prints on a mangle in his mother's kitchen in 1902.

Etching had one advantage; it did not necessitate the carrying about of bulky gear. I had not dared to sketch or paint out-of-doors. For a junior bank clerk to be seen with a sketching outfit in the streets would be, I knew well, certain to arouse the derision of my fellow clerks and would be regarded with at least suspicious curiosity by the higher officers of the bank, should it ever come to their knowledge.

All those belonging to the parochial banking world in which I was enmeshed were intensely preoccupied with the grim business of survival on their meagre salaries. They had their own shrewd and canny standards, and viewed with slight tolerance and vinegary scorn anyone indulging in unremunerative activity. To spend time and energy on the study or practice of art was considered as frivolous – the diversion of a trifler. Consequently, I went about the making of my first etching with all secrecy.

From the plumber Blaikie I bought a sheet of 18 gauge copper 4″×5¼″. With a file I made the edges true and put a bevel all round, finishing and polishing one side with fine emery cloth. Closely following Lalanne's directions I heated the plate and dabbed on the wax ground. After being blackened in the smoke of a candle it cooled to a fine matt surface. To protect this from accidental scratches whilst in my pocket, I covered it with a piece of cardboard to which I had fastened with thread a thick layer of cotton wool as a cushion.

On a sunny Saturday afternoon of July 1902, in a state of suppressed excitement, with a small mirror, my plate and two darning needles in my pocket, I walked down to the harbour, to the quay where the Shetland steamers tied up. This quay, known as Point Law, formed the tip of a tongue of land dividing the harbour into two arms of water. In the easternmost of these was tied up a fleet of herring boats, most of them of the 'Zulu' type, each with two tall pole masts and lug sails.

I picked a deserted part of the quay where were piled big

wooden packing cases. Sticking my penknife in one of them I hung my small mirror on it, so that, standing with my back to the fishing boats, I could see them reflected in the mirror.

Minutes passed before I had the courage to make a single line on the black matt surface. One contingency I had not foreseen: intense concentration made me involuntarily hold my breath; my pulse pounded so that I could not control the hammer-like motions of my hands, the impulses of which, although slight, would be sure to record themselves immediately my needle touched the wax.

I waited, trying to relax. I kept reminding myself that, although a mistake was difficult to cover up or rectify, the plate, as an object of expense, was not thereby spoilt; that I could wash off everything with turpentine. Gradually I became more controlled and once started I gained confidence.

The ease with which the needle, as it touched the black wax surface, made a copper-coloured line was almost uncanny. Eventually I finished, rewrapped my plate with care, walked home in a state of suspended elation, and straightaway immersed it in a bath of half nitric acid and half water.

Everything happened according to Lalanne, whose treatise I had handy, open at the page.

Bubbles grew on the copper-coloured lines. I took them off gently with a feather. Several times I removed the plate from the acid and painted out the lines where I wanted distance, trying to guess the depth of the lines by the feel of the needle in them. It was a messy-looking object by the time I decided to remove the wax coating. Turpentine and a wipe cleaned this off and suddenly there was my drawing in black lines on the copper. It was astonishing. But how was I to get a print?

So far as I knew, there was not in the whole of Aberdeen a copperplate press like the one Lalanne described. This was an elaborate affair, but the principle was simple – a very powerful squeeze.

It was just possible that the copying press in the bank would do the job. Surreptitiously I took my plate and the few accessories necessary and tried it. Nothing happened. The pressure obviously was too dissipated. It was mortifying to be defeated so near to my goal.

A week later it suddenly occurred to me that our mangle in the basement might be made to the job. It had strong wooden rollers.

If the top one were screwed down tight the spring pressure might be just sufficient.

I cut a piece of thick linoleum for a travelling plank and ran it a little way between the rollers. On it I placed my copper plate, inked and wiped; then the dampened paper; then three pieces of blanket. I screwed down the pressure all it would take and slowly turned the handles till the blankets were clear at the other side of the rollers.

Gently I peeled off the blankets and the paper. There, in front of my unbelieving eyes, was a perfect print.

James McBey (1883-1959)

First Exhibition

For some time the young McBey kept the details of his spare time activities from his employers at the bank lest their disapproval be elicited and lest his fellows mock his efforts. At the end of 1905, however, he dares to send two prints to the Royal Scottish Academy in Edinburgh.

At the end of 1905 I, greatly daring, sent two etchings to the Royal Scottish Academy, telling no one. One, 'Albert Basin', was rejected, but the other, 'Old Terry' – a number of herring fishing boats in the harbour of the Aberdeen suburb – was hung.

I received the unexpected intimation with mixed feelings. The elation I felt that my work was good enough to be hung alongside that of real artists was balanced by an uneasiness as to how the officials in the bank would regard the unbanking-like employment of my spare time should they come to know of it. I thought it advisable on the whole to keep dark my Edinburgh success.

A day later John Hutchinson – one of the inspectors – laid a folded *Aberdeen Free Press* in front of me, pointed to the tail of a paragraph, and said, 'Do you know anything about this?' I read the couple of lines at the end of the Royal Scottish Academy notice: 'Mr. James McBee, 42 Union Grove has an etching of "Old Torry".' My name was wrongly spelt.

'Yes, sir, that refers to me.'

'What is all this about? Do you make etchings?'

He was not disapproving, only curious. I confessed how I had worked quietly for years, rising early every morning and working for an hour or two before I set out for the bank.

'Where did you learn to etch?'

'From a book which I borrowed from the Public Library.'

'How many etchings have you made?'

'About twenty-five.'

'I want to see them. Bring them down one day and I'll show them to the Directors of the Bank.'

Although not popular with most of the clerks, he had a bigness, poise, and an independence outstanding in that office where timid standards ruled. Nevertheless his sympathetic attitude was unexpected and gave me a great sense of relief, even a mild elation. No longer was it advisable that I work in secret. My etching being exhibited in the R.S.A. was an armour against the sarcasm I feared might come from my fellow clerks.

When, subsequently, I brought him about twenty-five of my Aberdeen, Portsoy, and Edinburgh etchings, he took them to the Directors' Room. When returning them to me he said the Directors admired them very much, adding that he had hoped some of them, who were wealthy and considered themselves collectors and patrons of art, might have purchased several but that unfortunately no one had done so.

I now felt bold enough to send two etchings to the Royal Glasgow Institute exhibition. Both were hung.

James McBey (1883-1959)

Meeting A Scottish Painter

In this extract from his autobiography Eddie Linden describes his first meeting, in the French Pub in Soho, in the 1950s, with fellow Scotsman Robert Colquhoun. Colquhoun and his inseparable friend Robert MacBryde were both to die prematurely shortly afterwards and their work as painters is better known in death than it ever was in life.

'I'm Eddie Linden,' I said at last.

'Martin Green,' he said, 'publisher, and ex-left wing radical. I can smell that garbage a mile away.'

'Oh,' I said, 'so that's why you were so . . .'

'Aggressive? Yes, Eddie Linden. Something about you makes

me want to commit a major crime. I think I could get a great deal of pleasure entering a blade between two of your ribs to prick and even puncture your heart. All that enthusiasm for dreary nothing. Why don't you grow up and put your arse to the bloody wheel?'

'Did you used to be a socialist?' I said.

'I breathe publishing,' he said, 'but I pray socialist. You've been congratulating yourself for being a good, partyline socialist for years, haven't you, you frizzy-haired teaboy, and now you dare ask me if I *used to be* a socialist? Who are you? Karl Marx himself?'

'But you did say you were "ex-left wing". I wasn't trying to be rude. Why should I be rude to you? I don't even know who you are.'

'Who is this jerk?' said a man, turning round from the bar.

'Have a look for yourself,' said Martin Green.

'Who are you?' said the stranger, 'I've been listening to you talk to Martin for more than a minute and if I listen any more I'll throw up.'

'Who the hell are you?' I retorted, fearing that as I had lost so much ground I might as well lose it all.

'Look, sonny,' he said, 'I don't care how pretty you wish you were, I don't care how many times you bawled for your mama, I don't care what kind of mines you've been down, and what kind of trades union cross my heart you belong to. Get your stinking, snotty-nosed attitudes out of this pub, and learn to speak like a Scot.'

'You're drunk,' I said.

'Kill him,' he said, 'Martin, buy me another drink. Arrogance in one so young depresses me. And when it's Scottish arrogance as well, I fell like dying.'

'Of course,' said Martin, 'a large Bell's, Robert?'

'A large Bell's,' said Robert.

'I'm a painter. What are you?' he said suddenly turning to me.

'I'm a . . . I'm a . . . I'm a porter,' I said. 'St Pancras Station, and I . . .'

'No embellishments, rat-face,' he said.

'What do you paint?' I asked, 'Walls?'

'Walls,' he said, 'bricks, driftwood, fingernails, paper, canvasses. Why, are you some sort of joker?'

'You could say that,' I said, 'You come from Kilmarnock, don't you?'

'You could say that,' he said, 'I used to spank babies like you.'

'Now you get drunk to prove what a big man you are?'

'That's about it,' he said, 'and to escape people like you?'

'Everybody's being unfriendly tonight. Perhaps I forgot to wash?' I said.

'No,' he said, 'you didn't forget. You're still wet behind the ears.'

'Oh thanks,' I said, 'I thought you were going to be pleasant.'

'I am being pleasant,' he said, 'you wait till I'm unpleasant.'

'Is your name Robert? Mine's Eddie Linden.'

'Whisky,' he said, brushing my hand aside, 'pour a whisky down your throat. Green! Fill this boy.'

'Here you are, Robert. Do it yourself,' said Martin Green.

'Why the cheek. And to think I used to bite crocodiles. Here Eddie Linden, open your mouth, throw back your head, I libate you in the name of the dignity of Colquhoun. Drink!' And he poured the whisky down my vertical throat. I managed not to choke and said,

'Robert Colquhoun, may I buy you the drink you have just spent on me?'

'You may,' he said, 'you may. Green, do you think he'll last?'

'A snowball's chance in hell,' said Martin.

'I love that,' said Colquhoun, 'maybe I could paint it.' I sheltered behind some of the pub clients trying to buy him a drink. He grabbed me by the jacket and said, 'Come here, puppy. Do you see this?' He was looking at Martin Green.

'Yes,' I said.

'That has seen Spain.'

'In the tourist season?' I said.

'Nearly,' he said, 'in an ambulance.'

'Was he alone?'

'No,' said Robert, 'he was with his father, one or two corpses, and a few small sounds.'

'I'll get a drink,' I said, 'then I must go.'

'How one tires of these pups,' he said to Martin and turned away from me. I bought a whisky, pushed it across the bar towards him, watched his eye register the fact but make no other aknowledgement, and then left. The night air had never seemed so welcome.

Sebastian Barker/Eddie Linden (1929-)

To Joan Eardley

Pale yellow letters
humbly straggling across
the once brilliant red
of a broken shop-face
CONFECTIO
and a blur of children
at their games, passing,
gazing as they pass
at the blur of sweets
in the dingy, cosy
Rottenrow window –
and Eardley on my wall.
Such rags and streaks
that master us! –
that fix what the pick
and bulldozer have crumbled
to a dingier dust,
the living blur
fiercely guarding
energy that has vanished,
cries filling still
the unechoing close!
I wandered by the rubble
and the houses left standing
kept a chill, dying life
in their islands of stone.
No window opened
as the coal cart rolled
and the coalman's call
fell coldly to the ground.
But the shrill children
jump on my wall.

Edwin Morgan (1920-   )

The Burning Harp

A story for the eightieth birthday of Neil Gunn.

Two nights before Yule in the year of 1135 a farmer called Olaf and his wife Asleif and all their household were sitting at supper in their house at Duncansby in Caithness, when a kitchen girl looked up and said that there was a fire in the thatch. They all looked up; the roof was burning. Then Anna a dairy girl pointed; the window was all flame and smoke. 'We should leave the house now,' said Olaf. 'We are not going to die of cold, that much is sure,' said his wife Asleif. The door was two red crackling posts and a crazy yellow curtain.

'I think we are having visitors for Yule,' said an old ploughman who was sitting with an ale-horn in the corner. 'I am too old for such boisterous guests. I think I will go to bed.' While the women ran from wall to wall yelling the old ploughman stretched himself out on a bench and seemed to go to sleep. Olaf and Asleif kissed each other in the centre of the room. 'I am glad of one thing,' said Olaf, 'our son Sweyn is out fishing in the Pentland Firth.'

The whole gable end of the house burst into flames.

Outside there was snow on the ground and beyond the burning house it was very dark. A dozen men one by one threw their torches into the rooted blaze. They took out their daggers and axes in case anyone should try to escape from the fire. A thousand sparks flew about like bees and died in the white midden and the long blue ditch.

A man called Ragnar said, 'There are innocent ones inside, servants and children. We have no quarrel with them. They should be let out.'

Oliver threw a bucket of water over the door. He shouted, 'Servants of Olaf, and any children, you are to come out now.'

A few girls ran out into the night with glaring eyes and rushed past the besiegers and were lost in the darkness beyond. A boy came out. He turned and looked back at the fire once, then he ran laughing after the servants, rising and falling in the snow, wild with excitement.

'I don't think we should have done that,' said Nord. 'These servants will tell the story of the burning all over Caithness. You know how women exaggerate. People here and there will think poorly of us for this night's work. That boy will grow up and remember the burning.'

Now that the girls were out of the house all was much quieter inside. Even the tumult of the flames was stilled a little. In the silence they heard the sound of a voice praying.

'Valt the priest is inside,' said Oliver. 'I had forgotten that he might be here at this time of year. We would not be very popular with the bishop or the monks if Valt were to die. Throw another bucket of water at the door.'

Father Valt came out with a scorched cross between his fingers. There was soot in his beard. He said to Oliver and the other besiegers, 'God pity you, my poor children.' Then he turned and absolved the dead and the dying inside, and walked away slowly towards the church at the shore.

'We didn't get much gratitude out of that priest,' said Nord. 'In my opinion it was a mistake to let a man like that go. With Father Valt it will be hell fire for all us burners from now until the day he is able to preach no more. We will have no comfort at all, standing in his kirk.'

They heard a few faint harp-strokes through the snorings and belchings of flame.

'It is my opinion,' said Ragnar, 'that there is a poet inside.'

'Well,' said Nord, 'what is a poet more than a miller or a fisherman or a blacksmith?'

'From the sound of the harp,' said Oliver, 'from the way it is being played, it seems to me that the poet in there is none other than Niall from Dunbeath.'

'Well,' said Nord, 'and what about it? What is Niall more than other string-pluckers, Angus say, or Keld, or Harald?'

'Nord,' said Oliver, 'you are very thick in the head. I would keep my mouth shut. Niall is the poet who made the ballad of the silver shoals in the west. He also sang about the boy and the fishing boat – if I am not mistaken that was the first story he told. He was the one too who made us aware of the mysterious well of wisdom. He made that great song about the salmon.'

'It would be a pity indeed, I suppose,' said Nord, 'if the harp of a man like that was to be reduced to a cinder.'

'Nobody in Scotland sings with such purity and sweetness as Niall,' said Oliver. 'We would be shamed for ever if we stopped such a mouth with ashes. The world, we are told, will end in this way, some day soon, in ice and fire and darkness. But how can a harp stroke given to the wind ever perish, even though there are no men left on earth. The gods will hear that music with joy for ever.'

So another bucket of water was thrown over the threshold and the name of the poet Niall was called into the red-and-black dapple inside. Presently an old serene man carrying a harp walked from the burning house into the snow. He seemed not to see the lurid faces all about the door. Honoured, he sought the starlit darkness beyond the lessening circles of flame.

George Mackay Brown (1921-)

THE TRIALS OF AUTHORSHIP

Thomas Carlyle, born in Ecclefechan in 1795, went on to become one of Scotland's most illustrious sons. His magnificent magnum opus was The French Revolution. *Samuel Smiles, himself a Scotsman, born in Haddington, evidently had great respect for his resilience.*

The accidental destruction of Sir Isaac Newton's papers, by his little dog 'Diamond' upsetting a lighted taper upon his desk, by which the elaborate calculations of many years were in a moment destroyed, is a well-known anecdote, and need not be repeated: it is said that the loss caused the philosopher such profound grief that it seriously injured his health, and impaired his understanding. An accident of a somewhat similar kind happened to the MS. of Mr. Carlyle's first volume of his 'French Revolution.' He had lent the MS. to a literary neighbour to peruse. By some mischance, it had been left lying on the parlour floor, and become forgotten. Weeks ran on, and the historian sent for his work, the printers being loud for 'copy.' Inquiries were made, and it was found that the maid-of-all-work, finding what she conceived to be a bundle of waste paper on the floor, had used it to light the kitchen and parlour fire with! Such was the answer returned to Mr. Carlyle, and his feelings may be imagined. There was, however, no help for him but to set resolutely to work to re-write the book and he turned to and did it. He had no draft, and was compelled to rake up from his memory facts, ideas and expressions, which had been long since dismissed. The composition of the book in the first instance had been a work of pleasure; the re-writing of it a second time was one of pain and anguish almost beyond belief. That he persevered and finished the volume under such circumstances affords an instance of determination of purpose which has seldom been surpassed.

Samuel Smiles (1812-1904)

To an Aberdeen Poet Who Writes Solely in English

What ails ye at yer mither tongue?
Hae ye forgot the tang o' it?
The gurly guttrals, malmy soonds,
The dirly words, the sang o' it?
An wad ye cuist it a awa,
Like bauchles on a midden-heid?
Man, think agen afore ye sell
Yer saul tae saft-like English leid.

Wad ye forget the ballad-speik,
Melodeon's chord and fiddle's clink,
Forsweir yer grandad's weys o' life,
Swap uisge-beatha for Kola drink?
Say 'Shinty is too rough a game
And cricket's more my cup of tea.'
Weel, hyne awa fae Aiberdeen,
For feich, ye're owre genteel for me!

Helen B. Cruickshank (1886-1975)

CHAPTER 11

The Scot at Play and at Rest

Pleasures of The Flesh

Mrs, alias Lady, Agnew, Nether-bow.

This drunken bundle of iniquity, is about 50 years of age, lusty and tall, and she has followed the old trade since she was about 13. One thing she can boast of, that she is daughter of a late worthy Baronet, who was a brave General in the war before last. Being a disgrace to her relations, who are some of the best in Scotland, they sent her to the north, where she continued her business for a long time. She regards neither decency nor decorum, and would as willingly lie with a chimney-sweep as with a Lord. Her desires are so immoderate, that she would think nothing of a company of Grenadiers at one time. Take her all in all, she is an abandoned Piece.

Miss Moffat, alias Beeston, Fountain-closs.

This Lady is tall, black complexion, and about 30 years of age. She is very artful in her amours, and is almost worn out in the service. However, it is said, she does her business extremely well, as she still likes to mumble a piece of grisle.

Ranger's Impartial List of the Ladies of Pleasure in Edinburgh (1779)

Sensuality

Alas it is not practical to quote more than this short speech from Lyndsay's magnificent morality play, Ane Satyre of the Thrie Estaits, *first performed in 1554, in which Dame Sensuality seduces the young King.*

Luifers awalk! behald the fyrie spheir,
Behauld the naturall dochter of Venus:
Behauld luifers, this lustie ladie cleir,
The fresche fonteine of knichtis amorous,
Repleit with joyis dulce and delicious.
Or quha wald mak to Venus observance,
In my mirthfull chalmer melodious,
There sall thay fynd all pastyme, and pleasance;

Behauld my heid, behauld my gay attyre,
Behauld my halse, lusum and lilie quhyte;
Behauld my visage, flammand as the fyre,
Behauld my papis, of portratour perfyte.
To luik on mee luiffers hes greit delyte,
Rycht sa hes all the kinges of Christindome;
To thame I haif done pleasouris infinyte,
And speciallie unto the Court of Rome.

Ane kis of me war worth, in ane morning,
A milyioun of gold to knight, or king:
And yit, I am of nature sa towart,
I lat na luiffer pas with ane sair hart.
Of my name, wald ye wit the veritie,
Forsuith thay call me Sensualitie.
I hauld it best now, or we farther gang,
To dame Venus let us go sing ane Sang.

Sir David Lyndsay (1486-1555)

luifers: *lovers*
halse: *throat*
lusum: *loveable*

The Bonie Lass made the Bed to Me

When Januar wind was blawing cauld
  As to the north I took my way,
The mirksome night did me enfauld,
  I knew na whare to lodge till day.—

By my gude luck a maid I met,
  Just in the middle o' my care;
And kindly she did me invite
  To walk into a chamber fair.—

I bow'd fu' low unto this maid,
  And thank'd her for her courtesie;
I bow'd fou' low unto this maid,
  And bade her mak a bed for me.—

She made the bed baith large and wide,
  Wi' twa white hands she spread it down;
She put the cup to her rosy lips
  And drank, "Young man now sleep ye sound."—

She snatch'd the candle in her hand,
  And frae my chamber went wi' speed;
But I call'd her quickly back again
  To lay some mair below my head.—

A cod she laid below my head,
  And served me wi' due respect;
And to salute her wi' a kiss,
  I put my arms about her neck.—

Haud aff your hands young man, she says,
  And dinna sae uncivil be:
Gif ye hae ony luve for me,
  O wrang na my virginitie!—

Her hair was like the links o' gowd,
  Her teeth were like the ivorie,
Her cheeks like lillies dipt in wine,
  The lass that made the bed to me.—

Her bosom was the driven snaw,
  Twa drifted heaps sae fair to see;
Her limbs the polish'd marble stane,
  The lass that made the bed to me.—

I kiss'd her o'er and o'er again,
  And ay she wist na what to say;
I laid her between me and the wa',
  The lassie thought na lang till day.—

Upon the morrow when we rase,
  I thank'd her for her courtesie:
But ay she blush'd, and ay she sigh'd,
  And said, Alas, ye've ruin'd me.—

I clasp'd her waist, and kiss'd her syne,
  While the tear stood twinklin in her e'e;
I said, My lassie, dinna cry,
  For ye ay shall mak the bed to me.—

She took her mither's holland sheets
  And made them a' in sarks to me:
Blythe and merry may she be,
  The lass that made the bed to me.—

The bonie lass made the bed to me.
  The braw lass made the bed to me;
I'll ne'er forget till the day that I die
  The lass that made the bed to me.—

Robert Burns (1759-96)

Gie the Lass Her Fairin'

O gie the lass her fairin', lad,
  O gie the lass her fairin',
An' something else she'll gie to you,
  That's waly worth the wearin';
Syne coup her o'er amang the creels,
  When ye hae taen your brandy,
The mair she bangs the less she squeels,
  An' hey for houghmagandie.

Then gie the lass her fairin', lad,
  O gie the lass her fairin',
An' she'll gie you a hairy thing,
  An' of it be na sparin';
But coup her o'er amang the creels,
  An' bar the door wi' baith your heels,
The mair she gets the less she squeels;
  An' hey for houghmagandie.

Robert Burns (1759-96)

To the Editor of 'The Scotsman'

Palazzo Robinia,
Via Bustelli 2,
Ch-6600 Locarno, Switzerland,
July 15, 1984

Sir, – I have just come home after a two-week visit to Edinburgh and first of all I would like to thank all persons in and around your beautiful city who have been so very helpful and friendly to me.

However, when visiting Greyfriars Kirkyard last sunny Sunday afternoon I was very much displeased to see girls sunbathing on the grass of this world-famous burying place, amidst the old tombs of so many important Scotchmen. A policeman walked through the kirkyard but he did not seem to take any notice of this misbehaviour.

An hour later, visiting the National Portrait Gallery, I was shocked to see in there a young couple who were not properly dressed. Both in the shortest shorts you can imagine, she having a pair of mini-bra round the naked upper half of her body. Would it be too much to ask the authorities and wardens to see that visitors to museums are properly dressed?

Robert Murray Bakker Albach.

The Scotsman (July 21 1984)

The Benefactor

He'd taught her every single thing she knew.
At sixteen plus, he took her maidenhead
Expertly, with the minimum of fuss,
And gave her orgasm on the self-same bed.

Her spirit, like her body, got its due:
Her mind he moulded while her beauty flowered;
Till nothing lacked that he might be so bold
As teach her tolerance, his final dower.

Svengali with Pygmalion might vie,
But Casanova's gift he had to share
With all who offered, novice or adept.

When Galatea, free, gave him the air,
Incredibly, ungratefully, he wept;
Then, as an extra lesson, blacked her eye.

William J. Tait (1918-   )

Edinburgh Scene

we used to be typists
but the hell wi' that
now we live with these boys
in a two room flat

we've never washed for ages
we sleep on bits of sack
we've baith lost wir pants
and we dinnae want them back

the boys are a' big beardies
they think we're awfy sweet
we never know which one we're with
that's what it means to be beat

Alan Jackson (1938-   )

Zandra

The whole world's got problems, jimmie. Nobody's any exception.

I mean, take me – me and Zandra. Ye know who I'm talking about, don't ye? Zandra – big bird, blonde hair, nice legs, acceptable knockers, comes in here a lot, know who I mean? Aye. Zandra. Well, I never thought I'd ever get anywhere there, straight up I didn't. I'm no saying that she's out of my class or anything – but ye can never expect to win them all can ye? And I'd aye put Zandra down in the "definitely no chance" category. Still, it just shows ye, eh? My auld man aye had it that all ye really needed for the women was patience – he reckoned ye could score with the Queen, provided ye were prepared to bide your time and grasp the opportunity when it came! Aye, and maybe he was right enough and all.

I've known her for years of course – Zandra like, no the Queen! – as a matter of fact, we grew up thegither. Same stair, same street, same school, same damn everything, know what I mean? Her name's no really Zandra, it's Sandra – she changed the "S" to a "Z" when she took up the hairdressing. She's twenty-five years old and it's really quite surprising that she's no married yet – but then, Zandra never was too bright. No to put too fine a point upon it, Zandra's got the kind of mentality that makes a short plank look like a razor blade.

Now me, I'm different. I'm no saying I'm another Einstein or anything, but next to Zandra I'm a mental Colossus. There was a boy in here the other night cried me a "working-class intellectual" but he was probably just taking the piss – him being a schoolteacher and that. Still, I must admit that the level of my conversation tends to operate on an althegither higher plane from Zandra's – and that's a definite minus as far as she's concerned. I mean to say, what woman wants a man that makes her look stupid? Well, maybe some do – but no Zandra! It's like I was saying, she's no the type of bird I normally pull. The ethnic type – students and that – that's my scene, what ye might cry the folk-club style. Zandra now, she's no like that at all – more your Country 'n Western, if ye ken what I mean.

Anyway, it happened. Last Thursday night, it happened. Here's me, sitting in the *Ramsay Arms,* sooking away at a single malt whisky and reading a paperback copy of *Lord of the Rings,* when in walks Zandra on her lonesome. Now, right away, I thought that was funny. I mean, Zandra's the kind of bird ye normally see with her pal or her boy-friend or her mother – know what I mean? Seldom see her unescorted – nearly never.

Anyway, she gives a wee deek about the boozer and, no seeing anybody else that she kens, she comes owre to me. Now, I'll skip the opening chat, the pleasantries and all that sort of crap – I daresay ye're no interested in any case – and come straight to the point. I goes to the bar and I buys another whisky for myself and a vodka and lime for Zandra. When I gets back to the table, I finds her looking at the cover of the book.

'What's the book?' she says, as if she's no able to see for herself.

So I tells her.

'Aye, but what's it about like?'

'Hobbits,' I says.

'What's hobbits?'

'Wee men, about three feet tall, with hairy feet.'

'I don't know if I'd fancy that,' she says, and wrinkles up her wee nose. Then, she has a flash of inspiration and decides to make a joke.

'Ha. Ha. Ha,' says I, 'ye're the right wee comic the night, Zandra, right enough!'

She asks me the story and I try to tell her – but the thing is with Zandra, she's that bloody dopey, she can never hold more than two simple facts in her head at the one time for more than thirty seconds. So, after about thirty seconds, I gives it up, goes back to the bar and gets her another vodka and lime.

All this time, the auld brainbox is going round. Zandra bides with this other bird, Patricia – and I happen to know (because I once tried to lumber Patricia) that they normally stay in on a Thursday night. So what's the game?

'Where's Pat the night?' I ask, kind of off-hand and nonchalant-like, when I get back to the table. Right away I can see by her face that I've struck a sore spot.

'Pat's left,' she says, with a wee huffy sniff, turning her attention to a point far distant, at the other end of the bar.

'Is that right?' says I, with a modicum of surprise. 'Where's she away to?'

'Sanquhar,' says she. 'She's away back to Sanquhar.'

'Sanquhar!' says I – that's where Patricia comes from like. 'What for does she want to go back to Sanquhar?'

'It seems there's this fellae,' says Zandra, with some distaste. 'She's talking about marrying him.'

Well, that put a thought into my head, I can tell ye. I mean, if Patricia was away back to Sanquhar, it stood to reason that Zandra was on her lonesome in the flat as well as in the boozer.

'Oh Norman!' says Zandra suddenly. She's the only person I ken that cries me 'Norman' and no 'Norrie' – it comes of her knowing me since I was three. 'I ken ye were aye fond of her. I shouldnae have said nothing. Ye're bound to be upset.'

Upset? Huh, just because I tried (with a singular lack of success) to get next to her best pal a couple of years ago, Zandra has to build the whole thing up into Orpheus and Eurydice. Still, I reckoned there was nothing to be gained by putting her right on that score.

'Aye!' says I, with as heavy a sigh as I could manage. 'Fancy another vodka and lime, would ye?'

The rest is pretty academic – at least, as far as you're concerned, pal. If you think I'm going to sit here and tell you all the details – give ye a blow-by-blow account of how I managed the very tricky process of getting Zandra in exactly the right frame of mind to accept the game-set-and-match situation – then you've got another think coming. If you want that sort of thing, away and read Harold Robbins. He's better at it nor me.

Anyway, the next morning Zandra was right upset. It turns out that she was having this wee scene with a sailor – she cried him a 'ship's officer' but, knowing Zandra, he was likely just a matlow – and she was fair worried about what he'd say when she tellt him.

'I've got an answer for that!' says I, dead cheery.

'What's that?' she says.

'Never mind telling him!' says I – and that set her off again. Bawling like a bairn she was.

Seemingly, I'd got a hold of the wrong end of the stick. Zandra couldn't care less about the matlow – she'd taken the whole thing serious and was worried about how she was going to give the poor bugger the heave! Fancied me for years, she said, kept calling me her 'childhood sweetheart' and saying that now that she'd found out that I 'felt the same way' (her expression, no mine!) she'd have to do the decent thing by her sailor.

I've hardly seen the back of her since last Thursday. The only reason I've managed to dodge the column the night is because she's away to her Yoga class. She tellt me to be sure and be back by half-nine – but she's had that. It's my definite intention to get steamboats – no that'll solve anything, it never does – so's I can have a wee breathing space to consider the entire problem afresh the morn's morning.

The thing is, Zandra's got a brother – Sherman. Does that name remind ye of anything? A tank, maybe? Aye, well keep thinking about the the tank, pal – because that's Sherman. He's no nearly as clever as Zandra – but he's a lot bigger. Zandra and

Sherman are very close.

Like I was saying, jimmie, the whole world's got problems. I've tellt ye mine. What's yours?

Donald Campbell (1940-)

Golf

This, no doubt, expresses Buchan's own sentiments in John Burnet of Barns *and it surely will strike a responsive chord with so many readers.*

As for golf, I utterly failed to excel; and indeed it seems to me that golf is like the divine art of poetry, the gift for which is implanted in man at his birth or not at all. Be that as it may, I never struck a golf ball fairly in my life, and I misdoubt I never shall.

John Buchan (1875-1940)

Would you like to see a city given over,
Soul and body to a tyrannizing game?
If you would, there's little need to be a rover,
For St. Andrews is the abject city's name.

R.F. Murray, 'The City of Golf', The Scarlet Gown, *1891*

The Rules of Old-Fasioned Golf

1. Old-fashioned Golf shall be the game as inaugurated on Bruntsfield Links, Edinburgh, yesterday by Mr. George McNeill, J.P., chairman of the recreation and leisure committee of Lothian Region, by Mr. Finlay Neill, captain of the Bruntsfield Short Hole Golf Club, and by Councillor Donald Gorrie.

2. Mr. Finlay Neill shall be a retired joiner.

3. The players shall be accompanied by representatives of the Press and television, who shall wander in haphazard fashion upon the fairways, getting under the players' feet and becoming progressively more thirsty.

4. The object of the game shall be to publicise a new tourist

attraction launched by the recreation and leisure committee on a motion by Councillor Donald Gorrie. The cost of the project shall be £1,600 and the region shall guarantee it against loss for three years. The region shall keep its fingers crossed.

5. Bruntsfield Links shall be the world's oldest existing golf course; at least, the region shall hope so, as it will have printed lots of publicity material saying it is.

Method of Play

6. Messrs. McNeill, Neill and Gorrie shall be requested to turn up yesterday wearing Old-Fashioned Plus-Fours for the benefit of the photographers, but they shall fail to do so, not wishing to look absolute berks.

7. The photographers shall mutter a bit, but shall nevertheless use approximately 1,760 yards of film.

8. The clubs to be utilised shall be the mashie-niblick and the wooden putter as manufactured by Golf Classics of Dundee and St. Andrews. The ball shall be a sort of replica of the old-fashioned gutta percha missile.

9. These shall be hired to Old-fashioned Golfers for 50p plus £1.50 deposit from 1.30 p.m. to 4 p.m. Monday to Friday until September 15. After September 15 it shall probably be raining anyway.

10. Players, reporters and photographers shall gather at the first tee, upon which Mr. McNeill shall make a short speech. He shall say that he hopes the project shall be a big attraction to tourists coming to Edinburgh. And he shall add, to Lothian Region.

11. Messrs. Neill and Gorrie shall not make any speech.

12. The players shall pause before teeing off because of that idiot with the movie camera who shall be squinting at them through the contraption in their line of fire.

13. Mr. McNeill shall win the first hole by one stroke, much to his own surprise.

Local Rules and Definitions

14. On being requested by a photographer, any player shall repeat any stroke or adopt any pose, however ridiculous. The penalty shall be that their pictures shall appear in the newspapers.

15. This shall be known as a "birdie stroke."

16. Any player may be approached by a reporter at any stage of play, and requested to declare his age and occupation.

17. This shall be known as a "par quote."

18. Three veteran golfers shall stand at the edge of the first green with wrinkled brows, and shall wonder what all those old people are doing, running about with their cameras and notebooks and coughing unhealthily.

19. They shall be told. They shall say: "Tuts, whit a mob."

20. One of them shall say that he plays the 36-hole course every day, and that it is great for the asthma, although it hasn't cured his yet. He shall not give his name for fear of incurring the penalty stated in Rule 14.

21. This shall be known as "taking a stance."

Hazards

22. The following constituted hazards shall be present on the course and penalties incurred for involvement with the hazards are given in brackets: Park benches, unoccupied (one stroke); park benches, occupied (one stroke and profuse apologies); lamp-posts (£15.70p plus VAT); dog droppings (ten minutes).

23. On completion of play, reporters and photographers shall accompany regional publicists to Ye Olde Golf Tavern.

24. Some reporters and photographers shall stay there rather longer than others.

25. This shall be an additional hazard.

Anthony Troon (1935-)

Ladies Bathing

No place on the Firth of Clyde can ever be without charms and interest, and until Arran shall be covered again by the waters, it will always be delightful to look from Ardrossan. It consists at present chiefly of a single line of small houses, curving with the line of the beach; in front of the houses is the public road or street, and next the street the sea, which ebbs very little. The summer population consists mostly of strangers, few of whom have what, in Scotch Irish, are called self-contained houses, most of them cramming into the small, but clean, upper flats, which are let for bathers by the poorer people below. The whole place is respectably clean.

The ladies' bathing is conducted on the genuine Scotch principle of not being at all ashamed of it, as why should they? Is it not pure? and healthy? and ordered by the doctor? and anything wrong in it? So the ladies emerge, in full day, from their flats, in their bathing-dresses, attended by a maid, and a sister or aunt, the maid carrying a small bundle containing a towel and some dry clothes, the friend tittering. The bather crosses the road, and goes to the sea, which is never more than a few yards, or inches, beyond the road's edge. She then enters the water, and shivers, or splashes, according to her taste, conversing or laughing or screaming all the while, with her attendants ashore. But it is on coming out that the delicate part of the operation begins; for, as they don't walk home wet, and then dress in their own rooms, they must change their whole raimant before the public. For this purpose the maid holds a portion of the dry vestment over the dripping lady's head, and as the soaked gown descends to the heels, the dry is supposed to descend over the head as fast, so that the principle is, that, between the two, the lady is never seen. Ignorance is sometimes bliss, and it is very wise in the assistance never to tell the patient anything about it. But I wonder how, when they happen to be looking at a fellow-exhibitor, and observe the interest taken from every window, and by all the street, in the proceeding, they can avoid discovering that such feats are seldom performed without revelations, and that a single fold of wet linen adheres too accurately to the inner surface to require any other revelation.

But I never saw bathing performed by ladies in Scotland even with common decency. Why the devil can't they use bathing machines, or go into retired places, or wall or pale off enclosures? There was one bathing machine on the beach at Ardrossan, which was rarely used, and two in the inn court, which the landlord told me were never used at all. Portobello, however, (the most immodest spot in Scotland), shows that machines may be used so as to be no protection, but the reverse, for there they are used, nearly touching, by men and women indiscriminately.

Henry Cockburn (1779-1854)

Malcolm Bruce

Your cycling, cat loving, vegetarian, anti-nuclear, brown rice eating, sandal wearing, wood stove burning, real ale drinking, Scottish Ecology Party candidate for Newtown/Stockbridge.

Election Address

The Hunter Home from the Hill

Here is the Land of Venison.

I became aware of it in a little hotel which is tucked away slightly off the road in the shadow of a mountain. It is the kind of hotel which Englishmen of sober age regard as a foretaste of paradise because they are left alone to lie to each other about fish and stags. No one ever interrupts them (for they come mostly without their wives), and no one ever contradicts them (because that would be ill-bred, and, in addition, when every one is telling stories about fish or stags, who would dare to cast the first stone?).

It is rather a Spartan hotel. Draughts tear through it from back door to front. The hall is as full of walking-sticks as Lourdes of discarded crutches. Abnormal and improbable fish which seem to have been blown up with a pump by a reckless taxidermist lie in glass cases, suggesting to the generous and fair-minded that perhaps all fish stories are not apocryphal. There are deer slots mounted on wall brackets. The mild, slightly indignant eyes of stags gaze down at guests beneath perfect hat-racks of antlers. And there is no escape from them. Their glassy stare presides even over bedroom corridors.

In such hotels the casual guest feels himself to be an incidental nuisance, rather like the man who finds himself in an alien club while his own club is in process of redecoration. Conversation has a habit of lapsing in his presence. He feels that he is intruding. He is not in the secret. He is not a deer-slayer or a salmon-killer; he is merely an unpleasant reminder of the outside world.

At luncheon and at dinner it is difficult to avoid venison. Personally I hate venison. It is, to my thinking, the most overrated of all meats. I would rather eat bully beef out of a tin. It is strange that the Scots who can produce the most perfect porridge and soup seem nine times out of ten incapable of cooking meat, which is surely a much simpler thing to do. The Irish also cannot cook meat. Roast beef or mutton as served in an Irish hotel is the nearest thing to a rubber bathmat that has ever emerged miserably from a kitchen, always excepting, of course, venison in the Land of Venison. It is redeemed only by the red-currant jelly. Salmon is another story. The Scots cook salmon perfectly – when they can get it!

Luncheon in this hotel is a solitary affair. The dining-room is half full of motorists. The regular inhabitants are all out, either lying on their stomachs in heather or standing thigh-deep in water. But dinner! Behold the hunter home from the hill and the fisher from the loch!

They sit in a chill silence, terribly English, their past lives stamped on their faces, on the wide checks of their tweed jackets, or the twist of their evening bows: admirals, generals, proconsuls! The stranger looks at them, visualizing the grey lines of battleships, or the wheeling columns of infantry, the dusty squadrons of cavalry, or the arid plains and the white towns at the edge of alien oceans which formed the background of their lives. Now they lie on their stomachs in heather or wade into water and eat stonily in the evening, longing for that time when they will slink off to the little room behind the bar to drink the landlord's special Scotch and tell each other of the day's failures or successes.

Scraps of their conversation float out through a suddenly opened door.

'He was a twelve-pointer. I stalked him for three hours in the bed of a watercourse, then the wind changed. . . .'

'I cast over him. He was lying under a stone; an eighteen-pounder if he was an ounce, and, believe me . . .'

'Do you remember old Monty Maddocks?'

'The general?'

'Yes; the fellow who caught the big trout in the lounge!'

'When was that?'

'Eighteen ninety, wasn't it, Angus?'

The landlord taps his pipe out on the mantelpiece and after a reflective Scottish interval says slowly:

'Na; it wasna in eighteen ninety, 'twas in eighteen ninety-two, on the fifteenth o' September . . .'

Every one accepts this as if an oracle has spoken, as indeed it has.

In the fields of this part of Scotland are targets. They depict running stags. Sometimes, looking up, you can pick out, far away on the bare slopes of hills, moving brown creatures, uncannily cautious even to the naked eye. Through binoculars you see a herd feeding, lifting their heads to sniff the air, moving slowly behind the stag, which every now and then flings up his arched neck and gazes round him cautiously; as if conscious that the spiky splendour which he wears is hung about with death.

You wonder which old proconsul in check tweeds is crawling forward on his stomach to bring this wild beauty to the earth.

H.V. Morton (1892-1979)

The Country Gentleman's Tweed Suit

Those coming to stay at Blair Awfoll for a shooting weekend know that I won't tolerate scruffs. Got to look decent. Show a bit of form you know. Now anyone who has got any sense at all knows to possess a proper four piece suit.

The form is this. Arrive for dinner on Friday night from Edinburgh (I won't have people coming from Glasgow), having left your pin-stripe at the dry cleaners and having put on the jacket, waistcoat and trousers of your tweed suit.

Saturday morning dawns, and since you probably failed to undress the night before, all you have to do is swap the trousers for the breeks. Since dawn in Scotland is around 9.00, you stumble straight into the first drive, looking to others like a picture of sartorial sophistication. You button the collar around your neck after you have been waiting for an hour and three quarters without seeing a pheasant and you've noticed there's a nip in the air. Eleven o'clock: elevenses. Reach for your flask, if you remembered to pack it, inside your breast pocket. Three minutes past eleven every other guest has spotted your flask and is busily draining it. Three and a half minutes past eleven, the day's only flush of pheasants. Everybody's unloaded, swigging your whisky.

Lunch back at the Castle for defrosting. One more drive after lunch before it gets dark, by which time it is raining and sleeting.

Back to the Castle for a steam dry in front of the log fire. Then, after a perfectly marvellous bath (which you bagged first and got the hot water), you pull on your trousers (not your breeks) and come down for dinner. Struggle onto the bed several hours later (much the same as the night before) and wake up already dressed for church. Breeks on again after lunch for the afternoon walk, and trousers in the evening for the trip back to Edinburgh.

Moral of the story? A four piece suit is an all-in-one wardrobe.

Robin Chapman-Campbell (1947-)

The Highland Meeting

The Tour de France is not pursued with more tenacity of purpose than is the circuit of Highland Balls, Meetings and Assemblies. Plum-coloured doublets and diced hose are already hanging airing in the moisture-laden atmosphere of a Scottish late-Summer. Lace ruffs and the pleats of innumerable kilts are being ironed. From Loch Eriboll to Leeds, from Invershin to Manchester, the fledglings are polishing up their first pas de Basques and rounding off their first intricate figures of the dance.

From the first thud of the first grouse into the sodden heather the violins and accordions take their beat, and with the shortening days of autumn the rhythms of the reel and the strathspey leap across the bounding floors. From the Oban Meeting to the Skye Gathering; from the Garve Ball to the Perth Assembly; from the Tomnahurich Hunt Ball to the Aberfeldy Highland Soirée the gaily coloured caravanserai moves in unending procession. To go to bed before midnight is to be up betimes and few of the Balls finish before five or six o'clock. The best of all cover two successive evenings and the hardy Highlander will be off the next day and on to the next Assembly a hundred miles away.

There are few who will arrive at a Gathering on Saturday who have not been dancing on Monday, Wednesday, and Friday at the least. And the dancing has been none of your Palais glides, but Foursome Reels and Sixteensomes and Dukes of Perths and Petronellas and Hamilton Houses and Scottish Reforms. Each dance will have lasted a full twenty minutes and will have been danced twice.

It is not easy to be invited to a Highland Meeting. "It is hoped that all who accept the privilege of attending the Ball will respect the rule that no smoking is allowed in the Ballroom," says the ticket, which must be signed to prevent the attendance of any unauthorised person. There is, however, nothing at all to hinder the privileged from enjoying themselves enormously.

When a stray ticket came my way I was an emergency officer attached to a Highland Regiment and was thus able to borrow items of the essential uniform. A kilt believed to be of Macpherson tartan, came from the depot of another regiment. The adjutant had a pair of brogues which were too large but not excessively so when lined with sticking plaster. Major Sinclair had a kilt jacket and waistcoat of a splendid green. Major Mackintosh generously lent a sporran and some startling but effective red hose. The ensemble was impressive to a degree and, I think, reassured if it did not enthral my hosts. It is only cads who wear evening dress at Highland balls.

Upstairs the Petronella was about to begin. There were three double rows of alternate sexes drawn up the length of the ballroom, so we hurried in and squeezed into place. A hearty youth with a red neck and a large silk rosette numbered us off – for in this dance the alternate pairs start at once – and we were off. There is little *abandon* about the dancing at Highland balls due partly, at least, to the lack of available space. The bodily expression to which the dance should give formalised shape is reduced to a few curt nods, inclinations, and shufflings of the feet. This, however, is done expertly as if in conscious under-statement and there is little "pushing through" of the novices.

And so all went merrily as a marriage bell, with leaping and hooching and stamping and jumping, while through the chill Highland air the hours flew past heedless.

At about one o'clock the observant could see that a dichotomy had arisen between the dancers. As the queue at the supper-room door grew longer and longer they became divided into either rather haggard and weary Preprandials or beaming joyful Après-Champagnards. The former looked at their watches and shuffled downstairs. The latter pranced up them and flung themselves into the fury of the dance. A plate of cold chicken and salad, a trifle, and a few glasses of champagne make all the difference, and one returns to the ballroom purged of all doubts that the meeting is after all only a glorified Saturday night at the Palais and prepared to enjoy as many more hours as may arrive before the dawn. After supper one dances less but more gaily.

It is almost as pleasant to sit on the balcony as to dance. The stage is draped with various blue-green tartans. The proscenium is blanketed with heather. On the floor, and reflected in the tall wall-mirrors, is a mass of tartan and coloured dresses and kilts, which strangely sort themselves out from time to time into revolving circles and advancing lines. The dance of the molecules in a chemical equation.

After supper the supper-room remained open and the temporarily partnerless could pick up a kindred spirit and descend, easily, for another glass or two of champagne. But the most individual feature of these functions is the aroma of kippers which pervades the ballroom from about three o'clock onwards. Breakfast on this occasion consisted of "Clear Soup, Kippers, Sausage, Tomato and Potatoes, Coffee and Beer."

And so to the finale, which consisted of a Medley and Galop, the latter being a wild romp in radial lines round the floor. And then the dancers and the sitters-out and the few who had been standing around in the anterooms eating the last of the tomato sandwiches stood for the National Anthem. And so out into the morning at six twenty-five precisely. The last loungers-about and gazers-up-at-the-windows had gone to bed long syne and there were only two apologetic policemen who had waited all night for some one who had left a shooting brake on the wrong side of the road and without lights.

And so home to change for breakfast, but the true acolytes were already filling their petrol tanks and poring over their maps, while prostrate their ladies lay like Ophelias, drowned in sleep, across the back seats of their ancient Morrises.

Ronald Mavor (1925-)

Blows the Wind Today

Blows the wind to-day, and the sun and the rain are flying,
   Blows the wind on the moors to-day and now,
Where about the graves of the martyrs the whaups are crying,
   My heart remembers how!

Grey recumbent tombs of the dead in desert places,
  Standing stones on the vacant wine-red moor,
Hills of sheep, and the howes of the silent vanished races,
  And winds, austere and pure:

Be it granted me to behold you again in dying,
  Hills of home! and to hear again the call;
Hear about the graves of the martyrs the peewees crying,
  And hear no more at all.

R.L. Stevenson (1850-94)

Where Now?

I think the following death-bed conversation between a Scottish husband and wife is about the richest specimen of a dry Scottish matter-of-fact view of a very serious question: An old shoemaker in Glasgow was sitting by the bedside of his wife, who was dying. She took him by the hand. 'Weel, John, we're gawin' to part. I hae been a gude wife to you, John.' 'Oh, just middling, just middling, Jenny,' said John, not disposed to commit himself. 'John,' says she, 'ye maun promise to bury me in the auld kirkyard at Stra'von, beside my mither. I couldna rest in peace among unco folk, in the dirt and smoke o' Glasgow.' 'Weel, weel, Jenny, my woman,' said John soothingly, 'we'll just pit you in the Gorbals *first*, and gin ye dinna lie quiet, we'll try you sine in Stra'von.'

Dean Ramsay (1793-1876)

Andrew Gray

Here ligs Mess Andrew Gray,
Of whom ne muckle good can I say;
He was ne Quaker, for he had ne spirit;
He was ne Papist, for he had ne merit;
He was ne Turk, for he drank muckle wine;

He was ne Jew, for he eat muckle swine,
For forty years he preach'd and lee'd,
For which God dom'd him when he dee'd.

Glasgow Tombstone

Malcolm Donwie

Here lies interred a man o' might,
His name was Malcolm Donwie,
He lost his life ae market nicht by fa'in' aff his pony.

Tombstone, Cullen, Banffshire

The Optimist

Here lie I, Martin Elginbrod.
Hae mercy on my soul, Lord God;
As I would do, were I lord God,
And Ye were Martin Elginbrod.

Tae Jester

Here lie the bones of Alexander Weir,
His mouth it reached from ear to ear,
Tread light and softly on the sod,
For if he yawns – you're gone, by God!

Tombstone, Monzie, Perthshire

Beattie's Epitaph

Like thee I once have stemm'd the sea of life,
Like thee have languish'd after empty joys,
Like thee have labour'd in the stormy strife,
Been grieved for trifles, and amused with toys.

Forget my frailties; thou art also frail:
Forgive my lapses; for thyself may'st fall:
Nor read unmoved my artless tender tale—
I was a friend, O man, to thee, to all.

James Beattie (1735-1803)

A Premature End . . .

On the spot where Prince Charles Edward first raised his standard on the 19th day of August, 1745, when he made the daring and romantic attempt to recover a throne lost by the imprudence of his ancestors, this column was erected by Alexander MacDonald, Esq., of Glenaladale, to commemorate the generous zeal, the undaunted bravery and the inviolable fidelity of his forefathers and the rest of those who fought and bled in that arduous and unfortunate enterprise.

This pillar is now, alas! also become the monument of its amiable and accomplished founder, who, before it was finished, died in Edinburgh on the 4th day of January 1815, at the early age of twenty-eight years.

Loch Shiel; on a column marking the spot where Prince Charlie's standard was unfurled.

Bibliography

Aberdeen Journal, The, Aberdeen, 1802 and 1861
Allan, John, R., *Farmer's Boy,* London, 1935
Allan, John, R., (Editor), *Scotland 1938,* Edinburgh, 1938
Annals of Edinburgh, The, Edinburgh
Barker, Sebastian, *Who is Eddie Linden?* London, 1979
Blake, George, *The Shipbuilders,* London, 1935
Bold, Alan, *To Find the New,* London, 1968
Boswell, James, *A Journey to the Western Islands,* 1773, London, 1775
Boswell, James, *Journal of a Tour to the Hebrides with Samuel Johnson 1773,* London, 1785
Boulton, Sir Harold, *Prince Charlie in Song,* London, 1933
Brown, Catherine, *Scottish Regional Recipes,* Glasgow, 1981
Brown, George Mackay, *Greenvoe,* London, 1972
Brown, George Mackay, *Hawkfall,* London, 1974
Buchan, John, *John Burnet of Barns,* London
Burt, Edward, *Letters from a Gentleman in the North of Scotland,* London, 1754
Byrne, John, *The Slab Boys,* Edinburgh, 1982
Cameron, James, *Point of Departure,* London, 1967
Cameron, David Kerr, *The Cornkister Days,* London, 1984
Chambers, Robert, *Popular Rhymes of Scotland,* Edinburgh, 1841
Chapman-Campbell, Robin, *Catalogue of Some Traditional Clothes as Worn at Blair Awfoll, Home of Major Frost-Bye of That Ilk,*
Christie, Robert, H., *Banquets of the Nations,* London,
Cockburn, Henry, *Circuit Journeys,* Edinburgh, 1888
Cruickshank, Helen, B., *More Collected Poems,* Edinburgh, 1978
Daiches, David, *Two Worlds: An Edinburgh Jewish Childhood,* Sussex, 1974
Defoe, Daniel, *A Tour through the Whole Island of Great Britain 1724-7, London*
Farquhar, William, A. G., *The Fyvie Lintie,* Aberdeen, 1904
Fond, B. Faujas de Saint, *A Journey through England and Scotland to the Hebrides in 1874,* Glasgow (revised edn.) 1907
Fraser, David, *The Christian Watt Papers,* Edinburgh, 1983
Garioch, Robert, *Collected Poems,* Edinburgh, 1982
Garry, Flora, *Bennygoak and Other Poems,* Preston, 1974
Gibbon, Lewis Grassic, *A Scots Hairst,* London, 1967
Gibbon, Lewis Grassic, *Sunset Song,* London, 1933

Gibbon, Lewis Grassic, *The Scottish Scene,* London, 1934
Gray, Alasdair, *Unlikely Stories Mostly,* Edinburgh, 1983
Green, Stanley Roger, *A Suburb of Belsen,* Edinburgh, 1977
Gunn, Neil, M., *Highland River,* Edinburgh & London, 1937
Gunn, Neil, M., *The Silver Darlings,* London, 1941
Harris, Paul (Ed.), *The Rhythm of the Glass,* Edinburgh, 1977
Hogg, James, Letters to Sir Walter Scott published as *Highland Tours,* Hawick, 1983
Kesson, Jessie, *The White Bird Passes,* London, 1958
Kesson, Jessie, *Glitter of Mica,* London, 1963
Lang, Andrew & Lang, John, *Highways and Byways in The Borders,* London, 1913
Lindsay, Maurice, *Collected Poems,* Edinburgh, 1979
Linklater, Eric, *The Art of Adventure,* London, 1947
Lochhead, Liz, *Dreaming Frankenstein,* Edinburgh, 1984
McBey, James, *The Early Life of James McBey: An Autobiography, 1883-1911,* Oxford, 1977
MacCaig, Norman, *Collected Poems,*
MacColla, Fionn, *The Albannach,* London, 1932
McCormick, Andrew, *Galloway: The Spell of its Hills and Glens,* Glasgow, 1932
MacDiarmid, Hugh, *Complete Poems,* Dublin, 1978
Macdonald, Finlay, J., *Crowdie and Cream,* London, 1982
McGonagall, William, *A Library Omnibus,* London, 1969
MacGregor, Alasdair Alpin, *Auld Reekie,* London, 1943
McIllvanney, William, *The Papers of Tony Veitch,* London, 1983
Mackenzie, Compton, *Whisky Galore,* London, 1947
McLaren, Moray, *Understanding the Scots,* London, 1956
MacLaverty, Bernard, *A Time to Dance and Other Stories,* London, 1982
Maclean, Sorley, *Spring tide and Neap tide,* Edinburgh, 1977
Miller, Christian, *A Childhood in Scotland,* London, 1979
Mitchison, Naomi, *What Do You Think Yourself?,* Edinburgh, 1982
Moon, Lorna, *Dark Star,* London, 1929
Morton, H. V., *In Search of Scotland,* London, 1927
Muir, Edwin, *Scottish Journey,* London, 1935
Muir, Edwin, *Poor Tom,* London, 1932
Mulrine, Stephen, *Noise and Smoky Breath,* Glasgow, 1983
Murray, Charles, *Hamewith: the Complete Poems of Charles Murray,* Aberdeen, 1979

Ranger's Impartial List of the Ladies of Pleasure in Edinburgh, Edinburgh, 1779
Ramsay, Dean, *Reminiscences of Scottish Life and Character*, Edinburgh, 1857
Scott, Alexander, *Double Agent*, Preston, 1972
Scott, Sir Walter, *The Border Minstrelsy*,
Shaw, George Bernard, article in *The Author*, Autumn 1937
Sillar, Eleanor, *Edinburgh's Child*, Edinburgh, 1961
Simond, Louis, *Journal of a Tour & Residence in Great Britain, etc.*, Edinburgh, 1815
Smith, Alexander, *A Summer in Skye, 1886*
Smiles, Samuel, *Self Help*, London, 1865
Smith, Iain Crichton, *Collected Poems*, Edinburgh, 1981
Spence, Alan, *Its Colours They Are Fine*, Glasgow, 1977
Still, Peter, *Poems and Songs Chiefly in the Scottish Dialect*, Aberdeen, 1844
Tait, William J., *Collected Poems*, Edinburgh, 1980
Thom, William, from *William Thom: The Inverurie Poet* by Robert Bruce, Aberdeen, 1970
Toulmin, David, *Hard Shining Corn*, Aberdeen, 1972
Troon, Anthony, in *The Scotsman*, Edinburgh, June 27 1978
Wordsworth, Dorothy, *A Tour in Scotland*, Ed. W. Knight, London, 1896.

Index of authors

Allan, John R. 126-29

Ballantine, James 22-3
Barker, Sebastian 12-14
Biles, R. N. 50-53
Blair, Capt. Hamish 109-10
Blake, George 38-41
Bold, Alan 8-9
Boorde, Bishop Andrew 2
Boswell, James 80-82, 166-7, 185-6
Boulton, Sir Harold 171
Brown, Catherine 187, 196
Brown, George Mackay 102-4, 216-18
Bruce, Malcolm 235
Buchan, John 231
Burns, Robert 184, 223-5
Burt, Edward 96, 188
Byrne, John 46-7
Byron, Lord 2

Caie, J. M. 5-6
Calgacus 162
Cameron, David Kerr 131-3
Cameron, James 56-60
Campbell, Donald 227-31
Chapman-Campbell, Robin 237-8
Charles II 148
Christie, Robert H. 184-5
Cockburn, Henry (Lord Cockburn) 94-5, 233-4
Cruickshank, Helen B. 219
Cunningham, Allan 172-3

Daiches, David 154-7
Darling, Will Y. 189-93
Defoe, Daniel 164
Duncanson, Robert 162-3

Farquhar, William A. G. 193-5
Franklin, Benjamin 23
Freed, Arthur 80
Fyffe, Will 36

Garioch, Robert 204-8
Garry, Flora 130-31
Gibbon, Lewis Grassic 110-13, 187-8
Gray, Alasdair 96-8
Green, Stanley Roger 32-3
Grieve, C. M. *See* MacDiarmid, Hugh
Gunn, Neil M. 97-8, 102-3

Hanley, Clifford 56
Hazlitt, William 2, 5
Hogg, James 86-9

Jackson, Alan 227
Jacob, Violet, 14-15

Kesson, Jessie 122-4, 199-201

Lang, Andrew and John 63-6
Lindsay, Maurice 66-7
Linklater, Eric 201-4
Lloyd George, David 2
Lochhead, Liz 157
Lyndsay, Sir David 222-3

McBey, James 209-212
MacCaig, Norman 195-6
MacColla, Fionn 53-4
McCormick, Andrew 67-70
MacDiarmid, Hugh 28-31
MacDonald, Finlay J. 89-91, 98-101
McGinn, Matt 49-50
McGonagall, William 75-7
MacGregor, Alasdair Alpin 26-7, 152-4, 166
McIllvanney, William 42
Mackenzie, Compton 91-3
McLaren, Moray 3, 80, 163-4
MacLaverty, Bernard 176-81
Maclean, Sorley 82-3
Mavor, Ronald 238-40
Miller, Christian 149
Mitchell, James Leslie *See* Gibbon, Lewis Grassic
Mitchison, Naomi 12-18
Moon, Lorna 124-6
Morgan, Edwin 215
Morton, H. V. 71-4, 142-6, 151-2 235-7
Muir, Edwin 9, 55-6, 101-2
Mulrine, Stephen 198
Munro, Neil 4-5
Murray, Charles 133-4
Murray, R. F. 231

Nisbet, Eilidh 106-7
Nodier, Charles 148

Pichot, Amedée 148

Ramsay, Dean 150-151, 158, 241
'Ranger' 222

Saint-Fond, Faujas de 188
Scott, Alexander 10-11
Scott, Sir Walter 71, 74-5, 77
Seymour, Sir Edward 162

Shaw, George Bernard 201
Sillar, Eleanor 24-6, 158-60
Simond, Louis 148
Smiles, Samuel 218-19
Smith, Alexander 20
Smith, Iain Crichton 36-7
Spence, Alan 43-6
Stendhal 21
Stevenson, R. L. 32, 240-41
Still, Peter 136-7

Tacitus 162
Tait, William J. 226-7
Thom, William 135-6
Topham, Edward 20-21
Toulmin, David 115-22
Troon, Anthony 231-33

Watt, Christian 137-42
Wordsworth, Dorothy 96-7

General Index

Aberdeen:
  granite city 110
  high tea in 187-8
  joke factory 142-6
  Marischal College 110
  military riot *(1802)* 174-5
  student riot, Rectorial *(1861)* 168-71
  To an Aberdeen Poet 219
Aberdeen Journal, The 168-71, 174-5
Aberdeenshire, rural:
  Aikey Fair, How of Buchan 115-22
  Autumn; the land in 110-11
  feeing market 124-6
  Fun on the Green 122-24
  games, a country event 126-9
  harvest madness; the Hairst 112-13
  Lament for a lost landscape 131-33
Aberdeenshire poems:
  Bennachie 133-4
  Bennygoak 130-31
  Howe of the Mearns, The 114-15
  Last Tryst, The 135-6
  Mormond Braes 134-5
  Ugie Water 136-7
Aikey Brae 115-22
American visitors to Melrose 71-4
Arbroath Declaration of *1320* 162
Ardrossan, ladies bathing at 233-4
At the Orphanage 199-201
Ayrshire and Galloway; a traditional rhyme 62

Ballade of Good Whisky 195-6
Balmorality v; impact of 141
Barrie, J. M.; a comment by G. B. Shaw 201; by Linklater 202
Benefactor, The 226-7
Bennygoak, the Hill of the Cuckoo 130-31
Bloody Orkney 109-10
Blows the Wind Today 240-41
Blue Bonnets over the Border 77
Bonie Lass, The 223-5
Border Keeps 74-5
Border Warrior Knight, The 71
Bridie, James, with Edith Evans 203
'Brigadoon', the film defended 80
British, Briton; terms hard to define 3
Bruce's heart; the story 72
Burial in the Gorbals 241
Burning Harp, The; a Yuletide tale 216-218
Butchers of Glasgow, The 52-3

Cable car days 26-7
Calgacus faces the foe 162
Canadian Boat Song, The 173-4
Capital Sabbath, a 152-4
Carlyle's manuscript re-written 218-19
Censure from the pulpit 150-51
Church collection, the 158
Church-going 149-51
Clydeside from the river 38-41
Colquhoun, Robert, painter 212
Country Gentleman's tweed suit 237-8
Country without future, a 9
Covenanters' Grace; Burns' Selkirk version 184
Cuisine, Scottish:
  Aberdeen high tea 187-8
  Edinburgh, modern 189-93
  eighteenth century 185-6
  Highland hotel 235-7
  See also Haggis; Petticoat Tails; Shetland recipe

'damn Scotch' 4
Death of a Community 102-4
Deeside:
  before Balmorality 140
  after royalty came 141

Dinner at Inveraray Castle 188
Druids' Circle, Aikey Brae 119
Dundee: *The New Tay Bridge* 75-7

Edinburgh:
beauty of 20
Benjamin Franklin's arrival in 23
cable cars 26-7
childhood recalled 24-6, 158-60
effects of climate in 23-4
the Elect and the Damned 203-4
grace and talents of its ladies 20-21
indecorum of sightseers 226
a Jewish Sabbath in 154-7
ladies of pleasure 222
The Lamplighter 32
MacDiarmid's poem on 31-4
Sunday strictures 32
Sundays, 19th century 158-60
A View from Calton Hill 32-3
welcome to Mrs H. B. Stowe 22-3
Edinburgh Childhood, An 24-6, 158-60
Edinburgh after Flodden; the *1513* Proclamation 21-2
Edinburgh food and drink 189-93
Edinburgh International Festival *See Embro to the Ploy*
Edinburgh Declaration of Prince Charles Edward, *1745* 164-5
Election pamphlet, new style 235
Elgin; the 'shows' on the Green 122-4
Embro to the Ploy 204-8
Epitaphs 241-3

Feeing market, the 124-6
First Etching 209-11
First Exhibition 211-12
Franklin welcomed by Hume 26
French prisoners in Selkirk 63-6
Fun on the Green 122-4

Gaels; the Highland heritage 80
Galloway Fox Hunt, A 67-70
Galloway Grace 184
Games, The 126-9
General Discontent in Highlands 166-7
Gie the Lass her Fairin' 225
Glasgow:
Clydeside 38-41. *See also Trial Trip*
corrupting influence of 55-6
journalistic start in 56-60
living in a tower block 43-6
Saturday night bus journey 50-3
Slab boys in conversation 46-7
a small and great city 42
streets of Glasgow 53-4
Glasgow poems:
I Belong to Glasgow 36
Butchers of Glasgow 49-50
George Square 48-9
Glasgow Kisses 48
The Glasgow Underground 56
You Lived in Glasgow 36-7
Glencoe; the order for the massacre 162-3
Golf:
John Buchan's failure 231
Rules of Old Fashioned Golf 231-33
St Andrews 231
Good Ale 184
Granite City of Aberdeen 110
Greensleeves, a Glasgow cameo 43-6
Gude Buke, A 198

Haggis; the recipe 184-5
Harvest of the Sea; the herring girls' life 137-142
Hebridean alarms 89-91
Hebridean emigration 166-7
Hebridean shores 82-3
Herring Fishers 83-6
Herring girls on the Highlands 137-42
High tea in Aberdeen 187-8
Highland crofting community, a 97-8
Highland dwelling, a visit to 80-82
Highland emigration 166-7
Highland hospitality, kindly 96-7
Highland hospitality, malodorous 188
Highland hotel, sporting 235-7
Highland midges 106-7
Highland Meeting; the Ball 238-40
Highland poverty, 18th C. 80-82
Highland Sabbath 151-2
Highland travel by mail coach 94-5
Highland women 95
Highlanders; the real Gaels 85
Howe of the Mearns, The 114-15

I Belong to Glasgow 36
In Search of Scotland:
Aberdeen joke factory 142-6
Americans at Melrose 71-4
the land of venison 235-7
Sabbath in the Highlands 151-2
Inverness Courier, 1834; a censure of Sir Walter Scott 198-9
Invocation against the dark 160

Jacobitism, a glorious failure 163-4
James Bridie, dramatist 201-204
Jewish Sabbath in Edinburgh 154-7
Joan Eardley, To 215
joke factory in Abrdeen 142-6
journalism in Glasgow 56-60

Kelso Horse Show 66-7
Kilt, the:
at the Highland Ball 239

indecent garb 96
The Kilt's my Delight 4-5
kilt wearers, 'damn Scotch' 4
Kirk services:
censure from the pulpit 150-51
praying for sinners 149

Ladies sea-bathing 233-4
Lairds and factors 98
Lamplighter, The 32
Loch Shiel; MacDonald's column 243
Lord's Prayer, Scots version 160
Lowlands, the:
Blue Bonnets over the Border 82
Border Keeps 79-80
Border Warrior Knight 76
Dundee; *The New Tay Bridge* 80-82
French prisoners in Selkirk 68-71
Galloway Fox Hunt 72-5
Kelso Horse Show 71-2
traditional rhymes 62
visiting Melrose 76-8

Massacre of Glencoe; the order for 162-3
Meeting a Scottish Painter 212-14
Melrose:
The Monks of Melrose 62
visitors to 71-4
Mons Graupius; the battle speech of Calgacus 162

New Tay Bridge, The 80-82
Newspapers in Scotland:
The Aberdeen Journal 168-71, 174-5
The Inverness Courier 198-9
Mercurius Scoticus 204
The Scotsman 226

Orkney:
Bloody Orkney 104-5
Death of a Community 102-4
the Orkney Islands 101-2

Perth after the *1715* rising 164
Petticoat Tails; a shortbread recipe 196
Pleasures of the flesh, Edinburgh 222
Point of Departure; James Cameron in Glasgow 56-60
Poor Tom, debased by city life 55-6
Presbyterianism:
censure from the pulpit 150-5
prayers for sinners 149
Sabbath dress and strictures 148
an ungentlemanly religion 148
Prince Charles Edward Stuart:
his Edinburgh Declaration, *1745* 164-5
memorial erected at Loch Shiel 243
Puddock,The 5-6

Red Fellows, The 12-18
Rioting:
by Aberdeen students 168-71
by military in Aberdeen 174-5
in Stornoway 88
Royal Deeside 141

Sabbath; the Presbyterian Sunday:
behaviour and dress for 148
church collection 158
in Edinburgh, 19th C. 158-60
in Edinburgh, 20th C. 152-4
in the Highlands 151-2
matters of doctrinal debate 152-4
St Andrews, city of golf 231
Scot or Scotch 4, 5
Scotch inns, 19th C. 100
Scotch Oatmeal 193-5
Scotched 10-11
Scotland:
a country without future 9
'nothing there that looks like Scotland' 85
romance and reality. *See Introduction*
Scotland's first newspaper 204
Scotsman, The, a letter to 226
Scott, Sir Walter, censured 198
Scottish characteristics 2-3, 5
Scottish food and drink 185-93, 235-7
Scottish Nationalism 166
Scottish theatre 201-2
Scottish women:
barefoot on Sunday 148
characteristic 23-4
Glaswegian 54
herring girls 137-42
Highland 95
Selkirk, French prisoners in 63-6
Sensuality; from *The Three Estates* 222-3
Shaw, writing of Barrie 201
Shetland dish; sassermaet and brönies, a recipe 187
Shetland Lullaby, A 105-6
Shores (Hebridean) 82-3
Siddons, Sarah, in Edinburgh 201
Skye; the Macleods of Dunvegan 138-40
Skye Boat Song, The 171
Slab Boys, The 46-7
small and great city (Glasgow) 42
Song of a Small Nation 8-9
Spread of Ian Nicol, The 6-8
Stallion Man, The 98-101
Stornoway; a letter from James Hogg 86-9
Stowe, Harriet Beecher, welcomed to Edinburgh 22-3
Streets of Glasgow, The 53-4
Sunday. *See also* Sabbath
Sunday in Edinburgh, 19th C. 158-60
Sundaysong 157

Sutherland's refusal to enlist 168
Sweet Saturday Night; a bus journey 50-53

Talking with Five Thousand People in Edinburgh 28-9
Tay Bridge, The New 75-7
Theatre Royal, Edinburgh 28-29
Time to Dance, A; an Edinburgh rebellion 176-81
Tintock Tap 62
To a Midge 106-7
Trial Trip; down the Clyde 41-4
Trials of Authorship 218-9
Trustees' day at the orphanage 199-201
Tweed suit for country gentleman 237-8

Ugie Water, To 136-7
Union of the Parliaments 162

Venison, the land of 235-7
View from Calton Hill, A 32-3

Waverley Novels condemned 198
Wee, Wee German Lairdie, The, (George I) 172-3
Where Now? 241
Whisky Galore 91-3
Women. *See* Scottish women

You Lived in Glasgow 36-7

Zandra 227-31